"How do you create a monastic order in the 21ˢᵗ century? How do two women from the U.S.A. decide to live as poor among the poor and devote themselves to the medical needs of people in Honduras? What would the rule of such an order be? Join Sisters Alegría and Confianza on their journey into their vocation. Their emails home describe their daily life, their worship and their work. May they guide each of us to deeper commitment to Christ as we live into the challenges of our times!"

> **--Rev. Dwight H. Judy, Ph.D.,** Professor Emeritus of Spiritual Formation, Garrett-Evangelical Theological Seminary. Author of *A Quiet Pentecost: Inviting the Spirit into Congregational Life* and of *Embracing God: Praying with Teresa of Avila.*

"These stories are interesting, compelling and well-written. Readers are drawn into the stories of life as is lived by poor people in the third world and begin to understand their struggle to get through each day. At the same time we try to understand the story of two remarkable women who chose this setting to begin new lives of thoughtful prayer and worship, finding that loving one's neighbor is key to the new life.

"As an utter and complete unbeliever in anything mystical, I come to the philosophical question: how does one decide what to choose as a personal life mission both for the present and the future? The ability to reflect on our choices is what separates us as humans. I do not regret my choice of thinking rather than believing. I am wholeheartedly supportive of any book that makes me think this hard!"

> **--Russell B. Hanson,** blogger, author of numerous books on the history of Minnesota and Wisconsin, and co-author of dozens of scientific publications.

"Are there still people living saintly lives? I have been impressed that *Hermanas* Alegría and Confianza approach sainthood. Although I first became acquainted with them because of their work in family planning, I have come to admire them not only for their work, but also for their lifestyle and their sincerity. In reading <u>Giving Up Something Good for Something Better</u> I am reminded of the life that I had envisioned for myself—living and practicing medicine in developing countries. Instead, I have had a comfortable life in the

United States. This makes me enjoy living that dreamed-of life vicariously, and appreciate *las Hermanas* all the more. I recommend this book for anyone who wants to know how these two remarkable nuns live, and how they feel about their lives."

--Richard Grossman, M. D., M. P. H., member of Durango Friends (Quaker) Meeting, former clerk of Quaker Earthcare Witness and author of the monthly column "Population Matters!" for the Durango (Colorado) Herald.

"With delightful and insightful stories of daily country life from Limón, Colón, Honduras, the authors reveal deeper meaning in life stripped of convenience and committed to poverty, prayer, and service. You may laugh or cry while reading these vignettes, which document what it means to grow in faith. They inspire each of us to be conscious of our own spiritual journey."

--Rev. Alice G. Knotts, Ph.D., retired teacher, pastor, and author of several books including *Fellowship of Love: Methodist Women Changing American Racial Attitudes 1920-1968*, and *Allow God to Wear Your Face*.

Giving Up Something Good for

Something

Better

Sister Alegría del Señor & Sister Confianza del Señor

(Beth Blodgett and Prairie Naoma Cutting)

migas Press

Amigas Press
Box 755,
Cushing, WI. 54006

©2017 Amigas del Señor

ISBN-13: 978-1539888123
ISBN-10: 1539888126

Cover design by the Sisters and Russ Hanson.

Front cover painting, "Sisters in Christ," by Donna Metcalf, 2015, oil on canvas 16" x 20." Used with permission

Back cover photo by Amigas del Señor, looking southeast over Amigas del Señor Monastery, 2006.

For

David Nelson
Jyl Myers
Russ Hanson

The Encouragers

Also by the Sisters:

Amigas del Señor: Methodist Monastery

Table of Contents

Sisters Alegría and Confianza at Amigas del Señor Monastery, 2015

Introduction

Why, Who, and How
From: Sister Alegría

Writing a book requires a "Why?" Why not relax with your feet up, drinking a nice glass of limeade? Why not read some more—after all, who are you to teach? You should be learning. True, oh, so true.

We are all teachers, whether we choose to be or not. Everything that you do or say is a lesson. You are saying to everyone, "This is an option for you, too." You can't get out of teaching, but you do get to decide what you teach. In telling our stories, warts and all, Sister Confianza and I hope to be teaching ourselves integrity and humility. What we teach others, others are better qualified to say.

I was 58 years old when we founded Amigas del Señor Monastery. I remember a conversation from when I was 13, with a Protestant woman a generation older than I. I had brought up the topic of nuns and monasteries. "What do they do?" she asked.

"They pray."

"What good does that do?" she scoffed, ending the conversation.

I am so grateful to have found my vocation. There are tens of thousands of Protestants in the US who have a monastic vocation and have not realized it. I want everyone to have the satisfaction of saying, "Yes," to God and living that "Yes."

One of the great blessings of monastic life is that one lives with the concept of the whole Body of Christ. It is perfectly obvious that monastic life is not for everyone. (Remember the Shakers?) I want you to hear your own call from God and to answer it, with vigor and courage. And I want people to figure out their call before they are 58 years old. But still, better late than never.

You know persons who have a monastic call, I guarantee it. Maybe you, yourself, have a monastic call.

Charism is a word used in monastic circles. It answers, "What is unique about your Order, different from other Orders?" Part

1

of our charism is that we are *contemplatives:* our main job is to pray. Part of our charism is to let the world know that you don't have to be Roman Catholic or Orthodox to become a nun or monk. And we do poverty, rural Honduran poverty.

I like stories. I used to read a lot of novels. I don't read novels so much anymore. My life is like a novel. I find myself eager to turn the page to see what happens next. I hope you'll like these stories of five years in the life of our little Monastery, from July, 2008 through June, 2013.

Sister Alegría writes sitting in the hammock swing, 2015

As the foundress, I have the responsibility of writing the "Constitutions" or the "Rule." Well, that hasn't been easy. A few years ago I got up in the night to write. The next morning, Sister Confianza asked me on what I had been working. "The Rule," I responded.

"Oh, can I read what you've written?" she asked eagerly.

"Sure."

She looked in the notebook I had been using and her face fell. "But you always tell stories." What she held in her hand was a dull list of rules and a schedule.

It is true. Telling stories is my way of teaching—stories and more stories. I still haven't written a document that could be called the Constitutions. This book includes the Constitutions, embedded in the stories.

There are two voices in this book: Sister Confianza's and mine. We each write from our own perspective, and neither of us presents the other's personal stuff without her permission.

As the story begins, our names were Prairie Cutting and Beth Blodgett, so we use those names. In May, 2009, Prairie became Sister Confianza. In August, 2009, Beth became Sister Alegría. Those are the names we use from then on.

The bulk of the book is made of updates (edited) that we sent by email to persons who care about us. Each entry shows the date sent and the name of the writer. We began to be serious about this book early in 2015. Additions we've made are labeled like an update, with the name of the Sister writing but without a date. We hope we have learned from our experience; the *now* voice of each of us may seem very different from the *then* voice.

If you find yourself a little lost, look to the Glossary and the Geographic Orientation section at the back of this book. In fact, it might be good to go to the Geographic Orientation right now, read it, then return to read the rest of this introduction.

We have consciously included a few Spanish words and expressions. We want you to get a feel for what it is like to be an immigrant and for what it is like to be bilingual. If you have friends or acquaintances who are immigrants, you can be sure they will NOT tell you the whole truth of how hard it is.

This is not a work of fiction. These are true stories about real people. We have used the names they go by. You will notice a dearth of last names. Last names aren't used much in our neighborhood.

You will notice a lot of talking about food. Both Sister Confianza and I are interested in food. We like food. We also have had the desire that our poor neighbors eat (or at least have access to) an adequate diet. The poorer a country (or a family) is, the higher the percentage of income is spent on food. Haiti is the poorest nation in this hemisphere. Honduras is ranked as second or third, depending upon the year. Honduras is not independent in food production. In Honduras, producing food is a patriotic act (it helps the nation) just as, in the US, installing solar panels is a patriotic act.

We are hopeful that you will appreciate the lives of our poor neighbors, poor people in a poor county in a poor nation. These are folks that haven't had the advantages you've had: paved roads or streets (let alone sidewalks), electricity, public lending libraries, access to health care, a high school education. Unlike you, they live in a country that always loses ground instead of gaining ground with all international economic agreements, which are controlled by the rich to keep the rich rich and the poor poor.

When I was in college, I had an amazing US history professor. She told us that we were very fortunate that in the US, all of the presidents and secretaries of state (the most powerful persons regarding public policy) always had the best interest of the country as their priority. Not many nations have had that. Then she asked us what other value might also have served well. We all sat in stymied silence.

"They could have had the best interest of the entire world as a priority."

I was silent with all of the others. And I had considered myself a Christian.

Book Writing the Hard Way
From: Sister Alegría

Sister Confianza and I live on less than $200/month in rural Honduras. This is below minimum wage in this country. We live where public school teachers don't own automobiles or personal computers. A few weeks ago I mentioned to several women that in the US all of the public grade schools have electricity. They were very impressed. I think most of them believed me.

In 2011, we realized that what we have here in the Monastery is so good for spiritual growth we must share it. To quietly live our lives of poverty, chastity, and obedience would be selfish. Very few people actually believe our poverty. We are white; we talk, walk, and act like middle class Americans, which we were before we accepted the call to evangelical poverty. Poverty is our Peace Testimony. As James says, greed is the cause of wars. We accept, use, keep only our fair share. We do not hoard (save for a rainy day or for retirement).

We are writing a book, even though Sister Confianza accurately comments that "writing a book is for rich people," you know, people with electricity and computers.

We dedicate our material work on Fridays to book writing. Sometimes we can do that at home with paper and pens. But this Friday, we go to Tocoa to use computers.

We are up at 4 am to do morning prayers by solar-powered flashlight. Then we empty the night urine on the coconuts and pineapples to fertilize them, feed and water the five hens and one rooster. We eat a good, solid breakfast: cold bean soup with katuk leaves and lots of toasted corn tortilla fragments (like crackers in your soup).

4

At 5:30, we don our sun hats and backpacks, grab our umbrellas (for sun protection) and hike to the highway, a two-lane dirt road.

We watch several vehicles pass in the 15 minutes we wait. Then a pickup stops for us. We ride in the back, holding on to the metal frame, crouching when we want to escape the dust cloud. I love riding in the back of a pick-up truck, standing with my face to the wind. I'm Ben Hur, you know. At Bonito Oriental (Eastern Beauty) the pavement begins.

Once in Tocoa, the city, we walk another 3/4 mile to our usual internet and begin work at 8:05, amazingly early. The internet business has a water cooler—free potable water, chilled even. We drink as much as we want and fill a bottle to share with our lunch. Computers cost $1.40/hour.

Sister Confianza eats a big bean soup before heading out for the day, 2016

At 10:30 I'm hungry. We sign off and walk three blocks to the central park, stopping at the post office on the way. We use the public restrooms. Fourteen cents each. It would be 23 cents if we wanted toilet paper. Toilet paper is not a necessity today.

Introduction

We score tiny ice cream cones from a pushcart. The vendor has only one finger on his right hand; he's deft enough. Delicious. Twenty-three cents for each cone.

Lunch is homemade peanut butter between hearty wheat flour tortillas.

Back to the internet.

I edit Chapter Five, "Health Crisis," and enter words for the glossary. Sister Confianza prepares two maps: one of North and Central America and another of Honduras. We do a lot of communications besides the book work. Good effort.

It's 12:30, time to leave. We have a brief visit with our friends, Ingrid and Angel, at their dry goods/plastics store. We give them a pineapple from our yard. Angel gives us each a new straw hat (with red trim). Angel and Ingrid are middle class. A frayed hat should be replaced. We accept the hats with proper gratitude, but haven't decided what to do with them yet.

Next stop: groceries. We buy two pounds of raw peanuts, one pound of raw soybeans, one pound of bran, and two pounds of red beans.

Then the bank. We withdraw $1,325 and deposit it in Nurse Eloyda's account to buy medicines for her clinic and our public health clinic (which never has enough). We withdraw $150 on which to live for the next month.

We catch the first bus going our way. Sister Confianza sells copies of the Upper Room devotional. We get off at Quebrada de Arena (Sandy Stream). We catch the next bus going our way. In each of these buses, 25 people get to listen to one of the meditations, and two people buy a copy each.

At Bonito Oriental, we get off at the gas station—free bathrooms. We wait over half an hour. The Limón bus has still not arrived. I approach the owner of a pickup. They are going to Iriona (far past Limón). Yes, he would be happy to give us a lift. He cleans out the back seat of the cab so we can ride there. Then he buys cool drinks for everyone. A can of apple juice for each Sister. Wow!

We walk about three fourths of the way from the highway to the Monastery, when along comes Don Julio with Neri, his son, at the wheel. The pickup is overloaded as usual, but there is room in the cab. We are invited in and soon dropped off at our path. We make a date for them to bring us a sack (100 pounds) of chicken feed in the next week and a half.

Three minutes later, we are home, and it's not even dark yet.

1

Discerning God's Call

"What is mine to do?"—Judy Billings

Charlie Palmer
From: Sister Alegría

I was born in Dunn County, Wisconsin, in 1947, a big year for babies. Our family farm, where my mother, now 100, still lives, is near Boyceville, Wisconsin. One of our neighbors, Charlie Palmer, was an old man when I was little. His grandchildren were playmates for my brother, my sister, and me. Earl Daniel had not yet been born.

Beth at about age 9, when Charlie prophesied

7

One day, Charlie stopped on his way to town, just to chat with my dad. He didn't even come into the house. When Dad came in, his eyes were intense and puzzled. He told Mom, "Charlie says that all Christians are called to be poor." Charlie, his wife, his sons and daughters-in-law and the grandchildren were active in Boyceville Methodist Church, where my family was also active. This gave Charlie's words a little more authority, confusing as they were.

I never heard my parents refer to that day, that conversation, that doctrinal point again. But I didn't forget it.

We were all small dairy farmers, not quite poor, but certainly not wealthy either. Well, that's my parents' generation. Charlie was poor. He drove a small rattle-trap pickup truck that anyone would replace if they could. Such a rattletrap truck would make Charlie middling rich here in rural Honduras where I live now.

But back to rural Wisconsin in the 1950's: Charlie's younger son, Merle, had three children a little younger than I. They were my friends. Merle worked for the postal service as a letter carrier in addition to running his small farm.

One hot summer day, my mother, the family health officer, announced that it was too hot to work. We should go to Clear Lake. Dad, grinning, obediently went to dig worms, followed by Frank. Ann and I helped Mom pack the picnic and our swimming suits. We spent most of the day at the lake fishing, swimming, picnicking, and resting in the cool shade.

Arriving home, we had barely gotten through the door when the phone rang. This was in the days of party lines. Mom answered promptly.

Merle Palmer, in his early 30's, had died that day haying in the hot sun. I knew that the lives of my friends, Steven, Barbara and Mark, would never be the same again. I also knew that Merle Palmer died of greed. The doctor wrote "heart attack" on the death certificate, but I knew he had died of greed. Another theological detail I don't remember discussing in the family.

Like most prophets, Charlie Palmer was ignored in his place and time.

Pre-Monastic Life
From: Sister Alegría

My life was fairly mundane. While studying at River Falls State University (Wisconsin), I married another physics major. Getting married in college is just what was done. I bore two sons in that marriage, who are now middle aged.

8

I studied medicine at the Medical College of Wisconsin (Milwaukee, WI), where I also received my pediatric training.

After my first divorce, I married again. In the mid-80's I moved to Oregon, still married to that second husband.

In 1992, I recognized burn-out in myself and quit work and left my marriage. I began to pay attention to God more. My reading did not include the Bible. I conceded the Bible to those who publicly claimed it and used it as a weapon of hatred. I attended both Multnomah Monthly Meeting and Rose City Park United Methodist worship on Sundays.

Sometime in here, the stock market fell suddenly, but briefly. Instant awareness that it's all just paper, all of our little pretenses of material security. I spent many hours over a few years working through my relationship with material stuff. It took a while.

I was more or less supporting myself as a substitute pediatrician, filling in for a day or a week for my friends. I downsized. By now I was living alone in a small house (1,100 sq. ft.). I spent several weeks each summer at United Methodist Church (UMC) camps for children of all ages as a volunteer health care provider. Good stuff.

I was active in a movement to end the death penalty in Oregon. I felt strongly against military violence and saw my government as culpable. But how could we get our people to stop killing foreigners when they were willing to kill one of their own citizens? Once, I was on a pilgrimage with anti-death penalty activists. One woman asked me, "Where are all the anti-abortion people? When will they join us?!" I responded, "I suppose about the same time we join them."

May, 1999 saw my first medical mission to Honduras. Later that year, Multnomah Monthly Meeting (MMM) granted me a Clearness Committee related to dropping my income below the taxable level so that I could escape the responsibility of paying for all the exported violence. Some things went well in that Committee and within two weeks I was ready to sell my house without angst. Some things went not so well in that Committee. I gained clearness that if you are going to do something difficult, you must have a much higher level of readiness if you have to do it without support. So I worked on readying myself. I understood that I was being prepared for the Main Act in my life, but I still didn't fully claim it.

Did you know that the IRS considers it perfectly reasonable that you donate up to 50% of your taxable income? Who would think to go to the IRS for spiritual advice? I obeyed the letter of the IRS laws while violating the spirit as much as I could. I hadn't really chosen poverty, you see. I had chosen taxlessness; I still wanted my luxuries.

September, 2000, I became homeless. I was painfully conscious of having no one with experience to guide me. Various Friends opened their homes to me. I spent two to four months at a time in Honduras and continued volunteering at camps, beginning to feel somewhat comfortable in this Gypsy life. The late Alberta Gerould, an elderly Friend, asked me to consider her house my home, a beautiful roomy house in a nice neighborhood with nutritious and delicious food. After a few years, I began to get inklings that all was not well, that I should not be living at that level of material comfort.

I didn't feel "called" to do volunteer health care in Honduras. Should I do some serious discernment? Finally, I gave up the nagging worry. As long as I was doing it as a spiritual practice (i.e., without attachment), it was fine.

Beth laughs with a patient at an outreach clinic in Honduras, 2000

I studied Spanish; I didn't enjoy studying Spanish, but I did it. I copied in Spanish the whole book of Jonah; then I did it again. God's funny you know. Big Joker is one of the names of God. Sometimes I am the one who delivers straight lines for the Big Joker.

I gave up men. I knew that I should not marry again. I wasn't available.

Buying the Land, October, 2003
From: Sister Alegría

I was living at my friend Gloria Lacayo's house in Limón while volunteering five days a week at the Public Health Clinic (Centro de Salud). One day, Gloria told me that she had always wanted a mountain cabin—a get-away place. It just so happened that Chito had some land that he'd like to sell her along the La Fortuna road. She would be going out to look at it with him on Saturday. Would I like to go along?

Yes, I certainly would like to go along. I had traversed that road going on outreach clinics, but I had never stopped along the way. There was a stream.

The parcel of land was too large for Gloria. She couldn't afford to buy it all—four *manzanas*. I thought acre. I have since learned that a *manzana* is 1.7 acres. Yes, it is the same word as apple. It is easy to get confused in a second language.

Chito has a truck; we all went in his truck. Gloria was clear that she wanted the part of the land where the stream crosses the road. The stream is forded, not bridged. At that time, the locals considered the water safe to drink. As I write, I consider it to be contaminated with giardia, protozoa that causes diarrhea and general gut upset.

The property line to the south is over a biiig hill; we rode in Chito's truck. The west is bordered by the road. The north and east by the stream. We hiked to the peak of the high hill. The Knowing was there. It was as though God tapped me on the shoulder, saying, "This is the spot. Buy it for the Monastery."

So I did. The price was $250/*manzana*—an outrageously high price. Special price for North Americans. I bought two *manzanas* and Gloria, two. We purchased it in her name.

Less than a month later, she went out with the county assessor. He measured the land and told her that there was a lot more than four *manzanas*—more like seven. She should pay Chito for one more. She didn't have that extra $250, so I paid it.

This is sort of Honduran justice. The cost per acre was ridiculously high, so the way to make right the inaccurate low estimate of size is to pay for part of the increase. Chito still doesn't know the size. He was very happy with the extra cash.

11

I paid $750 for 60% of seven *manzanas*. A year later, Gloria officially "sold" me my land.

Ministry of Accompaniment
From: Sister Alegría

One spring I was at Wallowa Lake United Methodist Camp. One of my tasks was pulling thistles—an invasive species. I cleared a large area of the most-used part of the camp. In September of that year, I was back, this time with an Elder Hostel group. It was the Bicentennial of the exploration by Meriwether Lewis and William Clark et al of the Louisiana Purchase (1802-1805). That was the topic of the educational program; Wallowa Lake is quite close to the route they used.

The program included two hours of voluntary work by each "camper" to help the Camp. The need was for more thistle-pulling. Even though they had each signed up for the program agreeing to the work commitment, no one really wanted to do it.

One afternoon, before dinner, some spent 15 minutes pulling thistles, leaving them beside the trail.

I was furious. As a camp volunteer, I should gather them up and put them in the trash. The hired staff was busy preparing dinner.

Blythe Stanton, an expert at the Ministry of Accompaniment, held the title of Shepherd for this camp. She later confessed that this particular flock was singularly hard to shepherd.

I donned my heavy work gloves and, steaming (but controlling my tongue), I began to clean up the mess. It took three trips. Blythe walked with me all three trips. She said NOTHING. At the end of my task, I was no longer angry and I had learned the value and the power of the Ministry of Accompaniment. I humbly thanked her.

Back in Portland, I talked to almost no one about my plans for the Monastery. In the UMC, a few people indicated that I was crazy. The late Wayne Hill, retired pastor, would talk with me about spiritual growth and the dream/plan for the monastery. He announced, "No one would come." I was intensely grateful for his support, just as it was.

It was hard to tell family members what I was about to do. They love me and would like to have me around. We avoided the topic.

I spent a month at St. Brigid of Kildare Monastery (a United Methodist Benedictine Monastery for women) in Minnesota. Benedictines don't do poverty. That helped me clarify the call to material poverty—a level of poverty that I would not have been able to achieve in the US. I am continually amazed that so few people acknowledge a Divine call to poverty. High tech earplugs, I guess.

January, 2006, I had another Clearness Committee, all unmarried women of a certain age. I wasn't really seeking clearness. I wanted support. I got it.

The Monastery is *Amigas del Señor* (Women Friends of the Lord). At 6 am on Monday, February 1, 2006, Sister Confianza del Señor, then known as Prairie Cutting, and I boarded the Greyhound bus in Portland, Oregon, destination Honduras. We didn't know each other but shared a strong determination to found this monastery.

We had our blue habits, a Spanish Bible and a Spanish hymnal. Some other books were shipped separately. We wrote a book about those first few years: <u>Amigas del Señor: Methodist Monastery</u>, published by Quaker Abbey Press (an Episcopalian Quaker). Being new immigrants is hard.

We were both liberal Christians, used to avoiding all trigger words of Conservative Christianity. We learned those words with new meaning in Spanish. We claimed our job description: *monjas*, nuns.

How I Became a Nun at Amigas del Señor
From: Sister Confianza

Toward the end of the book of Genesis, we are told the story of Joseph, Jacob's favorite son, who was sold into slavery by his jealous brothers. Through a series of unusual events, Joseph eventually becomes the second-in-command to the Pharaoh of Egypt. After seven years of abundant harvest, a famine —foreseen by Joseph— strikes, and soon his brothers come from Israel to purchase grain he had wisely stored up. When Joseph reveals his identity to his brothers, they are shocked and afraid (after all, they were the ones who sold him and then told their father that a wild animal had killed him!). But Joseph reassures them, saying, "Do not be upset or blame yourselves. It was God who made all those things happen so that I would become ruler of Egypt and be able to save you and our father's family during this famine." In looking back over the events of his life, Joseph could see God's hand at work.

Like Joseph, I also see God working in my life in small and large ways when I look back over what has happened to me (though I wouldn't say I've been sent to save anyone). So many rather random and unrelated things came together to bring me to where I am today. I used to believe in coincidences. Now I believe in what someone has called "God-incidences." How did I become a part of Amigas del Señor? Through a series of rather ordinary life events and interests that I can now say God made happen.

As an infant, I was baptized by family friend Wayne Hill into the United Methodist Church, and grew up regularly attending worship and other church activities. By middle school I was clear I wanted to follow Jesus in my own life: to love God and others and to live by the teachings and example of Jesus of Nazareth. In high school and college, I got involved in local and regional church groups, and was particularly passionate about economic justice and equal rights for gay, lesbian, bisexual, and transgender persons. The question in the back of my mind was always, "How can I best serve God in this world, with the gifts and talents God has given me and the skills I develop?"

Prairie (middle) at age 13 with her sister, Autumn, and dad, Craig, 1995

I had a love for music from a young age; both my parents sang and played instruments. In fourth grade I had the chance to take up a band instrument at school. I chose the clarinet, and decided to stick with that single instrument to get really good at it, rather than try others (as I saw my friends doing) and just be OK at many. By tenth grade, I was the top clarinetist at my school. I had the privilege of private music lessons and learned solos for competition; sometimes I played them in church.

From at least eight years of age, I wanted to learn Spanish. I picked up words here and there and in eighth grade grabbed my first opportunity to take a Spanish class. I studied all four years of high school and continued in college. I wanted to go to Latin America, but spent a semester in Milan, Italy, instead because of the requirements for my major in music. In the summer of 2004, I spent five weeks in Guatemala. That whet my appetite to spend a longer time in one location so I could really immerse myself in the language and culture.

Prairie at college graduation with her mom, April, and grandma, Bee, 2004

After graduating from the University of Puget Sound in Tacoma, Washington in 2004, I joined the Lutheran Volunteer Corps (LVC) and moved to St. Paul, Minnesota. This gave me a chance to try direct service work, fulfilling Jesus' instruction to feed the hungry and clothe the naked. I assisted people in getting free groceries at the food shelf where I worked and accessing other resources to help with their other needs. About half the time, I could use my Spanish with immigrant families.

LVC allowed me to experience living in community—a definite call I felt for my life. Six of us volunteers (all with different kinds of jobs) lived in a house together and tried to live out the values of community, sustainability and simplicity, social justice, and faith. It was a good experience, but I wanted something more and deeper. I also found that while I could imagine doing service work part-time, it didn't work well as a full-time gig for me—too draining on my introverted personality.

In spring, 2005, I read a blurb in the "Connector," the email newsletter of the UMC in Oregon and Idaho. Beth Blodgett was seeking a travel companion to go to Honduras for several months that fall and do medical mission work and preparations on the Monastery land. I was certainly interested, but the dates conflicted with my LVC program, so I didn't respond. However, my mom saw the same announcement and forwarded it to me saying, "This sounds like you." With that, I decided to contact Beth.

We had a long and open-hearted email correspondence in which Beth told me about the plans for Amigas del Señor. We met once in person, and she invited me to come for a year in 2006 to help her found the Monastery. Though I knew nothing about monastic life, this fit my dream of spending extended time in Latin America as well as my desire to deepen my spiritual life, so I agreed to come. After one year, I found myself eager to stay on and see how things continued. In 2008, I felt a sense that this could be the life for me, and I became a Postulant. The next stages of my journey are told in this book.

In my search for how to serve God, I knew a few things. Though I had musical training, I didn't want to be a classroom music teacher. I couldn't see how playing in a symphony served others, as the audience is fairly exclusive. Being a church musician was out since I couldn't play piano or guitar. I didn't want to be a pastor like my dad, grandma, and grandpas. Nor did I want to have the kind of job that takes over one's entire life, like what I saw happen to my mom when she was the director of a church camp in upstate New York and we lived onsite. But as God would have it, I seem to be doing some version of all those things now! Being a nun is a 24/7 vocation. It is my whole life. I am doing the work of God, guiding myself and others in spiritual matters, and leading worship. I sing and play recorder, and after years of resistance now also teach music. I marvel at how God works and feel blessed to live in a supportive community, always seeking God's guidance.

Telling Time
From: Sister Confianza

I never considered myself a morning person before moving to Amigas del Señor. As a teenager, I loved sleeping in till 10 am on Saturdays. In college, I never took a class that met before 9 am. I've always found, though, that having a regular schedule helps keep me on top of things. On weekdays, I would get up with just enough time to get dressed and eat breakfast before going to school or work. I knew exactly how much time I needed to get ready (not long), and I hated it when summer camp counselors insisted I get up earlier than I thought necessary.

My wristwatch stopped working in January, 2006, and Beth concurred that I shouldn't replace it. We travelled together to Honduras by bus from Oregon through California, Arizona, Mexico, and Guatemala with just one timepiece: a digital alarm clock. As we began to form our monastic routine while living in a rental house in Limón, I wasn't eager to get up at sunrise; 5:00 just seemed too early.

In May, 2006, the President declared that Honduras would use Daylight Savings Time, so we set our clock ahead an hour. The experiment didn't go over well. When people made appointments, they would say, "Old time or new time?" (Not that Hondurans arrive at the designated hour anyway.) Pretty soon the Government rescinded, and we've been on what you call Central Standard Time ever since. However, the experience helped me let go of my time issues. With the sun rising at 4 am during those months, I recognized that time measurement is a human invention. The clock could say 5 or 4 or 12, but the sun will rise when the sun will rise! From then on I've gotten up in time for prayers at first light.

We also go to bed quite early—usually between 8 and 9 pm. My old desire to sleep in left as I found I easily got plenty of sleep at night.

When Beth and I moved out to the newly-built Monastery (constructed by Chito's nephew Mateo) in July of that year, we decided to set aside the clock and live more fully with the sun. I was excited to learn to live the rhythms of nature, watching the sun come up in the east and set in the west. It rises over the hills in a different spot each day, further north in the summer and south in the winter. I decide when to build our dinner fire based on how high above the west peak the sun is, with an internal sense of how much daylight is left. (We try to be finished eating and cleaned up before dark.)

Even without a clock, we can still "tell time" based on the shadows during the day and the location of the stars or moon at night. The house is more or less oriented to the four directions, with the front door facing west. Noon is when the roof's shadow hits the west end of the kitchen, which is separated from the living quarters by a breezeway. Checking against the clock or a visitor's watch helped me correspond the hour to how far out the shadow is from the house.

Rainy days are a different matter. Then we have to go by feel (e.g. if we're hungry, it must be lunch time). We've misjudged on

17

occasion and ended up cooking dinner in the dark or getting up long before morning. We go with the flow.

Amigas del Señor Monastery, 2006

After a while we gave away the alarm clock and obtained a wristwatch—not for telling time, but so Beth could calculate respiration rates at the clinic. During the five years of this book, we didn't keep a working clock in the Monastery. On days at home, we pulled out the stem to keep the watch from ticking, thereby saving the battery. When we went to town or travelled and it seemed important to know the hour, I surreptitiously read other people's watches. In worship and other spiritual practices, we try to relax and have a sense of sacred space and time, letting the Spirit guide us in how long to spend in activity, silence, and sharing. This is our ultimate goal: to live according to God's time.

Beggars
From: Sister Alegría

Monastic tradition includes having an almoner: a nun or monk with the specific duty of responding to beggars.

We wear hidden pockets in the front of the dress. It is awkward to carry all denominations of bills at once. We quickly decided to have one Sister carry the large bills: 100 and 500 lempiras. The other would carry the smaller bills: 1, 2, 5, 10, 20, and 50. I carry the larger and Sister Confianza carries the smaller ones, making her Almoner. Why Sister Confianza and not me? Because it would be easy for me, not a useful spiritual practice at all, but she was quite shy. She gradually grew into the role. She gives two to ten lempiras to any individual beggar.

Often, organized trips of teams to Honduras are told not to give alms. Good idea. They don't know how. I had learned how in my many months in Honduras before we founded the Monastery. With a long-term commitment to the country, one must learn. Jesus says to give alms, so we do.

Sister Alegría and a row of newly-planted pineapple sprouts
in the hillside garden, 2008

The every-six-weeks haircut, 2012

2

Learning Poverty

"Prayer and comfortable living are incompatible."—Teresa of Avila

Determined To Do God's Will
From: Sister Alegría

     One Sunday morning I was driving to Early Unprogrammed Worship at Multnomah Monthly Meeting in Portland, Oregon, heading west on SE Powell Boulevard. There was a conservative Christian Church along the way. At the entrance were two dressed-up middle-aged white men, hugging each other. It broke my heart. Every movement, every detail of their posture virtually screamed, "We don't know how to do this but we're going to do it anyway!" They were not guys who had learned from their fathers to hug other men. But in the last few years of the 20th Century, real men hug other men, so they would do it.

     Prairie Cutting and I didn't know how to be poor by world standards or specific rural Honduran standards, but we were determined to do it. God had called us to poverty. Our stuttering answer, *"Sí, Señor,"* is revealed throughout this book, but especially in this chapter.

Buying Medicines
From: Beth   Date: July 23, 2008

     Today, we are in the town of Bonito. It has a bank and an internet, both important for our needs today. We called Eloyda on Monday to make a medicine order for Centro de Salud. Today, we learned the cost ($764) and deposited that amount in her account. She'll send the medicines by bus. They'll be delivered to Andres' store in Limón, and he'll send them on to the public health clinic. There

21

are a few medicines we buy that the government either doesn't send at all or sends a fraction of what we need. Those are: Benadryl liquid, hexachlorophene soap, a good cough suppressant, and iron tablets for adults. The other medicines are less predictable about when we need how much. We order enough to share with the other two smaller public health clinics in the county.

We also withdrew $212 for our month's expenses. Of course, we don't need that much, except that the water tank still needs a repair and that will be costly. We are learning about poverty. We still have a lot to learn.

Garden and Sewing Progress and Home Improvement
From: Prairie   Date: July 23, 2008

Plans for the Monastery have always included raising our own fruits and vegetables. We want to have a balanced diet, but produce is expensive and the available variety is limited. As we live in an agricultural region, growing it ourselves is the obvious solution. Unfortunately, the soil on our land is poor and the hillsides are steep. Chemical fertilizers and herbicides are commonly used around here, but Beth and I are committed to organic farming. We often feel discouraged by the less-than-bountiful results from our efforts.

Since early this year we have wanted some manure. At the end of May, we paid a neighbor to bring us six sacks of it. It seemed like the next thing to do was hire someone to help us apply it and get other things going in the garden. June is the beginning of a rainy season and a good time to plant.

Beth and I discovered a house not far from ours where two men are living and caring for the property of a man named Elías, who lives in Limón. We talked to them, and they were willing to come work with us.

The question of paying people to work for us isn't an easy one. We feel called to live in voluntary poverty, alongside our neighbors who don't choose to be poor. Yet, we have money in the bank—more than we need. Part of our stewardship of the money we have is to put it back in the local economy or donate it. When we go to town, we try to buy snacks made by local people instead of packaged ones. We give to beggars and purchase medicines for the public health clinic.

When we hire someone, we try to pay a fair wage. We pay 100 lempiras (Honduran currency, about $5.50) for a five-hour workday, as compared to the 60 or so that the big oil palm plantation in Plan de Flores pays. We also feed our workers lunch and work with them, whether alongside them in the garden, or doing our house and kitchen work. This helps remind us that we are not hiring servants to give us leisure time.

The two neighbor guys have helped us about once a week since then, and now we are finally feeling caught up in our agricultural work. We got the manure put down on all the fruit trees, and used some to plant various types of beans for cover crops. The beans will protect the ground from the rain as well as enrich the soil and provide nitrogen-rich mulch. (Beans and other legumes "fix" nitrogen, a necessary nutrient, in the soil through bacteria that live on their roots.) The guys were also able to bring us some pineapple starts, which we planted along with some sprouts from the plants we already had. We now have nearly seventy pineapple plants in the garden above the creek.

Beth admires a ripe pineapple (view is looking south from the porch), 2008

To our delight, we recently harvested a few pineapples of the ones we planted two years ago. We are learning at what point the fruits should be picked: when they just begin to turn yellow. When we picked one while it was still green, it took two weeks to ripen and didn't have much flavor. One that we didn't pick ripened to a bright yellow on the plant and got partially eaten by a bird! (The part we could salvage was sweet and juicy.) We were also pleasantly surprised to learn from the guys that some *yuca* plants, which we had given up on, have actually borne some food, so we've been enjoying the addition of that tuber to our diet. Plus, one *plátano* (plantain) and one banana plant are currently putting on fruit, so we'll have something to eat next month from them. It gives me hope for the future; there is so much waiting involved, it can be hard to be patient.

The men also did some wood splitting, which freed up some of our time to work on sewing. At our Monthly Meeting for Worship with Attention to Business on July 3, Beth and I affirmed our unity on the fabric to use for blouses for Postulants, which we both are. We think it will serve for Novices as well. We bought six yards of the green gingham back in May and now have made us each a blouse. We also decided to try having just three blouses each, and will keep on sewing to make the rest of them from the new fabric.

Prairie at the treadle sewing machine, 2008

Up till now, we've each had four or five miscellaneous blouses that we brought from the US or made from other colorful cloth. Soon we will be wearing matching habits. The discernment has been slow on what the uniforms should be, and we are excited to have the discipline and simplicity of wearing the same outfit every day. It helps keep us from concerning ourselves about worldly things like fashion, and reminds us that we have dedicated our lives to God instead.

Another improvement the guys made for us was to build several benches. There is now one on each side of the back door where we do morning and afternoon prayers, and two among trees further from the house for meditation and other uses. It is an expansion of our living and prayer space and it is a dream we've had for a while.

It is nice to feel caught up on the gardening and on top of the sewing projects—which doesn't mean we slow down!

Sister Alegría sorts beans, 2013

There are always beans and corn to sort for cooking (we were grateful to buy fifty pounds of corn from a friend the other week who delivered it to our door on a donkey), hymns to pick and practice for our worship times, cooking, sewing, and firewood cutting and discernment on so many topics. All of this to support a life of prayer dedicated to seeking God first. May I learn to trust more fully in God's provision and strength.

How Poor are We?
From: Sister Alegría

Our neighbors/workers gave us a lot of advice from their own experience. We gradually realized that they assumed we would be buying and applying chemical fertilizers. We wouldn't be.

One day they encouraged us about passion fruit planting and care, telling us about Teddy Goff's shady arbor with passion fruit. I was puzzled. Teddy Goff is rich.

Oh! Our neighbors see us as rich; the advice they would give to us if they believed we were poor would be very different. Why would they believe that we were poor when we could afford to hire them?

Lost My Glasses
From: Beth   Date: August 27, 2008

Here we are in Bonito, with lots of news to tell you. But it is hard to do it. We hitched a ride in the back of a pickup truck. It was windy. My glasses left my head. I can find the ñ on the keyboard, so, hopefully, you can read what I write. But I can't proofread it.

I still have a pair of old glasses at the Monastery. When we return, I'll get them out.

The biggest event in August for me was my 8 day silent retreat for end of Postulancy followed by my Reception as a Novice on Sunday.

Planning a retreat for half of the Monastery is no small thing. Since we live as do most other poor Hondurans, there is a lot of physical work to do. First item for planning is to decide what work could just be left aside (gardening and sewing). Second, what work could I do and still be on retreat. We decide that sorting corn and beans, grinding corn, and washing dishes all qualified. These are all meditative and can be done without verbal consultation.

Prairie would do all of the meal planning, cooking, etc. As in the tradition of Little Brother Francis, she would be Sister Guardian during my retreat.

We start and end the retreat on Thursdays, which are our usual fast days, when we have midweek Unprogrammed Worship. We start the retreat with our usual August monthly day-long retreat. Prairie volunteers to lead it. She also leads the last day closing activities. It is a great privilege to live in a small monastery with so

26

much spiritual intimacy and it is such a privilege to watch this young woman grow before my eyes.

Back to the retreat: I participate in the three Programmed Worships each day, including reading aloud and singing. The silence is the rest of the time.

Novice means beginner. Well, now I am a beginner. It has been quite a stress on us poor pre-beginners.

The major work of the Postulancy is renunciation. That means to put behind yourself what is past, to make your life empty so there is room for God and God's will. Renounce is not the same as denounce. Denounce implies that there is something bad to be rid of. Renounce is often of very good things. An ordinary part of spiritual growth is giving up something good for something better.

Much of the time of my retreat is spent in reviewing and then ripping up my journals. Since I often put the most painful thoughts in the journal, it is not especially an easy spiritual practice. But that is my job and I do it.

We have a lovely ceremony for my Reception into the Novitiate. Prairie officiates. She also speaks for you when it is time for the congregation to promise to support and uphold me.

The scripture readings include Jeremiah 1:4-8. I read it. I am not saying that I read it in a clear, strong voice. No, the hanky is very handy to have.

We read Psalm 100. One must never miss a chance to remind ourselves that celebrating God is the main thing in prayer.

The Gospel is Matthew 22:37-38, the first and most important commandment, and the second which is like unto it.

Then Prairie reads advice from our old friend Deutero-Paul in his letter to the Ephesians about putting on the whole armor of God, a good exhortation.

The "sermon" is a talk given by Basil Hume to a group of his Novices a generation ago, very helpful. It is good to have at least one senior monastic present at such a ceremony.

Most of our hymns are from the Spanish hymnal *Mil Voces Para Celebrar*, and not available in English. We also sing the Spanish versions of "Here I am, Lord" and "Trust and Obey," a favorite from my childhood.

The creed is the Hispanic Creed found in the Spanish hymnal. We use a modified order of worship for baptism and renewal of vows.

Really, all of it is very cool. I put on my new habit. We have decided that the sleeveless habit is for Sojourners, Aspirants, and

Postulants.   Sleeved dress is for Novices and avowed Sisters. Discernment is a major spiritual practice for us.

After our worship and ceremony, we have a reception of sorts. Prairie baked snickerdoodles on Saturday afternoon. I made limeade. Special treats!

A New Dog
From: Prairie   Date: August 27, 2008

We have a new addition to the Monastery: a dog! We have been talking about wanting one for at least a year and a half. They are good for announcing visitors and scaring away wild animals (like the one that has eaten our *yuca*) or potential predators of chickens, which we'd like to raise.

Prairie and Belén, 2008

The last evening of Beth's retreat, Wednesday, August 13, some neighbor boys came over to visit. They had a small brown and black dog on a string, and after we'd chatted and hung out for a little while, they said they wanted to sell him. I told them that we'd be interested, but I couldn't make the decision on my own, and Beth was keeping silence until the next day. They said they could come back then, but they wanted to leave the dog with us for the night. So we tied it to a post on the porch. The poor thing yowled and howled when the boys walked away. I tried to comfort it for a while by petting and scratching him, but throughout the night he had crying fits.

The next afternoon when the retreat was over, Beth and I finally talked about the dog. The boys wanted 300 lempiras for it which is a lot of money around here (about $16, or three days' wages) but we had seen another puppy sold for that amount. It seemed this was just the opportunity we'd been waiting for, so when the boys returned, we paid them, and became first-time dog owners.

The dog is close to a year old. The boys said his name was Biónico. We weren't too pleased about that name. Since there is a tradition of changing one's name when entering a monastery, we started thinking of possibilities. We figured something religious would be good. Maybe an Old Testament warrior like Goliath or David, or an apostle like Pedro or Pablo. We wanted something that would be easy to say, but we didn't like all the baggage that came with the Biblical names... Then Beth had the idea of using a place name from the Bible. I said, "How about Belén?" (That's Bethlehem in Spanish.) It rolls off the tongue and even starts with the same letter as his previous name. So we tried it out, and it stuck. He was coming when called within 24 hours.

Our first big test was Monday, when we had to go to town. Back in April, the same neighbors had given us a malnourished puppy, but when we returned from Limón that Monday, he had disappeared. With Belén, we made sure he was tied up securely, and left food and water for him, as recommended by our Honduran friends. We also decided to work only briefly at the clinic so as to be able to come home as early as possible. He howled as we left, but he was happily waiting for us when we got back at noon.

For the first week, as recommended, we kept him tied up almost constantly, taking him out on a rope leash to go to the bathroom, and down to the creek with us. Several nights he had bouts of howling and whining. I was losing sleep from it, and I didn't know what to do. Beth had put me in charge of Belén's training and care, as I have a little more experience with dogs than she (my dad got a dog when I was in high school). I found myself a bit anxious and stressed, trying to figure out what to do with him when he cried or had other problems. One day when we went to the creek, I let him run loose. He went off in the woods and didn't come back when I called. We came back to the house without him, and I was overrun with guilt. After a few minutes, however, he came trotting back happily. That was a huge relief. It gave me a boost in confidence about his progress; he had already learned that this is home.

Now we are letting him off leash more often. Belén is generally well-behaved (he sleeps a lot on the porch), and he has a friendly disposition. We just don't know how to play with him! Beth and I practice with *"Ven*—Come" once or twice a day and we plan to start teaching him a few more commands as well. Some of the process is figuring out exactly what we want from him—what we want him to do (yes, bark to announce visitors; no, don't jump on us when we are having prayers...). We are using every resource we have from our memories and a little dog training book in Spanish. Happily, Belén seems to be a fast learner.

Another challenge is feeding him. Everyone around here says they just feed their dogs tortillas, though dog food can be purchased (not cheaply). We bought some to use as training rewards. We are feeding Belén a lot of *pinol* (toasted-corn porridge), but he prefers the tortillas. He's not consistent in the amount he eats either, but it is close to what one of us eats at a meal so that means we have to make significantly more food! And, of course, he gets the bones when we have chicken or fish on Mondays. (The meat gives us our vitamin B12 for the week.)

So there is much to learn—for the dog and for us—but I am truly grateful at how quickly he's coming along. It seems he is meant to be the Monastery dog, after just two weeks.

Ongoing Water Issues
From: Prairie   Date: August 27, 2008

The rains finally came in late June, and our 800-gallon water tank began refilling. However, because of the damage from a wildfire in April, there were drips all around the base, and they kept getting worse. We figured we were losing several gallons of water every day. Finally, at the beginning of August, we talked to Mateo about coming to repair it properly. (He had done a quick fix right after the fire.) We had to empty out the tank for that, and to our surprise it was nearly full. We saved some water in our wash tubs and buckets. Mateo put a nice thick layer of cement inside and out. When next it rained, we let the tank begin to fill up.

Then we noticed that the water tasted horrible. It had white particles and a slippery feel. We guessed it was cement residue, so one morning, I went in through the trap door on top to wash it out as well as I could, using some rainwater to rinse the walls and floor.

We started collecting rainwater from the downspout in buckets for use in the kitchen and bathroom.

Prairie peeks out from the trapdoor on the water tank, 2007

That was almost three weeks ago, and we haven't had any rain since! Now we are hauling five gallons of water a day up from the creek, bathing and washing our clothes down there, and praying, once again, for rain. The amazing part is that it is not a source of anxiety for me as it had been in the past. So, the tank is dry, and we go to the creek every day as just part of the routine.

Health Care
From: Beth   Date: September 24, 2008

A few weeks ago, I gave a consult to a 64-year-old woman, who had come in with her ten-year-old granddaughter. They live in a remote neighborhood of our county. On Sunday, they walked four hours to Plan de Flores. On Monday, they came for health care. On Tuesday, they walked back home. That is three days for two doctor visits.

The grandmother had a bladder infection. We were out of the three best medicines for her. I treated her with the fourth choice

31

antibiotic which is what I had. I find this very frustrating. It is frustrating trying to explain the systemic aspects of poverty. I have no idea how much money she has or doesn't have. I know that she may have invested her three days searching for health care only to receive an antibiotic that might not help her.

I do know that the ten-year-old was anemic. We did have worm medicine and iron drops for her.

The following week, a visiting medical team donated amoxicillin, Cefzil, and cephalexin to the Centro de Salud. We are very grateful. We are now back in action. They also donated a lot of ready to outdate anti-hypertensive drugs, which bummed out the professional nurse, who worries about our hypertensive patients. The rest of us just celebrated the antibiotics available again.

Eating as a Spiritual Practice
From: Prairie   Date: September 25, 2008

When Beth and I first moved to Honduras at the beginning of 2006, we had a lot of adjusting to do. One of the things that faced us daily was food. We were determined to learn to eat what Hondurans eat: beans and corn tortillas. Within our first month living in a little rented house in Limón we got a lesson on making tortillas with *maseca* (corn flour), pressing out the *masa* (dough), on circles cut from plastic bags and cooking them in a pan on the electric stove. We had challenges every time we made them: how wet or soft should the *masa* be? How hot the pan? We also had to learn about beans. The only kind available here are small red beans. Another challenge was learning to live without refrigeration. We heard that a pot of beans would keep if it were boiled once a day, but we tossed out several batches before we figured out they needed to be boiled morning AND night.

During those first few months in town, Beth didn't eat much at meals. She didn't really like the beans and tortillas. Sometimes she was sick and lost her appetite. Only recently did she tell me that she had wanted me to get enough to eat (she thought I was a pickier eater than I am) and she often gave me a larger portion of the more special foods to make sure I ate enough.

We bought vegetables as often as we could. The selection was limited and included: mostly cabbage, carrots, tomatoes, green peppers and onions. I remember many meals of scrambled eggs with peppers, onions and tomatoes — a dish we both really enjoyed. (Beth says she doesn't remember ENOUGH of those meals.) With no refrigeration, we thought we couldn't have leftovers. I sometimes felt like a garbage disposal, eating whatever was left at the end of a meal. Ironic how she thought she was helping me, and to me it felt like a burden. Beth lost a lot of weight during those months, and I was gaining.

When we moved out to the Monastery at the end of July, 2006, we had to learn how to cook all over again, using the *fogón*, a traditional wood-burning stove built by Mateo's wife Margarita. It was such a challenge building, starting, and keeping the fire going (besides finding and cutting firewood). We also learned to make flour tortillas which took us months to get comfortable with. In November of that year, we bought our first corn in grains and we slowly began to learn how to cook it, grind it, and make authentic corn tortillas. It was a lot of work, but they tasted good; we were really beginning to like the tortillas and beans.

In the months after moving out here, I gained more weight and filled out some. People commented on how good I was looking, and that the "country life" seemed to suit me. I began to understand that here, for a woman to be on the plump side is a sign she's doing well: the family has plenty of food, and she doesn't have to work too hard. I had a bit of an inner conflict, still thinking thinner is better. Beth says that to her doctor's eyes, I never got to the point of being unhealthily overweight, but I was close.

After returning from my visit to the US in June, 2007, I decided to change my eating habits. Beth had mentioned that a difference of 100 calories a day would mean a change of ten pounds in a year (whether more or fewer). I began to eat a bit less, stopping before I was completely full, and having fewer snacks. Beth had gotten sick and lost more weight while I was gone, so she was trying to gain it back. I tried to eat no more—or at least not much more—than she did.

Since we volunteer at Centro de Salud (the public health clinic) every Monday, we have the opportunity to regularly check our weight. I watched mine go down from 165 pounds in August, 2007, to 145 in March of 2008—that's twenty pounds in seven months. I had never intentionally lost weight before, and I was pretty pleased with myself.

I also noticed my developing muscle tone. Our active lifestyle includes splitting firewood with an ax, working with a machete, walking up and down hills, and other physical work. I have more upper arm strength than ever in my life, and more than I ever thought I might. When my weight got down to 145, I noticed that my forearms looked thin to my eyes, and my wrists bony, so I decided that that was probably a fine weight to maintain.

Prairie washes cooked corn, 2007

In October, 2006, Beth had made a goal of maintaining her weight at 135 to 138 pounds for one year, which she did. Since then, she has stopped weighing herself so regularly. She thought it wouldn't be bad to gain about five pounds during her trip to the US in February, but that didn't happen, probably because she was careful to only eat one dessert a day. Then, in mid-August, she checked her weight and it was at 128; she had lost weight unintentionally. We began to talk about how to help her gain it back and for us both to maintain our weights. Beth is unable to eat as much volume at meals as I am, so we talked about having more higher-calorie foods, like fried plantains. I had been averse to eating much fatty food. My first-world cultural training says that it is unhealthy, but the circumstances are different here. Our active lifestyle takes a lot of calories. When we lived in town, I tried to mix up just enough *masa* to make six tortillas for a meal: three each and no leftovers. Now, I want to make sure there are at least six tortillas for each of us and it is even better if there are leftovers for snacks! We have learned that foods can, in fact, be kept from one meal to the next without refrigeration. Toasting the leftover tortillas has them keep even better and they're yummy!

I told Beth I had been eating snacks. It turned out she had been being careful NOT to eat snacks, as a spiritual practice. We decided that if one of us wants a snack, to announce it. Then we can snack together as needed: a lesson in community living.

The last weekend in August, unbeknownst to me, Beth fervently prayed for God to provide some high-calorie food. That Wednesday, a neighbor who milks cows brought us a gallon of milk. (Pedro had borrowed money from us, and it was a way to repay the debt, bit by bit.) That Saturday, he sent three more liters. We were overwhelmed. The milk, of course, is whole, which is problematic because Beth has had high cholesterol. We thought a little less would be ideal—maybe two liters twice a week—but when Pedro came again on Tuesday with another three, we accepted it.

Sister Confianza toasts tortillas on the *comal*, 2012

Last Wednesday, Walter, a member of Pedro's household, came over with two liters. On Thursday, we visited a different neighbor who also has cows. She gave us some *cuajada* (fresh cheese) and promised to send milk the next day. On Friday morning, one of her sons arrived with three liters of milk. We were happy. We had just about finished boiling it (done twice a day to keep it good without refrigeration), when Walter arrived with two more liters of milk! We put that on to boil as well. Somehow, we drank it all before going to town Monday morning.

We've had quite a special diet the last few weeks, including pancakes, cream sauces and soup, *pinol* mush with milk, and cups of milk at meals or as snacks. Because of the cholesterol, we skim the milk as well as we can and give the cream to the dog. We've even given him some milk to drink. Already, my wrists aren't quite as thin. I may have to stop stuffing myself at meals again!

We have been so grateful and amazed at how God answered Beth's prayer. As it has been said, "Be careful what you pray for, for surely it will be yours."

Oil is Food
From: Sister Confianza

One of my reservations about using a lot of oil was that I thought it was expensive. We've since learned otherwise. Subsistence farmers, who eat only what they grow, don't have a major source of fat unless they are able to raise pigs or grow and process coconuts, though some shows up in the corn and produce like avocados. That means that cooking fat—here, usually shortening or oil from African palm—must be purchased with the limited cash one has. In that way it's "expensive"—because it must be bought.

Salt also must be purchased, though the unrefined salt only costs two lempiras per pound. There's a saying that one eats *"tortillas sin sal"* (tortillas without salt) when one is really cash poor.

At the Monastery, we do not grow our own staple foods; we purchase everything. In that way, we are more like poor people in the city. We eat proportionally more of the foods that cost less. Corn and wheat flours and sugar each cost ten lempiras (about fifty cents) per pound. Corn in whole grains costs half that much, and green bananas are also usually cheap, so we eat primarily those when they are available. Rice costs eleven lempiras a pound, so we eat less of it.

At one point, we calculated the cost of the cooking oil we buy. Though the price is 24 lempiras per pound, it is much more calorie-dense than grains, and thus is actually a cheaper food! So we chose, more like the urban poor, to use more oil in our cooking—until 2011 when we admitted that it was causing acid reflux for Sister Alegría.

Food (In)security

From: Beth   Date: September 25, 2008

I have not been completely open with you about one thing: my weight. My mother gets these updates and she worries. But I've been thinking things over and feeling guilty about keeping secrets. I have, therefore, decided that at 91, she is a grown-up and can "take it."

It is a struggle to keep my weight up. Poor people don't eat rich food. Rich food is costly. We eat a pretty good diet. We have a good friend, Judy Billings, a dietician who gives us lots of free consults by email. We are just coming off a month of a well-balanced diet.

The problem is calories. Beans are usually cooked without oil. Corn tortillas are prepared without oil. Rice is usually fixed with a little oil, but rice has jumped in price and we don't eat it often. It is quite possible to eat boiled green bananas, beans, and corn tortillas and have no fat in the diet for a few days.

We live a very high calorie life. We are active. Some days are 2,000 calorie days. I don't eat that much in a day. Overfilling my stomach is miserable.

So, the day after a very active day (e.g., Mondays, in which we walk 2-6 miles, much in hills, and half with backpacks of groceries), I am in calorie deficit. We do more sedentary work on Tuesdays and cook higher calorie foods that day.

Poor people are skinny in Honduras. Our sometimes neighbors called the nursing mother in their group, *"la flaquita,"* "skinny."

When we realized that I had lost about 4 pounds without intending to, we had to relook at our whole food and cooking situation. Bad management. We hope to do better. The idea is that monastics think about God, not food. Well, they shouldn't waste away while doing that.

Fortunately, we now have two neighbor families giving us whole milk. I have regained more than a pound in two weeks. As long as these neighbors last and the cows don't go dry, we expect to be consuming a lot of milk!

My grandmother used to say that she didn't want to be a skinny old lady. I remember those words. Now I am a skinny old lady. In Honduras, 60 is *"la tercera edad,"* "the third age," and I turn 61 next week. As we were sorting through our consternation about the weight thing, it was said, "Maybe we are called to be skinny."

Yes, maybe we are, called to be skinnier than we already are, which, by Honduran standards, is already on the thin side. We are learning more about what it means to choose poverty. It is a slow process.

The Community Table
From: Sister Alegría

I once read an article in <u>National Geographic</u> written by an anthropologist who lived with the Pygmies in central Africa. The men go out to hunt, singly or in groups. Once, the men found no game, but they did find a large bee tree. They gorged themselves on honey and honeycomb, arriving home with protruding abdomens and no food for the extended family. No one challenged their assertions that they could find no food.

That is an extreme case. I (or we, the small subgroup) take care of myself first. It is opposite to our monastic values, where all have equal access to whatever food we have. We have a community table. We all eat or no one eats. It's quite simple, once you get your mind around it.

Occasionally, I have written in my journal: "There was enough food." That's means, "We ate everything, there was nothing left." With Teresa of Avila we say, "If God wants us to eat, God will send us food." By definition there is always enough.

Sisters Alegría and Confianza sing grace at lunch, 2012

Knives and Neighbors
From: Beth   Date: September 25, 2008

As Prairie and I transition from excess and wealth (our state before coming here) to our chosen material poverty, we notice the aids we have used in that transition. One of the aids was a pair of folding knives that my mother gave me before leaving the States. We have used them quite a bit in the kitchen. We had just worn out the clasp on one of them and we had begun to think that we might be ready to go without them. We hadn't decided yet. They were quite a nice luxury, after all.

On Monday, September 15, neighbor Walter came over. He brought two liters of milk and he split some firewood for us. We were grateful. Three times Walter asked for a loan of money. Three times I turned him down. He said that his son was sick and he needed money to take him to Bonito to buy medicine.

September 15 is Independence Day. That's why we were home, clinic closed. I told him he could bring the child over and I would do a consult and I would bring the medicines back on Tuesday when we returned from Centro de Salud. OK. But they didn't show up.

Later that afternoon, I was washing dishes and noticed that the two knives were missing. There was no question about how they had disappeared.

So, after noticing how vulnerable we felt in the face of this theft, we had to decide what else we felt and what we wanted to do about it.

We didn't have long to wait. On Wednesday, Walter came again, with two more liters of milk, and ready to work for us for the morning.

OK, but first, I told him that we knew he had taken the knives. He began to deny it, but I asked him to just listen and not to say anything. (Child development: if you ask a child to confess, you are really asking him to lie to you, and how does adding a lie to a theft help anything?)

I had not planned what I would say, but I told him that my mother had given us those knives to help us as we left our nation to start a new life in a new country. I told him that she didn't know that a Honduran kitchen wouldn't usually have knives like that. It was a powerful and spirit-filled time.

Then I showed him the work to do to start the morning. He kept a wide berth from the kitchen door. We all worked in the garden and we ate lunch together as we would normally do when someone works with us. A lot of hard physical work got done.

The stolen knives are now a resolved issue in my mind. I would never have guessed two years ago, that such a thing could happen. A theft on Monday, a resolution on Wednesday. Maybe this monastic stuff works.

Walter worked for us again on Friday. We all worked together in the garden. We got a lot done. I think about the Book of Ezra. The Israelites came back from their exile ready to rebuild the temple. The neighbors came over offering to help build the temple. The Israelites said, NO, we have to do it ourselves (i.e., you aren't good enough to help build the temple). The neighbors were instantly converted to enemies who did all in their power to thwart the construction and more.

By the way, Walter was a very good student as I was teaching him the lunch prayer to sing. "For health and strength and daily bread, we give you thanks oh Lord." It's nice in Spanish. He didn't learn it completely, but he made a good start.

I'm sure you have neighbors, too, who give you cause for gratitude and discouragement, maybe, like Walter, even in the same day. And, of course, we are the neighbors who give him cause for gratitude and discouragement in the same day.

An Invitation
From: Prairie   Date: October 22, 2008

Back in June, Beth and I went to Plan de Flores to find a girl we'd met at Centro de Salud named Maylín and to invite her to visit the Monastery. When we visited with Maylín that day, she asked us when she could come. We said, "How about next Monday?" We suggested she could come meet us at Centro de Salud in Limón, and we would all come back to the Monastery together. Maylín thought she'd come for two or three days. Before leaving, we blessed her by putting a hand on her head and shoulder and praying over her, something we have learned in the Honduran churches. She smiled.

During the next few days we did some house cleaning and set up a bunk in anticipation of her visit. On Monday, June 30, we went in to work as usual, keeping our eyes open for Maylín. She didn't show up.

The next week, we went to Limón wondering if we'd see Maylín. When she didn't show up by the end of the workday, we decided to go to Plan de Flores and to track her down to see what was going on. We hopped a bus to go the twenty minutes in the opposite direction from home.

Maylín was at her aunt's house where she lives. She hadn't expected us, so we waited in the living room while she bathed and changed her clothes. Two men came in with beers and they sat down to watch TV (Mexican soap operas that we were now familiar with from our first visit). Outside a young man was lying on the ground, passed out. When he started puking, a woman went out with a broom and she sent him home, then she cleaned up the mess. We realized that they sell alcohol there, like a bar. Beth was disconcerted and she later said, "That is no place for a sixteen-year-old girl to be growing up. She is basically being trained to hook up with a drunk."

When Maylín finally came out, we talked only briefly. She gave some excuse about why she didn't come the week before, but said she might come "anytime." That's the line people here use when they think something is a nice idea, but they aren't promising anything. We told her she was welcome to come any Monday to Centro de Salud. Then we left. Only afterward did Beth start to think of other questions she might have asked or things she could have said to Maylín.

We have not seen Maylín since, but about a month later, Maylín's cousin came in for a doctor visit with Beth. "Do you have a message for her?" she asked.

"Yes," Beth said. "What is the purpose of your life?"

On the 1st of October, the new caretakers at Elías' property visited us. The family moved here from Las Hicoteas, the town just east of Plan de Flores. As we were chatting, the mother asked about "the girl from Plan de Flores who wanted to be a nun." We explained that she had never come.

Beth and I were impressed that the news of Maylín had spread. We realized that our "recruiting" trip to Plan de Flores did more publicity for us than anything we might have planned ourselves. The message is getting out that there are options for women besides having babies at a young age.

Update on Maylín
From: Sister Confianza

The possibility of being a nun may be a little more well-known than in the past, but it still isn't the choice girls make around here. About a year after we visited her, Maylín came in to Centro de

Learning Poverty

Salud for her first prenatal check-up. Like so many of her peers, she became a single mother as a teenager.

In March, 2016, we ran into a woman who introduced herself as "Maylín's mom." "She always remembers you," she told us. Maylín has two kids now, a boy and a girl.

Dry Compost Toilet Great Success
From: Beth   Date: November 25, 2008

As you know, we are learning by doing. Lots of times we learn what not to do. But once in a while, it just all works.

The dry compost toilet was installed in August of 2006. (Many rural homes don't have a latrine of any kind.) One hole for urine which goes out a tube to be used for fertilizer. Another hole for poop, paper, and whatever other compostable stuff you want to toss into it.

We used one of the twin seats for a year and a half, then switched to the other, and let the waste sit as directed for several more months before "harvesting" the compost. This month we opened it up. Beautiful rich compost!! We are thrilled.

Another Wild Week in our Life
From: Prairie   Date: December 10, 2008

On Sunday, October 19, Walter and his younger brother came over. We hadn't seen him for several weeks. I had felt slightly uncomfortable around Walter ever since his first visit when he took the knives, but we had a friendly chat, and they gave us some *plátanos.*

The next day, we met Walter on the road as we went to Limón to work in Centro de Salud as usual. When we got home in the afternoon, I noticed that the bathroom door was open. Had we not latched it well? Then I saw that the latch on the front door had been pried off. "Beth," I said, "Our house has been broken into." The dog, Belén, was still tied in his spot outside the door, unharmed and as happy to see us as usual. We wondered what he had seen and experienced.

We stood outside for a moment, uncertain of what to do. In the States, one is told not to enter the house in such a situation. There, you would call the police, and they would come and check it out. We, of course, don't have a phone, and our experience here is that the police aren't interested in such things. So, we walked around the house to make sure there was nobody still around before going in.

Prairie puts ashes down the dry compost toilet, 2006

The place was a mess: storage boxes pulled out and things strewn about. Only the bookshelves were left untouched. There was a stick of firewood inside—defense against the dog, we guessed. That evening and the next morning we cleaned up and we noted what was missing: the guitar, three unused mattresses (from the empty bunks), the digital camera, a machete and files, yards of fabric for blouses, and some odd things like my wrist braces and bottles of sunscreen, mosquito repellent, and glue. My first suspicion was Walter, but I had no concrete evidence. I wondered if I was judging unfairly. We're open with everybody about the fact that we're not home on Mondays.

We were disappointed to have been robbed a second time within twelve months. At the same time, it felt like we were being relieved of unnecessary material goods, and thereby moving closer to living in true poverty. It also crossed my mind that the fewer things we have, the less there is to steal, or be attractive to thieves. Even so, we figure that being gringos, we are automatically seen as rich and that may never change.

On Wednesday, we went to Bonito Oriental. We bought a new machete and files which seem to be essential to this life (in truth, we still haven't finished sharpening it to use; we're getting by with the one that wasn't stolen). On our way there, we stopped in Limoncito to tell Mateo about the robbery. He wasn't home, but we talked with his wife Margarita.

After telling our story, we asked what was up with them.

"I'm going to be left *sola*," she told us.

"What do you mean?"

"Mateo is leaving for the US—on Friday."

Only two days away! His brother in Houston had sent for him, meaning he would pay for his way to go *mojado*, (wetback: illegally through Mexico). Margarita said that in 23 years of marriage they'd never spent even a week apart. She didn't like the prospect of being left to run everything alone (including a property with cattle), even with young adult children to help. We were concerned for Mateo's safety and for the loss of a friend and helper. Beth told Margarita to give him a message: "He needs to give you enough kisses in the next two days to make up for the year he plans to be gone." Margarita blushed and we headed off.

On Thursday afternoon, Mateo showed up at our house. "So you're going to the States," we said.

"No," he replied. "I decided not to go. The job my brother had lined up wasn't going to pay enough, only $200 a week." We agreed that was too low.

He had come with a different purpose; he had news about our robbery. The thieves were, in fact, Walter and company. They had been seen in the bed of their boss's truck Monday afternoon strumming the guitar. Mateo said these same folks owed him and Omar, their boss, money. The two of them had given them advance pay for work that was never done, so they were going to try to track them down to get their money back and to see about the stolen items as well. We thanked him.

On Saturday, Mateo's brother-in-law and worker, German, came by. He said that he had newly harvested corn if we were interested in buying some. We were; we wanted a hundred pounds. Then he just hung around for a while, as seems to be Honduran custom when visiting. Finally, for something to talk about, Beth mentioned the robbery. That brought him to what was apparently the other reason for his visit: Mateo and Omar wanted to know if we could pay for the gas for them to go find Walter and company, whose hometown is a couple hours away by car. I wasn't too certain about it, since for one thing, I didn't really want the items back, and I wasn't comfortable with Mateo and Omar taking the law into their own hands. (Actually, Mateo does have a special license from the police that gives him at least some local power. There are guys like that in the smaller communities, including La Fortuna). But, as Beth said, they would be able to confront those guys in a way that would make sense culturally (unlike anything we might do), and this was a way to support friends. So we agreed. But we didn't know how much to give. German said he would talk to Mateo and come back later with the info.

German didn't return that day. Instead, on Sunday morning, he rode up on a burro with the *quintal* of corn for us. This was slightly problematic because we don't do business on Sundays. We worked it out to pay his partner, Doris, when she came in to Centro de Salud for her prenatal visit the next day. German said that the reason he and Mateo hadn't come back Saturday was that there had been a murder in La Fortuna and Mateo had to drive some of the family up there. German's eyes were wide and he stuttered as he told us the story: a father and son of the Cruz family were killed. Was this the son who had robbed us last year?

The next day we learned more when we got a ride to Limón with someone coming from La Fortuna. He had a bull in the back of his truck which belonged to the Cruz widow. She was planning to sell it and to move out of town. The driver was able to tell us the name of the son who had been killed —he wasn't one of the ones who had robbed us. The murders were apparently vengeance on the family for a murder we had heard rumors about a couple months earlier, likely perpetrated by a different son. The criminals themselves are still alive. We are saddened for the family and for the whole community of La Fortuna and for others affected. Violence is a vicious cycle.

All of these events left us reeling emotionally. We were grateful for our monastic routine which helps keep us centered and for relative quiet the next week.

We heard nothing more about any of those things until November 25, when we went to Bonito and again stopped at Mateo and Margarita's. Mateo and Omar had tried to contact the robbers, but their phone number had changed. They decided these guys were too dangerous to try to confront in person. Margarita was looking very happy to be at home with her whole family together. Life goes on.

Adalaida

From: Beth   Date: December 10, 2008

Carlos is the new caretaker at Elías' place. He and Adalaida have three kids. (The former caretaker, who helped plant pineapples and build benches for us, got fired for a five-day drinking binge in town.) They seem to be higher achievers than the usual caretaker. She had 19 chickens she was raising to sell and 2 half-grown sheep. I think Adalaida was pretty shocked to see the shack in which they were expected to live and the long, treacherous path to get there. Adalaida never attended public school; she taught herself to read, using the Bible as her textbook. They moved here from Hicoteas, where she was a Sunday School teacher for the little ones. Like us, they have no family in Colón.

Adalaida had an ovarian cyst which required surgery and caused her a lot of pain. She was very sad about this tumor. When people here tell about a surgery, they say something like "she resisted the surgery," meaning that she survived the operation! Trepidation! Adalaida had never had surgery before. She wasn't sure where she would go to recuperate. It was obvious that she wouldn't be able to walk down to their little house. When people are sick in remote parts, they are carried by hammock. It would be pretty scary on that steep clay slope.

Well, Elías had a house built (but without a kitchen or a good packed dirt floor) near the road. Ah, step one. Adelaida would use the cattle shelter for a kitchen for a while.

We offered to have her come here for her post-operative resting. One day she and the two little ones came over to see the place. It seemed like she didn't have a better option. She might not be able to walk from the road to the Monastery, but at least the hammock style carrying would be doable. The surgery was scheduled for Tuesday, November 11, in Tocoa.

On Monday, November 10, we ran into Carlos in Limón and chatted a bit. He didn't seem sure that the operation would actually happen. He talked a lot about the financial challenge of feeding the children while Adalaida would be in the hospital. Of course, he would be there with her. It is not considered safe to go to the hospital without a family member to look out for you. As we walked home, I wondered, "What was that all about?" Lots of indirect communication here. Sometimes I get it, sometimes I don't.

The next afternoon, I got it. The children showed up about 3 pm. Manuel, the 13-year-old, got right to work cutting us some firewood. Prairie and I went to the kitchen. They were here for dinner. Each day we fed them large breakfasts and large dinners. At that first dinner, the three-year-old ate five corn tortillas, one and a half cooked green bananas, a half cup of beans and some tomato sauce. He and I ate the same amount at that meal and at several others. When he wanted a snack he would sing *"tortillilla,"* a nickname for tortilla. Then we would offer him one and he would eat it up. At the end of the week, we learned that they weren't eating lunch.

Saturday, we were running out of food and no news from Carlos and Adalaida—and no mechanism for getting any. Then the mill (what you would call a food grinder) broke. Home-ground corn is our major staple. At least one third of our calories come from it. We send Manuel to Limoncito with a grocery list and some cash. Corn flour was on the grocery list. It costs twice what corn costs.

Mid-afternoon, he arrives. We were concerned. He was concerned, too. He had tried telephoning his dad and a different person answered the phone. We all eat our very late lunch. Then they go home.

Prairie and I make the big dinner and they don't show up. They are children, after all. We eat and then quickly walk to their place (taking the flashlight along). No one at the house, but we could hear the children's voices. Then we heard a man's voice. Carlos was back and they were working together.

Carlos tells us about the surgery, the traumatic experience of being in the hospital, seeing all the sick people and hearing them call for help. The doctor showed him Adalaida's tumor—about the volume of three grapefruit. He was thoroughly grossed out. The post-operative pain was pretty bad.

The dinner is all ready, so we all troop back to the Monastery (about 1/3 mile) in the dark. And they eat.

We are very ready for our day of rest. A quiet day. At dinnertime the children show up again. Dad went to Limón and he hasn't returned. We feed them, of course. I tell them not to come on Monday as we leave early and get home late.

On our way to Limón on Monday, Rosa tells us that she bought a chicken from Carlos the day before. He had to get cash to get back to Tocoa. He had asked Elías to bring Adalaida in his truck, but Elías refused. He would be willing to bring her from Bonito. But if she could get on the bus and get to Bonito, she would be able to go all the way on the bus. Carlos was pretty disgusted.

Before going to Centro de Salud, we take the mill to Samuel, the mechanic, who fixes it easily and quickly and doesn't charge us even one lempira. We are very grateful for his friendship. This is not the first favor we have received from him.

Adalaida stays a few days with a friend in Tocoa (where the situation was bad and she was obviously a burden). Then, Elías does bring her—to his own house. That situation is even worse. These families are of different races and there is a lot of distrust. She was hungry most of the time, since the first food was served about noon.

By now, it is another Monday and we are on our way to Limón. As we are walking toward town, we meet Elías with Adalaida. We climb into the back of the truck. She will be needing help. The truck slips and slides in the wet clay, finally coming to rest in a precarious position six inches from a very steep embankment.

Elías goes off for Carlos and we just hang around. Carlos helps Adalaida walk a little up the slope until they can get the truck into a safer place. Finally, we all reboard. We are still not sure if she is going to her own place or ours. They drop us at our place and we tell Carlos that we are "at their service."

We start a fire to cook beans and corn. We end up going over to Adalaida's place three times that day, mostly taking food. Tired.

On Tuesday we go to Bonito. We are almost out of cash and need to get to the bank. That's the day that we try to send you this news. No internet.

Wednesday, we go again to visit Adalaida. Prairie is sick by then (sinusitis and overwork). The family is doing pretty well on their own, so we can take care of our own stuff again.

Citizenship in the City of God
From: Beth   Date: December 10, 2008

It is fascinating to live in a new country, especially during elections. This November, Honduras had their important primaries very near to the time that the US had its national elections. It has given me a lot to think about. Perhaps you will have thoughts to add to my essay on Citizenship in the City of God. I wrote it before knowing the results of either worldly election.

Citizenship in the City of God
Living in the Monastery means accepting citizenship in the City of God. As a Christian, one is already a citizen. There are many forces in the world to divide one's loyalty. With Paul, with Priscilla, with Aquila, we risk

censure for declaring that Jesus is our commander-in-chief. Jesus is our president, our prime minister, our emperor. The law we wish to obey is the will of God. We do find it convenient when that doesn't conflict with the laws of the nation in which we reside. But that convenience is a luxury. We are not promised thornless roses in this garden.

Our loyalty must not be divided. Our Master warned carefully about that. It is our job to listen.

The Reign of God is a come-as-you-are party. The church is the only organization in the world whose membership requirements include being a sinner. And so, we sinners band together hoping that the tiny strength each of us receives from God can be shared and we can all benefit—that we can learn to be good citizens.

Our citizenship classes are called Spiritual Formation. It takes a while. We learn patience with ourselves and with one another. We notice all the people, organizations, causes, even nations that would compete for our loyalty and our service. Just noticing helps to put them in perspective.

Each day we pray "may your kingdom come, may your will be done." This is our pledge of allegiance as citizens of the City of God. It is our daily promise to seek and to obey the will of God.

Christmas in Honduras
From: Prairie   Date: January 15, 2009

I really wanted to make tamales for Christmas, which is the tradition around here, so the Thursday before Christmas we visited the neighbors and asked Adalaida if she could teach us. She was willing, and we made plans for her to come to our place on Tuesday, the 23rd, to do it. It would be an all-day event: boiling corn, grinding it, making the filling, wrapping the corn *masa* and the filling in already-boiled plantain leaves, then cooking the whole thing. She gave us a list of ingredients to purchase.

On Monday in town we got recommendations from other friends about what is good in tamales—spices, green pepper, chicken or pork, rice, potatoes, etc.—and on the quantity of meat to buy. (Making tamales with Adelaida, we expected to send home plenty for her family as well.) We normally purchase one pound of chicken or fish per week, but this time we got a three-pound chicken.

To our delight, we came upon a truck selling vegetables in town. When we try to purchase veggies, we're always being told, that "the truck comes on Tuesdays," so the selection is usually poor, but because of the holiday, the truck was in Limón on a Monday. We splurged, spending 104 lempiras ($5.50) on two pounds of carrots, two pounds of cabbage, a *pataste* (think summer squash), one pound each of potatoes and onions, half a pound of beets, a stalk of celery, two green peppers, and even a cantaloupe! We'd love to buy that much every week if we had the opportunity, since we aim to eat our five servings each of fruits and vegetables a day for a balanced diet. (Only the onions and celery don't add much nutrition.) It really felt like a Christmas gift.

We got a ride part of the way home with Elías. He told us that Carlos came to him the day before to ask for his December pay early, then called today to say Adelaida had already left for Hicoteas, the town where they lived previously. Beth had predicted that they would be moving once Adelaida was well enough after her surgery, since they had a difficult relationship with Elías. That meant no tamale-making on Tuesday. Instead we did regular activities like washing laundry and worship planning.

Though we were a bit disappointed to not have tamales, our Christmas celebration wasn't dampened by not getting to see our neighbors. On Monday when we were at Centro de Salud, we talked with our friend, the nurse Juana Nidia. She was looking sad that day and told us that because of work she'd decided she couldn't go to La Ceiba to be with her family for Christmas; she lives alone in Limón. We invited her to come out to the Monastery. To our delight she accepted.

In the late morning of Wednesday the 24th (*La Nochebuena*, the "Good Night", when the big celebration is here), Beth and I walked down the *desvío* to meet Juana Nidia. She has a motor scooter, and rode it as far as Rosa and Chito's; we planned to meet her there. We were a little over halfway when we heard a motorcycle and saw someone in blue. It was Juana Nidia in her work uniform; she'd gotten a ride that far with a police officer. So we all walked back to the house together.

We had a lovely 24 hours together. Juana Nidia seemed to relax and enjoy herself, as she changed into a comfortable dress and we all chatted about Christmas traditions and other things. She gladly participated in our prayer times, including the special Christmas Eve service at midnight. (Juana Nidia's watch confirmed that our inner clocks are pretty accurate: we got up at 11:40 for that service.) She even joined us for our Spiritual Formation/Bible Study of the Gospel of John.

Since we didn't have tamales, Beth and I had the idea to make *pastelitos* for dinner on Christmas Eve. We'd never made them before, but Juana Nidia had, so we all work together. We mix cooked rice, green pepper, potato, and shredded chicken for the filling, and place a little of that in the center of uncooked corn tortillas. Then we fold them over, press the edges together, and deep fry them. Delicious!

Christmas morning we eat Italian chicken soup, along with apples and grapes—special holiday fruits that Juana Nidia brought. Afterward, we hang out telling stories and singing carols till she is ready to go at 10 am. We accompany Juana Nidia on the walk all the way to Chito and Rosa's. She gets her motorcycle and heads off with a couple of tamales from Rosa. Then Rosa offers us each one and we happily accept. We get our Christmas tamales after all! They are pretty good—filled with pork. We then sing for her, (and later for her mom, Eva) "Hark the Herald Angels Sing," which we'd memorized in Spanish. It feels like a milestone for us to be able to do it in two-part harmony, and they seem to enjoy it.

Finally we head home, but not before Eva gives us cans of fruit juice, and Rosa gives us a care package of three more tamales, some of her delicious pork, and white bread for dinner. That evening I am so full my tummy aches, but I am happy. It was a lovely Christmas celebration.

Adiós, Belén
From: Prairie   Date: January 15, 2009

Ever since we acquired the dog in August, we struggled with taking care of him, as neither Sister Alegría nor I had much experience with dogs.

Every Monday, when we went to Limón, we left Belén tied up at the house; we didn't want him following us to town. He even stayed tied up the day we were robbed in October. But the weekend after that, when German came to sell us corn, Belén got aggressive and barked menacingly at him. I tied him up behind the house, but he chewed through the nylon cord—twice. The next Monday we decided not to bother tying him up, since he'd now figured out how to escape and we didn't have anything stronger to hold him.

For several weeks, he walked with us as far as Chito and Rosa's house, about half way to Limón. They kindly kept him tied up at their place while we'd go into town, but they recommended we get a chain. We really didn't want to do that if we didn't have to.

In November, when the neighbor kids came over for meals, Manuel, the 13-year-old, would play around with Belén, and the dog soon started following them home. At first, he'd come back for dinner and to sleep, but gradually spent more and more time at their place, even overnight. (It certainly made Mondays hassle-free for a few weeks.) They milked cows, and sometimes gave the dogs milk or the whey from making cheese. We noticed Belén bulking up. We knew we couldn't compete with the mush we were feeding him.

We began wondering if we should keep the dog. We had taught him to come when called, but as he spent more time at the neighbors, he obeyed less. Every week—almost every day, it seems—we were questioning what to do about him (tie him up or let him run?), what best to feed him (maybe he'd digest tortillas better than mush), how to train him (what were our goals exactly?). Our neighbors told us what a great dog he was: he would sniff out wild animals that make good eating, and once killed an animal that would have attacked their chickens. But to us, he was only a headache. We don't have chickens for him to guard, and we didn't even enjoy his company all that much.

Then a friend mentioned in a letter the need to have an assertive dominance in order to train the dog to behave well. So in mid-late December, we resolved that we would take control of our situation, reclaim the dog, and start training him properly. But first we'd have to go to the city to buy a chain, and we couldn't do that till January.

Christmas week, the neighbors moved away. On Christmas Eve, Belén spent the night at our house and was still there in the morning, for the first time in a week. It felt like a true gift. He stuck around for several days, and he began to learn to sit on command for treats and his dinner.

Then one morning he left and didn't come back for dinner. We guessed he had gone to Rosa's, but the next Monday, she said she hadn't seen him. Someone else said he'd seen Belén with the new caretaker at Elías' property. We were thrown into questioning once again. Maybe it was time to sell him. Beth came up with the clincher: if the point of the dog is to guard the chickens, and the point of the chickens is to have eggs and reduce our grocery bill, it wasn't cost-effective. We spend 100 lempiras on fruits and veggies a week (when they're available), but only 20 on eggs. The time, money and energy we were putting into training and care of the dog (not to mention worrying about him) and the as-yet-unpurchased chickens would be better used trying to raise fruits and vegetables.

We resolved to find a buyer for the dog, figuring our new neighbors would be interested. Of course, we didn't even have Belén in hand, so our search included finding him. We waited. On Thursday, after eight days away, Belén reappeared, but only stayed one night. I was stressing some about the whole thing, wanting to get it all resolved before we left for our trip on Monday, but I tried to give it to God again. I'd been praying for clarity and guidance for weeks.

Saturday afternoon as we took a break from our Spiritual Formation class, we heard a familiar sound—Belén had returned! Beth and I looked at each other. "Shall we go to the neighbors'?"

"Yes."

"Right now?"

"Yes."

We put the dog on a string and we went to Elías' property. We could hear male voices, and we saw two guys chopping with machetes. Beth said to them, "I'm told you like our dog," and one guy asked if we were selling him.

"Yes."

"How much?"

"I hadn't thought of that yet. Are you offering?" Then Beth said, "What we'd like more than money is manure for our garden."

Silence. We waited. I suggested she tell them how much we'd paid for the dog, but she said it was their turn to make a move (I have no experience in bargaining). Finally the guys started talking to each other and they eventually came over to the fence where we were standing.

"So, you're selling the dog."

"Yes." We told them how he's a good hunter, though he likes to wander all over. Beth said, "We paid 300 Lempiras for him and we're not trying to turn a profit, so we'll sell him for the same." The man paid us and we wished them well. We felt hugely relieved and satisfied.

I hope that with Belén gone, I will be able to concentrate on better things, instead of having my mind occupied with worries about the dog. May peace reign at last: quiet at the Monastery and in my soul.

Interesting Visit
From: Beth   Date: January 15, 2009

Learning Poverty

We had an interesting visit in early January. It was a Sunday morning and we were just beginning our Programmed Worship when our friend Polo showed up with *Hermano* (Brother) David in tow. David is a preacher. Well, let me tell you he is a preacher. He is a compulsive preacher. It made for a very interesting worship experience.

Hermano David had lost his Bible in a flood. His dwelling was full of water waist high and he got himself out, but not his stuff. So we gave him the Bible that I had inscribed for Prairie in 2005.

Yesterday, we tried to replace it in La Ceiba. Well, we couldn't. The Bible Society store doesn't carry the cheap copies, only the more costly ones—usually with tiny print. I say tiny because reading by kerosene lamp light is not so easy with small print. Again we make a little progress in material poverty.

In agricultural news, we have a 6 ½ foot-tall six-month-old papaya plant in the urine bed. It seems very happy there. We are ecstatic with our success. The highly acid soil (pH 4.5) became neutralized to a nice agriculturally friendly 6.0 in a year. The high nitrogen content of the urine is well appreciated by the papaya.

We have planted papaya before, but we have never had a plant grow to this size before. We may actually get fruit. I'll let you know. (When we were in El Pino, our friend Salvador gave us a follow-up lesson on papaya-raising.)

Year-end Financial Review

From: Beth   Date: January 15, 2009

This is how the money was spent in 2008 (in dollars)

```
EXPENSES
Food                        $1,043
Household expenses             866
Immigration                     83
Communication                  781
Agriculture                    118
Medical care (ours)            599
Clothing                        51
Library (ours)                 325
Transport to/in USA          1,008
Property tax                     2
Total cost of living        $4,876

Alms                         3,145
TOTAL EXPENSES              $8,019
```

Financial management is a spiritual practice as much as is any other activity in the Monastery, just as it should be in any practicing Christian's household, any church, Monthly Meeting or other religious organization. Abba John the Little (over 1,600 years ago) said, "We have abandoned a light burden, namely self-examination, and taken up a heavy burden, namely self-justification."

Self-examination is a core monastic practice. We simply choose the light burden over the heavy burden. Our friend, Teresa of Avila says, "What are you killing yourselves for?"

I invite you to accompany us in our self-examination of the 2008 financial management of Amigas del Señor.

- Food: Food is basic in poverty. Jesus taught us to pray for our daily bread. Why would he do that? Because his followers were very poor and had no worldly confidence that there would be food each day. To me the line between destitution and poverty is drawn according to the risk of malnutrition. Each month, food is the first item on the financial report. Perhaps, one day we'll be more spiritually advanced and place alms first on the list. But this year, we notice where we are. We pray for our daily bread and get it.

  Our expenditure for food in 2008 was the same as in 2007. This stability, in spite of dramatic increases in food prices here in Honduras, represents our growing experience. Being new immigrants means not knowing anything (like how to prepare the available food, when fruits and vegetables are in season, where the best prices are—the list is endless). There has been a small, but very small, increase in home grown food.

- Immigration: That immigration still ranks as a category reminds us that our legal status is still very questionable. When we concern ourselves about the worldly risks, we remind ourselves that we have a lawyer. Then we remind ourselves that we live on faith (in God, not in the lawyer). We are not yet legal residents.

- Library: "Library" expenses are for our Monastery library. We were delighted to increase the library a lot this year and yet we notice the "missing" things. We have given away items that are no longer of value to us. This is the area in which we are in greatest risk of falling to the temptation of accumulating beyond what is appropriate for a poor monastery. We wonder if the library expenditures will be less in 2009.

- Alms: We use the word "alms" to mean money spent to help other people. When we added up the total expenses, a large amount of money was spent in the US (transportation, books, medical care). Alms came in at 39% of total expenditures. Hmm, something to think about. This is important. To spend the majority of the budget to maintain ourselves does not fit with our calling any more than it would for a local church congregation. We have determined to give with a freer hand in 2009.

  The overwhelming majority of our alms bought medicines. Of that, the majority was to help the local public health clinic in its service of our poor county. Some bought medicines for Clínica Metodista in El Pino. Another large chunk bought notebooks and pencils for poor children in the county public school system. The rest was alms to individuals, offerings to churches, and books for the public library.

  Direct giving of used items, groceries or cooked foods to others we have not documented as alms. It would have seemed legalistic and counterproductive.

- Income: We have talked about expenditures; maybe you are curious about income. Income is monetary donations. Thank you! We also have received from friends in the States gifts of books, stamps, dried fruits and nuts, pens, envelopes and miscellaneous other things, most of them useful. Gifts from Honduran friends have included food, lodging, rides and other favors. We do not estimate the value in dollars or lempiras of the non-money gifts.

We do not give publicity to donors. One friend sent us $1; another sent $1,000. We are grateful for both. One of the purposes of a monastery is spiritual growth, not only of the monastics, but also of their contacts in whatever setting. In general, public praise is detrimental to spiritual growth. One of our friends feels so strongly about this idea that her donation is not even reported to the IRS.

Doing fiscal management as a spiritual practice feels like one of the ways in which we are re-inventing the wheel. Maybe we don't need to re-invent this wheel. If you are willing to share your (personal or group) self-examination of this spiritual practice, we would benefit by it. Write to:

Amigas del Señor
Limón, Colón   Honduras

Still Waiting
From: Sister Alegría

No one wrote. The invitation is still open, the mailing address is still the same. That's right, no numbers.

Being Immigrants
From: Sister Alegría

Immigrants look, listen and notice. That's what we've done. One thing we noticed is that in our little neighborhood there are two classes of people: bosses/owners and hired workers. Oops, we have chosen to live at the economic standard of the hired workers and we were hiring people! We also noticed what is expected of the bosses/owners. If a man got hurt working with us one day, it would be our responsibility to provide transportation to healthcare, pay the bills and make sure he and his family still eat until he can work again. Wow. We stopped hiring workers, except Daniel. Daniel is different; you'll hear more about him later.

Sister Confianza and Ceniza tend the fire, 2012

The Sisters at Lauds, 2012

3
Monastic Formation

"We want to be obedient as Christ was obedient to his Father's will;
we want to be poor because he was poor;
we want to be celibate because he was celibate."—Basil Hume

Our Third Anniversary
From: Prairie   Date: February 18, 2009

Sunday, February 1st, was the third anniversary of Amigas del Señor (technically of the day Beth and I left Portland, Oregon, to travel to Honduras to found the Monastery in 2006). We began making plans for the celebration in December. At the same time, we were thinking about New Year's. December 31st is a big holiday around here, celebrated like Christmas with *tamales*, family get-togethers, and church services. Was it a holiday we should celebrate at the Monastery? No. We decided celebrating Christmas—all twelve days of it plus Epiphany on January 6—was more important. Yet, we like the idea of what New Year's means: a day of new beginnings and a chance to look back over where we've been and rededicate ourselves to the life we want to lead. We decided that February 1—Founding Day—would be Amigas del Señor's New Year's Day.

For the first time, we did a review of the past year as a spiritual practice, with deep listening and sharing. We began on Thursday, January 22, and had an hour-long session almost every day for two weeks until we felt we'd covered everything (we'll start earlier next year to try to finish before February). We would sit together on the east bench, under a pine and the overhanging branch of a *nance* tree, overlooking the hills, or on the bench at the back of the house where we do prayers. One of us would share memories of the last year as the other listened. Then the other might expand on the topic with her own memories, or, after some silence, share a different memory, sometimes in chronological order, sometimes by topic. We reviewed things that happened in 2008 including my sister Autumn's visit during Lent; Beth's trip to the US; the fire; the damaged water tank and going to the creek to bathe and wash clothes; the robbery; feeding the neighbor children; and buying (and selling) the dog. We named the lessons we learned and the ways we've grown spiritually and personally. We looked at challenges we've had and celebrations. We laughed and cried, and felt God's presence with us. It was really a wonderful practice, and I feel like I am entering the new year renewed.

Beth and I wanted to invite friends to our Founding Day celebration, although we had our reservations. We sometimes feel like we aren't very good hosts in this culture. It would involve feeding our guests, and since February 1 fell on a Sunday that would mean more work for us on our day of rest. I had to face my tendency to be less than generous. Finally we came up with a plan where, if anyone showed up, we could serve a simple lunch of rice, tortillas, beans, and tomato sauce, as well as have plenty of Tang to go around.

The Monday before Founding Day, when we went to town, we made it a point to invite some of our friends. About six people and their families expressed interest in attending. The prospect of guests got us excited, so we bought extra groceries that day for the event.

We had plenty of preparations to do the rest of the week. There were our regular tasks of washing laundry, gathering firewood, and feeding ourselves; and our regular spiritual practices like daily Spiritual Formation exercises and prayers, plus *lectio divina* and the Yearly Review. We wanted to cut down weeds in the yard to have a presentable space for our guests. Plus, we had to prepare our special worship services! I tried to be fully present in each task I did to avoid feeling stressed about all the things to do, and with God's help that seemed to work. I was also pleased with how the worship planning went. Each time Beth and I talked about it, the ideas about what we wanted to include (songs, scripture, themes) gelled a little more.

On Saturday in the late morning, after a session of Yearly Review, we had a hymn-sing and prayer time to participate in the monthly prayer vigil of the First United Methodist Church of Hermiston, Oregon, where I am a member. In the afternoon we had our weekly Spiritual Formation class. However, as it was getting late and we still had worship planning to finish, we decided not to do the second half of the program. We postponed it and our daily formational exercises a whole week, so we could finish our Yearly Review. (I guess we did get just a bit overwhelmed with the tasks of the week, but it was easy to come to a solution.)

That night after Compline, we entered the Grand Silence as usual. In the middle of the night we got up for the New Year's service. It included hymns for the occasion as well as a liturgy to welcome in Jesus with the New Year, culminating with the Wesleyan Covenant Prayer, asking God to use us as he wishes, instead of seeking our own will. Try praying it yourself:

Wesleyan Covenant Prayer
I am no longer my own, but thine.
Put me to what thou wilt, rank me with whom thou wilt.
Put me to doing, put me to suffering.
Let me be employed for thee or laid aside for thee,
exalted for thee or brought low for thee.
Let me be full, let me be empty.
Let me have all things, let me have nothing.
I freely and heartily yield all things
to thy pleasure and disposal.
And now, O glorious and blessed God, Father, Son
and Holy Spirit,
thou art mine, and I am thine. So be it.
And the covenant which I have made on earth,
let it be ratified in heaven.
Amen.

On Sunday morning Beth and I woke up excited. At breakfast, we experimented with a recipe for gingerbread pancakes, which we could serve like cookies later. We had Unprogrammed Worship and then hung out, doing a crossword puzzle.

The day turned out to be overcast and a bit rainy, so we weren't surprised when no guests showed up. At 11:00, the hour of our usual Sunday Worship, we began the Founding Day program, just the two of us. I found myself a little nervous about it all, it being such a special event. Beth and I both flubbed the words of our opening song, but we beamed as we sang a series of upbeat choruses we'd memorized. The worship service included a special time of intercessory prayer for six congregations in the US that have supported us in one way or another in the founding of the Monastery. Beth gave a Spirit-inspired sermon on David and Abigail (check it out: 1 Samuel 25). We concluded with Holy Communion, using a liturgy we'd put together emphasizing that everyone is welcome at God's table. That was a milestone; it was the first time we didn't use a liturgy written by someone else. Our elements were corn tortillas and orange juice, which is what we figure Jesus would have used if he were in Honduras.

Since there were no guests, Beth and I ate the gingerbread pancakes for lunch ourselves (they tasted delicious, like authentic gingerbread!) and drank Tang. It was truly a special celebration, and what feels like the beginning of some good traditions. We've had three years of amazing growth and education, and, by God's grace, will have many more.

The Life Cycle of a Habit
From: Beth   Date: February 18, 2009

Last week Prairie got out the sewing machine to mend her nightdress. It already had nine patches on it; a tenth would have made the surface area of the patches on the front larger than the unpatched area. Time to consider replacing the nightdress.

How does having a nightdress fit with monastic poverty? Most Hondurans do not wear special nightwear. They wear regular clothes to bed.

Our habits are simple light blue denim cotton dresses worn over blouses. We each have three. "Why three?" you ask. Because Teresa of Calcutta (who also lived in a tropical country) tried two and couldn't make it work.

We patch the habit as needed until its state offends feminine monastic modesty. Habits are worn in rotation without regard to age, fading, stains, or patches. One of the ideas behind wearing habits is to be fashion free. Most people with involuntary poverty (and middle class, too) have as many clothes as they can and are careful about which ones are worn for which occasions. We have as few clothes as we can and wear the same ones everywhere. The twenty-first century nun in her habit is always dressed for the occasion, whether she is doing household chores, worshiping or is out in public. We are perhaps the only people in the county who wear worn, stained or patched clothing in public as a choice. The others who do are the drunks, the beggars and the truly destitute. When we have new habits we look rather wealthy, when we wear old ones, we take our place with the drunks, the beggars and the truly destitute. We're all the same, after all.

When a habit is retired, we cut off the belt and it becomes a nightdress or a towel. Our habits last longer when we don't wear them 24 hours a day. Towels are a rich person's affectation in Honduras. Most people just grab an item of clothing if they want to dry themselves. Not drying prolongs the refreshment of bathing. In "cold" weather (70's), it is nice to have something with which to dry oneself. Last week, the towel that I was using was a retired habit; it was the obvious choice to replace Prairie's nightgown. We cut the old nightdress in half (each part looking like a paper doll's dress), one of which would be my new towel. I chose the front—more patches, therefore, more absorbing capacity. The other half was put aside for patching material. This week, my pants needed to be patched and I cut a piece from the other half of Prairie's ex-habit, ex-nightdress to mend them.

We also hang a hand towel (part of an old habit) on a nail in the porch just outside the kitchen door. Very useful. Not to mention the hot pad and tortilla cloths made of old habit fabric.

Finally, after habit, nightdress, towel, patching material, the cotton fabric becomes mulch. We haven't yet come up with a good use for the old tie belts.

No, this wasn't the most exciting part of our last week. The most exciting parts of our lives, we have a hard time believing ourselves. There is no reason for us to expect you to believe them. Let's just say that Mateo is coming out to repair the water tank again.

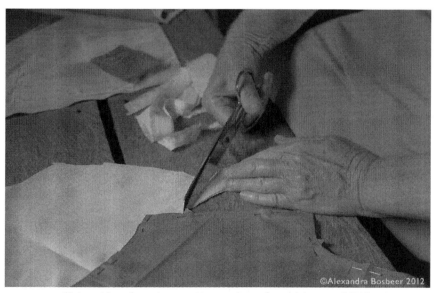

Sister Alegría cuts a pattern piece for a blouse, 2012

Simplicity and Poverty
From: Sister Alegría

It looks all very straight forward and easy the way I wrote about recycling habits. It was a complex discernment to get there.

Simplicity and poverty are usually completely congruent; they lead one to the same decision. Not this time. Simplicity (as modeled in Carmelite and Trappist Monasteries) means you sleep in the same habit you wear all day. Poverty means you try to make your day habit last as long as you can so it need not be replaced as often.

Simplicity and poverty in disagreement. We did a lot of discernment. Fortunately, neither of us had a preconceived idea of what we should do. We still wear old habits for nightgowns. When rainy nights are really cold, we wear the blouse, the nightdress, the habit, the pants, the kerchief, the long sleeved blouse and socks to bed. It doesn't get that cold very often.

Doña Amelia
From: Beth   Date: March 4, 2009

The Friday before my last update to you, we walked to La Fortuna to visit Doña Amelia, my friend, who has been sick in bed for five months. She is 82 and is probably dying. This looked to be my last chance to see her. She "gets it" about the Monastery. It is not a gift one can give by wishing it; it either is or it isn't. It is a very precious gift to me. I didn't tell you about this visit last time because I just wasn't ready. It is hard even today.

The walk to La Fortuna takes two hours, but it was mostly overcast, so it went smoothly. There is a new road, hanging perilously off the side of the mountain when you get to town. Instead of fording the river twice, we ford a small stream twice.

Doña Amelia is thinner than her usual skinny self. She tells me that she is dying and she thinks it is God's will for her. She wants rest for her soul and for her body. She is a good Catholic. She asks us to pray for her soul. Then she prays to God for mercy and so sweetly says, "I can't remember my sins." I suspect most of them were pretty long ago.

We stayed with her for two hours. A neighbor sends her fresh milk every day, since she is sick. Her son and daughter-in-law take care of her and her 11 year-old granddaughter, who has no local parent. They gave us each a small cup of sweetened hot milk. Amelia also drank a small cup of nasty herbal remedy tea while we were there. I don't have any idea what her diagnosis is. I decided to stay out of it. Prairie and I sang for her. Finally, we tore ourselves away, leaving with a prayer/blessing.

We stopped to visit Doña Rosa, another friend. She was having a busy day, but took time to chat a bit and gave us each a can of fruit juice and let us use her bathroom. She told us that there are two other elderly ladies that are sick. So we decide to visit them, too. Why? Well, the last time I had visited Doña Amelia, I found her with an eye infection that had left her blind for three months. She had received a treatment that should have worked, but didn't. I sent medicines from Centro de Salud a few days later and she was cured. Poor old ladies don't leave the neighborhood to seek health care that might or might not help.

Next stop, Doña Argelia. Doña is a title for older ladies (I am often called Doña, but Prairie, never) or rich ladies. A child led us to her house. Doña Argelia was bright eyed and on her feet in the kitchen. She is about 4' 10" tall with a dramatic kyphosis (humpback). She was absolutely charming and brimming with health, but she walked poorly. A closer look revealed dramatic varicose veins, left, worse than right. Eleven pregnancies will do that to you. She also had several ulcers on the left leg. She washes them every day and they usually don't hurt. That's good; pain usually indicates that they are infected. A lively little mouse with a long tail frolicked on the floor—in broad daylight. What kind of a mouse is this? So, you're thinking support stockings. Me, too. Also, I'm thinking mouse traps. Both ridiculous dreams in this context. We bid farewell to our delightful hostess (politely not mentioning the mouse, just as we didn't mention the rustling of the mouse in Doña Amelia's house).

Another child leads us to Doña Martha's house. She is co-mother-in-law with Doña Amelia. She is in her early 60's. A charming lady. In November she went to Trujillo for a big medical work up, even a chest X-ray, and was sent home without a diagnosis, but some pills. This is bad news. Either the diagnosis was unspeakable or incurable or both. Well, both seems to be the case. She is a skeleton. She, too, tells me that she is dying. Like Doña Amelia, her mind is clear, at least as clear as it can be when she is so sick. She has a fever and every breath costs huge amount of effort. She is exhausted all of the time. We don't stay long. When we do our prayer/blessing, she drifts into sleep and then arouses herself to bid us good bye. She obviously did not have much time left.

This was not exactly our favorite way to spend the day. We were ready to leave. We stopped at the stream and drank a lot of water. Then we stopped at our friend Pastora's house. She gave us a sour-orange drink. Very nice. Then on we went.

Impulsively, we decided to visit Francisco and Santos on the way home. It was only half an hour each way out of our way. It was already mid-afternoon, but we did it. We stayed a while and they also gave us each a sweetened drink. Then one of the boys looked at his watch and said it was 4 pm. We needed to get going if we wanted to get home before dark. As we were leaving, we met Polo, David (you know, the compulsive preacher), and a young man with a guitar. There was going to be a worship service at Santos' house that night. Santos' household has 12 people, so it would be a well-attended worship!

We moved quickly. We did most of our afternoon worship as we walked, only stopping to read a passage from Galatians. We got home just before full dark. I started the fire while Prairie peeled a couple of oranges for us to eat. We cooked by lamplight and ate heartily. Did prayers and went right to bed. We had been on the road for over 11 hours without lunch.

Some folks think of fasting as penance, but we think of it as a spiritual practice of keeping body wants/needs in perspective. In rural poor Honduras, the capacity to fast is simply an essential survival technique.

Water Tank
From: Beth   Date: March 4, 2009

The Monday after our walk to La Fortuna, Daniel (Doña Amelia's son, who is our local agricultural consultant and helper) had permission to come cut some *ocote* (grease wood, very good for starting fires and can be used like a candle—but with nasty black smoke). Since we live amongst the type of pines that produce this valuable stuff, we are generous with it. He would borrow a horse.

When we got home from Limón, we noticed big pieces of *ocote* in the yard and piles of horse manure—too much for one horse. Then we noticed that the back draining valve of the water tank was broken off and lying on the ground!! There was a regular drip from the tank opening! The loaded down horse would have walked past and just broke off the spigot in the process. A piece of firewood had been whittled down to a make-shift plug. Most of the water was gone, but we figured that 100 gallons were left. It was coming out about two gallons an hour.

Wednesday, we came to Bonito to email you. On the way we met Mateo and told him our troubles. He would look it over. But later that morning, his nephew, the mayor's son, was kidnapped for ransom. Mateo had more important things on his plate than our water tank. Rumor said that the ransom was to be half a million dollars. Good grief! Apparently, they thought the mayor would publicly steal the county treasury!

On Friday, Daniel came over. He said that another person had also been there cutting *ocote* on Monday. He would have recognized the mare if it had been from La Fortuna, but he didn't, so he figured the person was from Limoncito. The foal was also along. That explains all the extra horse manure.

Daniel told us that Doña Martha was feeling a little better. She might even recover. She had been moved over to Doña Amelia's house. They were now together, with their two children taking care of them. I think about this couple, caring for their two dying mothers together. How hard! We sent some oranges, just bought in Bonito, with Daniel.

The next week, Daniel told us that Martha had died the day he was at our place. He attended the *velorio* (wake). Wakes are the thing. I'm not even sure if funerals are done much. The body is buried the day after the death. Only the very rich have their relative's body embalmed. Burial must be rapid in this tropical place—stench.

We learned that the kidnappers released Mateo's nephew without getting a ransom—four days later.

As days went by, the leak slowed down. We figure that the wooden plug swelled up. We also got a fair amount of rain. Now the leakage ranges between four and fourteen gallons a day. We're not sure about the reasons for the variability, but the tank is gradually filling. It is pretty close to the top now.

This Monday, Mateo gave us a lift to town. He had seen the tank and says that a pipe needs to be purchased. He hasn't done it, obviously. We are really close to the end of the rainy season. In fact, today could be the last day for the next two to three months for any significant rain—or last night might have been. We have decided to leave the tank the way it is until it is completely empty or the rainy season comes.

Doña Amelia is still hanging in there.

Lent

From: Prairie   Date: March 4, 2009

February 25 was Ash Wednesday, the first day of the season of Lent (the forty days before Easter, not including Sundays). In our time here at the Monastery, Beth and I have come to appreciate the church calendar and the chance it gives us to reflect on various aspects of Jesus' life and important Christian themes over the course of the year. Advent and Christmas were easy to adopt, as the Incarnation—God's solidarity with humans in Jesus, and also residing in our hearts—makes so much sense to us. Lent, on the other hand, has been more difficult, with its traditional focus on Jesus' suffering and death, and the idea of suffering and penance as good ways to get closer to God. We come from a cultural and religious milieu in which feeling good and being comfortable are high priorities—even goals—in life. Yet, the forty days Jesus spent in the wilderness—a time of fasting and temptation—speaks to us. I particularly have connected with the idea of Lent as a time to do extra spiritual practices and have a more disciplined life, to focus more on God. So it seems we are getting closer to an understanding of the season and developing our own monastic traditions.

Our first year, we didn't observe Lent in any way. We had barely moved down here, and felt like we were struggling—suffering—enough just to learn to live. By the second year, we'd moved out to the Monastery on the mountain and decided to add a number of spiritual practices for Lent. They included doing *lectio divina* (spiritual reading) three times a week and fasting for a meal on Thursdays, both of which we incorporated into our regular schedule after Easter. Last year, Beth was in the US during all of Lent, and my sister was here with me. (We didn't look at the date for Easter before purchasing the plane tickets. What kind of nuns are we?) Now, as we began our fourth year together, we came up with a nice variety of practices to do for Lent.

Beth and I normally have two or three books going for shared reading. While it doesn't have a set place in our schedule, often we will read to each other while cooking or washing dishes, and in the evenings. For Lent, we put down Guns, Germs and Steel (we're trying it in Spanish), and a book on the history of Christian doctrine, to read two others: Teresa of Avila's Life (which we're reading in the original Spanish, but keeping an English translation at hand), and Good News to the Poor: John Wesley's Evangelical Economics, which is an interesting look at what the founder of Methodism thought was our Christian duty concerning wealth and the poor (live small and give generously to help those in need). Besides our daily Spiritual Formation, which is currently a study of the Gospel of John in Spanish, we've added a study on healing ministry.

Since our second year, we have had a regular fasting practice on Thursdays, which has developed as we've learned how to do it. However, during much of this past fall we didn't skip meals because of physical vulnerabilities—the challenge to keep our weight up and stable, and various episodes of overwork and illness. After the

Christmas season was over, we introduced it again, not eating breakfast on Thursdays. As our weight and health seem to be doing well now, with Lent we are eating just one meal in the mid-afternoon on Thursdays. We usually do a reading at the hour of the omitted meals, and during Lent we are reading a book on Prayer and Fasting by a Bolivian Evangelical. Thursday mornings we also have Unprogrammed Worship and another practice, like our once-a-month business meeting and monthly retreat days.

This Lent we are also having a silent work day each week—a chance to conscientiously focus our minds on God throughout the day, and experience that monastic tradition of the union of work and prayer.

We're pretty excited about the smorgasbord of practices, and I think this Lent will be interesting as we continue to deepen our faith and relationships with God.

Monastic Formation
From: Beth   Date: March 25, 2009

The big news is that last week, Prairie completed her clearness process and will be entering the Novitiate the end of May. I thought you might like to know what that means in this monastery.

Amigas del Señor is a pretty traditional monastery. Since a few friends have casually commented about the Benedictine order, I hasten to explain that we are not Benedictines (although some of our good friends are). Our governance is the main difference from older monastic traditions. We use Quaker process of discernment for decisions. It is often quite slow, but sometimes amazingly fast. Practice helps, of course. Most other monastic orders have top-down power structure. Perhaps they would use different words to describe themselves. Things always look different from the inside than from the outside.

The basic monastic guidelines, often called vows, are Chastity, Poverty and Obedience. We're not into vows. The Master said, "Let your yes be yes and your no be no. Don't swear." True Quaker practice means that anything you say has the same force as a solemn vow. Perhaps that's why Proverbs recommends so little speaking.

Celibate chastity is to avoid conflict of interest. No excuses about the family's needs or the spouse's desires versus what God is asking. Monastic chastity is a deliberate choice to direct one's sexual and romantic energies into one's availability to God. Some orders of nuns even wear wedding rings; we don't.

Poverty in this monastery means that each of us has no personal property. It also means that our standard of living is at the poverty level. For example, we live below the Honduran minimum wage. Most families in our county live below that wage. We do not live at the lowest level, destitution. Malnutrition is ordinary at that level.

Religious celibacy requires poverty. To give up lifetime partnership with another human (generally considered a good thing) for God makes sense to those with a monastic call. One gives up something good for something better. To give up this positive good of ordinary human love and to replace it with material things is to take several steps backward.

Obedience, obedience. Oh, how we have searched for a word with less baggage!! So far, we have not found one, but we are open to suggestion. Obedience to whom? To God, of course, as understood by the discernment process of the Monastery. A daily practice of trying to align one's personal will with the will of God is living obedience. This is a little different from pleading with God to follow your will—although this doesn't keep me from praying for fruits and vegetables.

We've been thinking a lot about these values as Prairie comes to the end of her Postulancy.

The rich Christian monastic heritage offers many variations of dedicated religious life. We also have taken tips from the Buddhist monastic practices, especially the acceptance of short-timers (a few years), whom we call Sojourners.

The time of Postulancy is a time of looking back with open eyes at what one is leaving behind in the world—a time to decide if one can renounce one's past life. Note: not Denounce, but Renounce. One gives up something that was (probably) good for something better—you know, the usual method of spiritual growth. It is also a time to consider if you (like Abram) are called to receive a new name in your new life.

Reception into the Novitiate is the rough equivalent of getting married and starting your professional career on the same day. It doesn't get much bigger than that.

The outward signs of this inner commitment include taking a new habit, cutting off the long hair and (probably) accepting a new name.

At Sister Alegría's Reception into the Novitiate, Sister Confianza wears a fading Postulant habit, Sister Alegría wears her new Novice habit, and both wear green gingham blouses, 2008

The haircut is an old monastic tradition. The archetypal symbol of a woman's sexual power is her long hair. Cutting it off is a disavowal of the use of that power and a disavowal of the call to fashion and worldly beauty (not to mention the simplicity of personal hygiene). We do not cover our hair. Monastic tradition has included the covering (hiding) of the hair of nuns. It was part of the religious and secular repression of women. Feminine power of any type was too scary and feminine sexual power was absolutely terrifying!

The Postulant habit is a jumper—a dress without sleeves, worn over a green gingham blouse. The Novice habit has sleeves—symbol of increased responsibility, putting on the yoke that Jesus offers. It is worn over the same blouse as the Postulant wears. We are now scrambling to catch up on our sewing.

Please pray for Prairie at this very important time in her life.

Entering the Novitiate
From: Prairie   Date: April 15, 2009

*____*____*____*____*

Amigas del Señor Methodist Monastery
is pleased to announce that
Prairie Naoma Cutting
will enter the Novitiate
on Pentecost Sunday, May 31, 2009

She will take the name
Confianza
(cone-fee-AHN-sah)
which means "confidence" and "trust"

*____*____*____*____*

Becoming a novice is a big step in my life, comparable to getting married and starting a career. It's a very exciting time for me! If you wish to honor this special occasion with a gift, consider one of the following options:

1. **Help the poor in your community.** Donate time or money to feed the hungry, clothe the naked, or otherwise help those in need where you live.
2. **Help the poor in Honduras.** Donate to the Monastery's "Alms" fund, which we use to give alms, purchase medicines for the public health clinic, and help with other needs that we learn about.
3. **Help me pay off my student loans**, a debt of about $5000.

Thanks for your love and prayers.

Covenant of Caring
From: Sister Alegría

Besides Sister Confianza's Reception into the Novitiate, we had another joyful landmark that May. We entered into a Covenant of Caring with Multnomah Monthly Meeting of Friends (Quakers). Multnomah has been my Meeting since early 1995 when I began attending regularly.

Monasticism surges when the church is in need of reform. This is an observation of the history of Christianity and it is a factor in the founding of this Monastery. In the 90's, I was discouraged with the United Methodist Church in Oregon. "Can I be OK in this church that isn't OK?" was one of my queries to myself. I began to worship with Friends, putting aside for a while my Methodist roots.

The UMC had offered me a mirror that I didn't want to look at. I wanted to see myself as better, more spiritually advanced, more compassionate, wiser, more Christ-like than my coreligionists. I wasn't better, more spiritually advanced, more compassionate, wiser, more Christ/like than other United Methodists and I just couldn't stand it.

Multnomah has been a great blessing to me. Soon I noticed the value of the practice of quiet non-judging without the harsh criticism that had infected me. Each Sunday I went to Early Worship at Multnomah, then drove to Rose City Park UMC to warm up with the choir for late worship. I was a double dipper. I am still a double dipper. It is a great blessing. I figure that if Jesus can be fully Divine and fully human, I can be fully United Methodist and fully Quaker.

When I had visited Oregon in 2008, I asked that the Meeting take the Monastery "under its care." We have Unprogrammed Worship (silent waiting on the Lord) twice a week. It made sense to me. I felt isolated and a long way from home. I wanted support.

Slow Quaker process fits well in Honduras, where everything is slow for other reasons. It took a year to craft the Covenant of Caring. Here's a copy:

A Covenant of Caring

Multnomah Monthly Meeting and Amigas del Señor Monasterio Metodista in Honduras enter into a "Covenant of Caring" to foster and share spiritual support and strength.

We see our covenant as a unique, supportive, loving, inspiring, evolving and committed relationship.

Some attributes of our covenant are:
- An ongoing care for our shared spiritual connections and concerns.
- A sharing of joys and concerns through frequent communication including letters, photographs, audio tapes and videos.
- Occasional visits to Portland and to the Monastery near Limón.
- The designation of a day or two each year to formally hold our Covenant in the Light.

Also, we are adding to the "job description" of Worship and Ministry Committee words to this effect: "participating and nurturing the Covenant of Caring with Amigas del Señor Monasterio Metodista in Honduras."

I chuckled over "audiotapes and videos." We had no electricity, nor equipment for making or listening to/viewing such things. We decided to accept this gap in understanding between rich (Multnomah) and poor (Amigas).

We had asked to be taken under care of the Meeting (a subordinate role) and were offered a Covenant between equals, separate equals. A milestone. Amigas del Señor accepted as an autonomous institution, beloved by but separate from its parent Meeting and churches. Our neophyte monastery was growing up.

We formally approved the Covenant of Caring in our May Meeting for Worship with Attention to Business. We had decided in our first year of monastic life to use Quaker process and Quaker governance. We held our first Meeting for Worship with Attention to Business in January, 2007. We don't have an abbess or a prioress. We chose and choose to leave hierarchy aside.

On Discernment about Habits
From: Sister Alegría

In the May, 2009 monthly Meeting we decided that four blouses—four HABIT blouses—should be available for each Sister's use. We found that during the rainy season when clothing dried very slowly, three blouses were inadequate. We still didn't have that many. We were still sometimes using blouses of miscellaneous colors, including a bright red one from my pre-monastic life.

A "Nervous Bride" and New Neighbors
From: Sister Alegría

We were engrossed in preparations for Prairie's Reception into the Novitiate. She reopened conversations on topics we had discussed before and listened avidly. Religious celibacy and its responsibility suddenly applied to her in a new way, for example. Deep conversations. Lots of practical preparation, too. A retreat to prepare, house guests for whom to provide, a Reception program to plan. She focused on the program so much, I reminded myself regularly about nervous and controlling brides. It drove me crazy. "

74

There won't be a program if there is no retreat, and there won't be a retreat if you don't leave me alone to plan it." I may not have said those exact words, but the thoughts were there.

Then there was the rest of life.

The last two weeks of April, we worked extra days as health care providers during the annual immunization campaign.

In mid-May, we decided to visit whoever was the current caretaker at Elias' place. As we neared the house, we heard children's voices and saw clothes hanging on barbed wire fencing. A kitchen, roughly three-and-a-half walls with zinc roofing, had been added to the 16 by 20 foot house.

Berta, age 23, is our new neighbor. They've been there for six weeks. She was hoping we'd visit but was too timid to visit us. Heidi, age nine; Martín, age seven; Ana, age five; and Omar, age three, are her children. Martín, the dad, is not at the house. Berta is friendly and welcoming. The children readily engage with us. Berta had in her hovel a beautiful set of elegant royal blue cooking pots. We admired them and were impressed. These pots are financially out of reach, but here they are, in her house. She enjoys them a lot: "I just really wanted them."

The house looks a lot better. When Adalaida lived there, a four inch wide, one foot tall stump was still in the floor. The floor was simple dirt, and sloped at least one-and-a-half feet from north to south in the house. Berta said that when she arrived, "I didn't know what to do first." She is working on the floor. They have carried sack after sack of heavy clay soil to level the floor. She moistens it just enough and spreads it out with her hands. She does a little every day; it is hard on her hands—the grit in the clay burns if she sticks with it too long.

We invite her to stop by at the Monastery anytime. Oh, she must be on call at the house. When Martín is out working, he might return to the house, thirsty or hungry, and she must be ready to take care of him.

Martín milks the cows. Berta makes *cuajada* (soft fresh cheese). She sends some home with us in a plastic container, commenting delightedly, "Now you'll have to come back to return the container." She really wanted more visits.

I'm A Novice!
From: Sister Confianza   Date: June 23, 2009

Pentecost Sunday, May 31, was a very special day for me, as you can imagine. We had invited many of our friends from Limón to attend my Reception into the Novitiate, but as the hour approached and no one showed up, it was just as well—that meant my sister was off the hook for translating! Instead, we had a beautiful intimate service with my family. Beth was the emcee, and led us in worship as we sat in a circle on the porch. She even gave a sermon about wrestling with God—something at which I have demonstrated much skill! My mom April, dad Craig, sister Autumn, and Aunt Becky were here and they all participated. Each one did a scripture reading or prayer. Scripture selections included:

Psalm 84 (living in the house of God)

Jeremiah 9:4-5, 7, 11-13 (God's promise to his exiled people)

Acts 2:1-22, 36-42 (Pentecost)

Genesis 32:24-31 (Jacob wrestles with God)

Colossians 3:8-17 (Clothing ourselves in the good things of God)

My parents, who are United Methodist ministers, reaffirmed my baptism; and at the end, all of my family members, as well as Beth, gave me a blessing. We sang Jesus' Great Commandment (Matthew 22:37-39) and many other wonderful songs. My family and I sang two musical selections in four part harmony, which was an extra-special treat for both Beth and me. Tears flowed freely throughout.

It was a hot day (my family's visit seemed to be during the hottest week we'd had in a year!), and we had a couple of stretch breaks during the service—I think it lasted close to three hours! The most formal moment was when Beth asked me the question of commitment and the most informal was as she gave me a haircut and everyone took photos.

The new Sister Confianza's long hair is cut off, 2009

After the service, we celebrated by making and eating *pastelitos* (savory fried pastries) and limeade Tang, plus some treats my family brought. It was so wonderful to have them here for five days—to me, well worth the preparation ahead of time and the exhaustion afterward.

This is the question Beth asked me:

¿Vivirá este año del Noviciado dedicada a Dios y confiando en el proceso de este Monasterio para discernir la voluntad divina, viviendo una vida profética de pobreza material y castidad en obediencia humilde?

Will you live this year of the Novitiate dedicated to God and trusting in the process of this Monastery to discern the divine will, living a prophetic life of material poverty and chastity in humble obedience?

This was my answer:

Por la gracia de Dios quien me da las fuerzas para hacer todo, lo haré.

By the grace of God who gives me the strength to do all, I will.

I'd like to thank everyone who has sent me encouraging words and gifts; it has made this time even more special, knowing there are so many people thinking about me. Novice means beginner and there is much to learn, but I go forward into the unknown, trusting that I am in God's strong hands and that he will guide and care for me.

Ordinary Time
From: Sister Alegría

Sometimes overweight people bemoan the caloric temptations of the Christmas season. A wise one has said, "The problem is not what you eat between Christmas and New Year's, the problem is what you eat between New Year's and Christmas." Whether it is weight control or spiritual growth, the real results come from the day-in, day-out living, not the special events.

Sister Confianza's Reception was on Pentecost. The next day marked the beginning of Ordinary Time in the church calendar. Exhausted and stressed, I entered Ordinary Time determined to be faithful.

While Sister Confianza's family visited we gave each of them the title of honorary nun, so that we could stick with our two-by-two

77

rule. That worked well. On Monday, I saw patients at Centro de Salud (nurse Wornita is also an honorary nun), and Sister Confianza showed her family around town until they left on a late-morning bus.

When the ordinary work was done and it was time to make our way back to the Monastery, we had to notice that Sister Confianza was really tired. I told her where to rest while I walked a half-mile, each way, to get the mail. I abandoned her. Not a good idea. It was a time to stick together.

We went to Wornita's house where she could lie down and rest. She slept for over an hour. Wornita gave us a cool drink and we returned to the Monastery in the ordinary way, walking and hitch-hiking.

We had said that we go two-by-two (just as Jesus sent us out). But, we made lots of little exceptions here and there. The exceptions were usually in the interest of efficiency.

We had had a big event, a major milestone in the life of our monastery. A solemn acknowledgement of a growing commitment. We had to notice that our young monastery was in need of reform. We did a lot of talking, self-encouraging talk, we-can-do-it talk, and made a new, deeper commitment to traveling two-by-two. We travel two-by-two.

Sisters Confianza and Alegría walk the highway
from the *desvío de* La Fortuna to the *desvío de* Limón, 2012

A New Name

From: Sister Confianza   Date: June 24, 2009

God called Abram and Sarai to leave their homeland, and when they said yes, he gave them new names: Abraham (Father of many nations) and Sarah (Princess). After Jacob wrestled all night, God renamed him Israel (One who struggles with God). Jesus told Simon that he was to be called Peter (the Rock), for the Church would be built on him. When Saul responded to Jesus' call to evangelize to the Gentiles, he began using the Greek version of his name, Paul. When a person enters religious life, he or she may take a new name. It was a question for me to ponder during my Postulancy: if I entered the Novitiate, would I take a new name and what would it be?

Don't get me wrong. I love the name my parents gave me. They considered giving their children Biblical names—then they noticed that names in the Bible all have meanings in the original Hebrew. Instead they chose names that are words in their own language. My Dad is from Minnesota, so they named me Prairie. My middle name, Naoma (a variant of Naomi from the Bible), was in honor of a family friend.

I liked having a unique name (I've only met one other Prairie), even though I sometimes got teased as a kid with "Prairie Dog" or "Little House on the Prairie." It also fostered a place in my heart for the grasslands of the American prairie and its conservation. As a teenager I accepted my name as my own. Turns out God had something more in store for me.

I took the question of a new name seriously, and one of our Spiritual Formation courses helped me with it. The exercise was to consider what I saw or I wanted in my relationship with God— like faith, hope, or patience. For me, it was trust and confidence: *confianza* in Spanish. I'd been discovering in the previous year that I can trust in God to provide for my needs, and I wanted to have more self-confidence to be the me God created me to be. So, as I discerned that I am, in fact, called to the religious life, I decided that taking a new name would be an appropriate outward symbol of the inner change and my dedication to God. Therefore, during my Reception into the Novitiate, I took the name Confianza.

In Honduran churches, people call one another *Hermana* (Sister) or *Hermano* (Brother), just as the early Christians did, for we are all children of God. Beth and I have decided to adopt this custom in the Monastery, and are practicing calling each other *Hermana*. In town, children address us as *gringas,* many people call Beth *Doctora,* and I am sometimes *la muchacha* (the girl). In the weeks since my Reception, Beth, the staff at Centro de Salud, and our other friends are learning to use my new name, and I am learning to respond. Whatever title or name is used, we are committed to answering when we are called.

We're Residents!
From: Sister Confianza   Date: June 27, 2009

As of yesterday, June 26, Sister Beth and I are legal Honduras residents! Getting the five-year permit was a complicated process.

As United States citizens, we can visit Honduras legally for 90 days with the visa stamped in our passport on arrival. Another 30 days can be added with a visit to the Immigration Office. Then one must leave the area and return for another 90-day stamp. Beth and I went to Belize and Guatemala a few times in the past to do that. In September of 2007 we made one of those trips, and then were ready to start the process to become residents. We contacted a lawyer in Tegucigalpa recommended by a missionary friend, and at the end of October made a trip to visit him. We'd collected all the necessary papers, including our birth certificates and criminal background checks from the US. The only thing left was to get a letter from the Honduran church that was sponsoring us. We confirmed that during the time that the lawyer, Enil, was working on the residency, we'd be legal in the country without leaving.

During the last year and a half, Beth and I called Enil every couple of weeks to check on the progress. It wasn't always easy to catch him at the office, since we can only make calls when we're in Limón on Mondays or at another town. He always asked if there was a phone number where he could reach us, but, of course, there isn't. So things were going fine, going fine. Then a glitch: the Methodist Church could write the letter, but as an organization it wasn't properly registered with the government. After a few months of that, Enil said he would talk to a friend and get another church to sponsor us as a favor. We were grateful. In May of 2009 we called Enil and he said, "by the end of the month." When we called him at the beginning of June, Beth's had come through, and mine was on the way!

Enil said he would send the papers through an airline to La Ceiba, and we could pick them up and go to the Immigration Office there. We came to El Pino (a town west of La Ceiba with a Methodist church where we stay) Monday afternoon after working at Centro de Salud. On Tuesday we went into the city, figuring we could finish up the residency: pick up our papers, go to the Immigration Office to pay a small fee, and be done with it. Well, it was a nice idea.

We went to the airline office and picked up the envelope. Beth's hands were trembling, so I had to open it. There they were: a document for each of us on the *Dirección General de Migración* (General Direction of Immigration) letterhead, asking that we be given residency. "Whereas, whereas, whereas, therefore let it be resolved that 1, 2, 3..." We'd been waiting eighteen months for this!

Next we headed to the Immigration Office. We went up to the window and presented these pages with our passports. The employee, Amanda, said, "OK. Just bring me two passport size photos, photocopies of these documents and your passports, and the letter from the church. Also, you haven't been leaving the country every 90 days, so you have a big fine."

What? I thought we were legal during the time our lawyer was working on this. Amanda explained that he was supposed to have submitted a particular paper to show that we were in process. It would have allowed us to pay $20 per month for us to stay. Beth had 12 and I had 18 months past our legal time, so that would have been $600. Instead, according to the fine schedule, we owed about $1,200, not to mention the lawyer's fee and we only had $1,380 in the bank! Moreover, the computer system to register us at Immigration was down, and we'd have to come back another day to try again. We were in shock, and left to call Enil.

Que barbaridad! "What a barbarity!" he said, but confirmed that whatever Amanda told us was the law. He promised to send the letter from the church the next day.

We scrambled to figure out how we could do it: We would drain our bank account to pay the fines, pay the lawyer by writing a check on our US bank account (which did, thankfully, have the funds) and stick around as long as needed in La Ceiba to get this finished up. We spent much of the day Wednesday walking around town to collect all the other papers and photos that were needed, and on Friday returned to the Immigration Office. Amanda filled out the bills while we filled out the short application form. Then we walked to the bank a quarter of a mile away to pay the fee (that's to help avoid government corruption) and returned a couple hours later.

Amanda was ready for us. However, her computer wasn't. She took Beth's photo with a remote control camera, but when Beth went to sign on a digital pad, it didn't work. The computer had to be restarted and it was slow. This time though the computer system still wasn't working on the other side of the room where Honduran citizens were waiting, but Amanda's did! "I live on miracles," she told us.

Monastic Formation

Beth finished hers up, and I did mine. Then we both got our fingerprints taken. Finally, Amanda filled out little papers that give us ninety days in the country while the rest of the application is processed. By that time, our special ID cards will be issued and we can come pick them up. Thankfully, there are no late fees or fines anymore, so we can return when it's most convenient for us. Praise the Lord!

Military Coup?
From: Beth   Date: June 30, 2009

This has been a pretty wild time, politically, this last week.

First of all, if you have any concern about our personal safety, rest assured that Sister Confianza and I are fine and not in any danger. We do not circulate in the halls of power.

As well as I can tell what has happened is the following:

Mel (politicians are called by their first name here) won the presidential election in 2005 and is not eligible for re-election. Constitutional law. He is a fairly popular president, very personable and there are remarkably few complaints about his government.

Here is the sticky part. His mentor is Hugo Chavez, the president of Venezuela. Chavez' government has resulted in a higher standard of living, a reduction in hunger and loss of civil liberty in Venezuela. He has confiscated property of international companies (e.g. Coca-Cola). He has started a few national television stations, radio stations and newspapers. He has closed down several of the private media organizations. He seems to be president for life.

The government here, under Mel Zelaya, started its own newspaper. It is a nice newspaper, free, colored pictures, well-written. You read a few articles and you feel good about the government and its programs. He also started a national radio station.

Mel made a movement for a national "poll" of opinion. This would not be a binding law, but a direct going to the people for their opinion. If the people said yes on this opinion poll, the option of a constitutional assembly to rewrite the constitution could be put on the ballot in November. The ballots for this poll were printed in Venezuela and shipped here.

To rich people, this looks like a power grab—the first step towards gaining another chance to be president and then more manipulation for further time as president. However, it appeals to anyone who thinks that the constitution should be amended on any topic. The constitution, for example, does not properly recognize the

Garifuna people in the opinion of many Garifunas. This would mean completely rewriting the constitution.

There were demonstrations in the streets, thousands of people in Tegucigalpa and San Pedro Sula, the biggest cities. Schools and businesses were closed. Fear. Folks stocked up on groceries

Last week, Mel fired the head of the military. The Supreme Court reinstated him and said that he no longer answered to the president (who is the commander-in-chief) because of that firing which it called illegal.

The high election tribunal declared that the poll is not legal. Sent UN election observers home. There are processes for amending the constitution and for calling a constitutional assembly, but they are not to come from the office of the president. This poll was declared unconstitutional and illegal.

The head of the military refused to take back his job. "I'm too old for this crap." (The short version of his attitude).

The Congress, unanimously, fired the president. As I understand it they have the legal right to remove him from office for cause. (Key: for cause.)

The Supreme Court issued an edict to the military to confiscate all of the poll materials, forbade any government agency or building to be involved with the poll, and ordered the military to prevent the poll from occurring.

Mel and supporters responded to this edict by rushing to the warehouse to rescue the poll materials and move forward as well as they could towards the poll, which was scheduled for Sunday, June 28.

In the middle of the night, the army entered the presidential palace, took Mel and put him on an Air Force plane, sending him to Costa Rica. We have no idea how that was all arranged. Supposedly he wrote a letter of resignation, but there is reason to believe that if he did, it was with a gun to his head.

The poll officially didn't happen. Mel has a lot of supporters and in smaller towns, it went forward, including in Limón.

The Congress installed Roberto Micheletti as president (again unanimously). He was the president of the congress—the role of "vice president" in terms of presidential succession. Micheletti had run for president in the primaries last year. He lost. Micheletti is of the Liberal Party (same as Mel).

There were two days of curfew—9 pm to 6 am. No violence. As well as I can tell, there has been no bloodshed.

We got a newspaper yesterday morning on our way back to Limón. When we saw all of the pictures of military, we realized that you would be curious.

Our bus from La Ceiba to Tocoa stopped a mile from the bridge into Tocoa where the police had their road block. There was a protest. Only foot traffic. The protesters were calm, blocking the bridge, carrying "walking sticks" and an occasional machete. There was a speech going on, but we walked through, not stopping.

We walked about two miles to Tocoa, seeing along the way two bus workers. You know transportation is in a mess when bus workers are walking!

Most of the conversations that we had with people on the street indicated that they supported Mel. In the city, before the big events, there were some conversations against Mel. We do not have the pulse of the people. Some say that the power establishment (except Mel) was united because they all represent the rich and powerful, no matter what else they say.

Looked for internet and couldn't connect. Got to the bus terminal and it was almost empty. Caught the first bus going sort of our way. Got to Corocito. Another bus to Bonito. Arrived about 4 pm, knew there would not be another bus. Dark sky with clouds; rain started. Our only possibility of getting home would be a lift all the way to our road. We walked over to Juan Donald's house. He is the local Jesuit priest, whom we met a few months ago. He offered us hospitality any time that we wanted it. Yesterday, we accepted. Walked 3/4 mile to his place and were welcomed with food, water, showers and beds. We were very tired, hungry, and dirty. Gratitude.

This morning our biggest concern was that you might be worried about us. We're not worried.

We do not expect to return to internet until the first half of August. We are well.

But, yes, keep praying for us and for the people of Honduras.

And All Things Shall Be Made New
From: Sister Alegría

In the Zen Buddhist tradition, the taking of a new name is all about habit energy. You are to be conscious that you are being made new. Learning to use the new name reminds others that you have been made new.

The change of habit (in this case I mean dress) means that we must sew new ones to replace the old ones. We only managed to get two done for Sister Confianza before her Reception into the Novitiate. Her third one was not completed until July 9th. Until then, she wore her sleeveless Postulant habit when it was the only one clean.

That same day, we finished my first white blouse for my First Profession that would be coming up in August. Blouse making is more complicated, but this particular blouse making was a struggle. We had received the gift of two rummage sale white sheets for blouses. One can make clothing from used sheets, but one does not expect it to last very long. One sheet was lightly worn. The other more worn. When one is poor, one accepts what one is given. When one is a nun, one is grateful for all gifts.

I confess, I was not grateful. I was not grateful, but I was fully committed to wearing white blouses as a Professed Sister, so the work began.

Prairie (Sister Confianza) irons, 2006

We cut out the pieces, sew several seams, then wait. Our iron gets its heat from wood coals inside. We need both the light of day and coals from a fire. Usually the ironing step occurs in a morning right after breakfast, while there are still good hot coals. Then more seams, more waiting, more ironing. A blouse is not made in a day.

Sister Confianza's old pants also wore out and were replaced (yes, the same method) in August before my Profession.

Garden Work and a Visit to the Neighbors
From: Sister Confianza's journal   Date: July 18, 2009

Yesterday was quite a day. The plan was to work in the garden, so Beth and I made a quick but hearty breakfast. When I stepped out of the house to take the dirty dishes to the kitchen, there was Daniel! It had been months since we'd seen him, but we'd sent him greetings with his nephew on Monday. Luckily there were a couple flour tortillas left so we could feed him.

Daniel's being here meant we could get two to three times the work done than what Beth and I would have by ourselves. We were able to plant a bunch of legumes in the garden as well as plant *camotes* (sweet potatoes) by using pieces of the vines we already have. Back at the house, he and Beth dug up a few guava seedlings that had sprouted up behind the toilet and dug two holes for planting them in the evening. They also planted a barrier row of pigeon peas to the west of the toilet.

I bathed and made lunch and we ate. Daniel didn't stick around too long which was good because we were tired. Then Beth bathed and we napped.

We wanted to take two of the guava seedlings to Berta's family, so we did our Spiritual Formation exercise before afternoon prayers. Decided to take the Bible and do prayers there since on our first visit Berta had requested it.

When we got to their house, only little Ana and Omar were around, playing in the hammock, but we could see Berta coming across the hill. She and Heidi arrived shortly, carrying boards on their shoulders for the bathroom wall. (There's a big cement pad next to the house with a blue ceramic toilet in the middle.) At the same time Martín and Martín arrived from the other direction carrying *chata* starts and a rifle.

They all were busy for a while getting drinks, etc. Berta gave me a cup of coffee and Beth a pineapple drink. She also served us fried *plátanos* with *cuajada*. Then Martín started work with the chainsaw on a pine log nearby to make posts for the bathroom.

I was thoroughly impressed by the authority and obedience in the family. Martín would ask a kid to go get something, and he did. Then he said "quick" and the kid started running. When Berta didn't respond to a request promptly, Martín said her name and she jumped up. The wood cutting was a whole-family affair. Berta has authority over the kids as well—so far, I've never seen them use violence or the threat of it—and the two parents do things for each other and share ideas. Fascinating to watch.

Beth and I watched the action up close for a while. It was apparent that they were too occupied for worship. Before leaving, Beth asked about getting manure from them. Martín said, "Go for it—there's lots in the corral," and the two girls walked over with us. We'd brought a sack just for this, and filled it up. A bit heavy to carry home, but it will be a boon for our gardening.

We did Vespers as soon as we arrived back at the Monastery. Happily, we didn't have to cook dinner. We put the laundry to soak in the washtub, and planted the two guavas as dusk settled in, then ate leftovers on the porch. Even though we were rather tired—Beth especially, but my lower back and knees also ached—we did music and chatted before evening prayers. Beth was particularly pleased with all we were able to do in the day.

First Profession
From: Sister Alegría   Date: August 7, 2009

This month, I make my First Profession. It means that I move from being a Novice to being a Sister. It is one more official step in the process of no turning back. It is intensely personal and profound. This is one of those precious times when I am forcefully and graciously reminded that today truly is a new beginning, a reminder that all of the Reign of God is there for me, all I need to do is to notice and accept it, again, today—and tomorrow.

One never makes an informed decision; the costs and the rewards reveal themselves along the way. It is a great privilege to live in the Monastery and to become a Sister. I get to say with the Psalmist, "I will dwell in the house of the Lord forever."

The name I have chosen to take is Sister *Alegría* (ah-leh-GREE-ah). It means happiness, joy. I seriously considered Sister *Paciencia* (Patience). I can certainly use more patience. But the name evoked a long-suffering, downtrodden Sister, so Alegría moved into the lead. It is a name that I will be happy to live with. Of course, I will answer to what I am called. You are not obligated by my monastic decisions, only I am.

Monastic Formation

My Profession Day is Saturday, August 29. I wish that you could be here with us. Please hold us in your prayers that day. I pray for you as I hope you pray for me that we can each say with our brother, "My meat is to do the will of him who sent me."

Guests and Special Events
From: Sister Alegría

We had invited local friends to our special days, and they had not come. We didn't know the whys and wherefores. I was not willing to do that again. We planned a private First Profession ceremony.

Now we understand a little more. Poor people don't give parties. Rich people give parties, and it's all about the food. Meat must be served. A chilled drink, preferably soda pop, must be served. Ideally, there would also be a decorated cake. OK, choosing to live in poverty means that we don't give parties. Lesson learned.

Profession Week
From: Beth   Date: September 9, 2009

Profession week was a week to remember. Sometimes we would rather forget. The Saturday before, Berta and her four kids came over early in the afternoon. They borrowed money from us to buy groceries as their boss hadn't paid them on time. They stayed for dinner.

Sunday they came for lunch and dinner. We normally do not cook a noon meal. We make enough at breakfast for two meals, then put the lunch into the still-warm oven and eat sort of warm food at noon. We do this simply to save work. Well, our day of rest became a big cooking day. We cooked and cooked. They are all good eaters. That meant that we started Monday without the usual Sunday's rest and we still had a lot of Profession Day service to plan. Sigh.

Oh, yeah, then there was the firewood emergency. Having guests on Saturday and Sunday meant that all the cooked beans were used up. We had to cook beans on Sunday—a long fire that used up almost all of the firewood.

Then there was the laundry emergency. We usually have four blouses each, but I only had three right then. When we got home Monday night from our day in Limón, we still had enough wood to cook dinner. We also cooked a little food to have a cold breakfast. No firewood left at all. It was very hot and when we bathed, I had to put on my nightgown (it was almost time anyway) as I had no blouse to wear. Sister Confianza washed one for me while I worked in the kitchen.

Tuesday morning is usually wash day, but not wood cutting day. We started with washing two blouses so that when we finished our hard work and were all sweaty we would have clean (even if not dry) blouses. Then we cut firewood, what we could get with the amount of time and energy that we could expend on it. We also did the laundry and all else that needed to be done.

We had trouble finding suitable standing dead trees and ended up cutting firewood three mornings in a row. We kept trying to do the planning. The planning had progress, of a sort.

On Thursday, we each simply despaired that Profession Day could be anything other than disaster.

On Friday morning, we each woke up with determination and a new calm about the whole thing. It would be fine.

Friday, Berta's family showed up for lunch and dinner again. We just fed them and enjoyed their company. The program had been planned, there was enough firewood for the weekend, and we had scored some nice vegetables on Monday so that we would have special food for Profession Day (*pastelitos*, complete with potatoes and onions, topped with shredded cabbage—oooh). I casually let the dad know that the Profession Day would be a private affair.

Profession Day:

We were both very tired, but it was a lovely day and a lovely program. We were grateful not to have invited guests. We made our *pastelitos* for a late lunch, drank our *nance* fruit drink and were happy to rest. We had considered going swimming as a celebrative activity. We considered dancing some of the Dances of Universal Peace dances that we enjoy. Resting seemed the best celebration of all.

Sister Confianza sang a solo—a poem of Teresa of Avila, put to original music by Sister Confianza. Teresa of Avila is a special mentor of mine. One doesn't get a better Profession Day gift than that.

Now I am officially Sister Alegría.

As we settled into our nice Sunday morning, Berta's family showed up—even Dad this time. They arrived during our morning "church" service (which is after our Unprogrammed Meeting for Worship), so we included them. Then they stayed for lunch.

They are delightful people, but guests for several meals for four days out of eight was a little too much for us.

Sisters Alegría and Confianza, 2009

The Gift Not Given
From: Sister Confianza

A dark cloud of negativity fell over us after my Reception into the Novitiate and contaminated what should have been a joyful time with Sister Beth's upcoming First Profession. I failed in love during those months. I was in pain from my parents' lack of acceptance of my vocation, and had second thoughts about becoming a Novice. My inner turmoil erupted against Beth. I was hurtful instead of kind, critical instead of appreciative, a boor instead of a loving Sister. Beth persevered in her path and guided me even in her pain. That September we were able to begin anew, re-founding the Monastery on Love.

A prayer of thanksgiving would have been appropriate at my Reception or Sister Alegría's Profession. Here is a belated one.

<u>Thank You</u>
I thank you, God, for Sister Alegría. Thank you for her joy, for her wide toothy grin and her open-mouthed laugh, for the sparkle in her eyes and the laugh lines around them.

Thank you for her life and all she has shared with me about it. Thank you for her storytelling and the way she finds lessons in the smallest things. Thank you that through them I have learned to appreciate stories and their teachings.

Thank you for being with her even when she didn't know it, and for bringing her through the hard times and trials. Like your son Jesus, she has suffered much at the hands of others; let her suffering also be redemptive. Forgive me the wounds I inflicted on top of those from her past. Give her healing that she might know true joy. Let the suffering cease.

Thank you for calling her to be a nun, and for persisting until she heard. Thank you for all the life experiences that helped her recognize what her call was and what it wasn't, and for your patience as she made her way step by step.

Thank you for sending her to Limón and showing her the place to found the Monastery where she was to live. Thank you for connecting the two of us and for guiding me through my interests to say "yes" and come to Honduras with her in 2006.

Thank you for all that Sister Alegría has taught me: about monastic life, about human nature, about medicine, about sewing and cooking, and more. All I know about monastic life I learned from her: from her mouth, her experiences, and the books she shared with me. I am here because of her. She made the experience available, invited me, and accepted me over and over again, even when I flailed about and hurt her with my judgment, criticism, self-centeredness, and unkind words and actions. Thank you for giving her patience, compassion, and wisdom in dealing with me. Forgive me for all I did—and didn't do—that hurt her. I failed to be appreciative, kind, loving, and compassionate. She was all that for me.

Thank you for my vocation that she saw before I did. Thank you for her invitation to join the Monastery, and for my joy at the idea of it. Thank you for the Amigas del Señor monastic life made possible through your call to her.

You are our rock and our salvation. Our foundation is Love. Thank you for bringing us through the hard times, and guiding us in re-founding ourselves in you and your love.

The Sisters walk from the Monastery toward the stream, 2012

4

Berta

"Love your neighbor as yourself."—Jesus of Nazareth

Learning to be Neighbors
From: Sister Alegría

    Berta, (Henry) Martín and their children almost dominated our thoughts over these next few months. We were eager to go deeper in our understanding of the people who live in our economic class here. Berta was our teacher. Her children were fun and liked to sing with us. They visited often.
    By September, we formally decided in our Meeting for Worship for Business that we would not loan them money again. First it was 200 lempiras, then 300 lempiras. Then another 500 lempiras. This last was actually somewhat of an emergency. Remember those beautiful blue pots and pans? They had been purchased "on time" and were not yet paid for. If (Henry) Martín didn't deliver the money, a collector would come to the house.
    We also decided to do more of our formal spiritual practices early in the day, so that we would be able to whole-heartedly welcome our neighbors when they visited.

Health Care
From: Sister Alegría   Date: September 30, 2009

    We have had a rash of babies with congenital heart defects this year. Last year, we had only one, but it was a severe problem and she died earlier this year. She was a precious child.
    A woman in her early twenties delivered her fourth baby at home in Limoncito. When the baby was one month old, she brought her in because of cough, but she still nursed well and was obviously

growing. On physical exam, she had a loud heart murmur (not the nice kind) and she breathed 120 times per minute! Normal is 40.

I made a referral to the hospital, saying that she needed to take the baby that very day. She had no money. We gave her 200 lempiras ($11) in such a way that she didn't know it was from the Monastery. The time before when something like this happened, we sent the Mom to the mayor's office and he gave the money. But this time, the mayor wasn't in.

Mom insisted that she had to go home to get clothes first. So she hitched a ride home, then another to Rosa's place to wait for a bus. She was headed to Trujillo, where the state hospital is located, and where her sister lives.

At about 4 pm, we stopped at Rosa's on our way home (a little later than normal). The Mom and baby were still there. There are no buses this late in the day. Baby was still stable. I figured she wouldn't get to Trujillo that day. But less than ten minutes later, a big palm oil truck (carrying the "nuts" from which the oil is made) passed us with Mom and baby in the cab. Just another ordinary miracle.

By 9 pm, they were in the Pediatrics Department and an IV was put in. She was in the hospital for four days and sent home with an appointment there for follow-up. "But they didn't give me any money for transportation, so I didn't go." Mom was told that her daughter had pneumonia, but no mention was apparently made of the heart disease, even though I had made a big point of it in the written referral.

It is now a month later, and the baby has a cough again. This time she breathes only 90 times a minute (still pretty far from normal, but lots better than last time). So I treat her as an outpatient for her pneumonia.

Mom wants a consult, too. Her menstrual period is irregular. She is taking birth control pills, but irregularly. We (Juana Nidia and I) decide that she should, indeed, take birth control pills and we instruct her to take them daily. Perhaps you are aware that birth control pills can reduce the amount of mother's milk. It is true. But this woman's babies have come one right after another. I have to say, as a pediatrician, that the risk to my little patient with heart disease would be higher with a too-soon pregnancy, than it would be if the milk supply decreases. We must make hard decisions here.

We'll see what happens. General medical practice in rural Honduras is often a little too interesting. It is unlikely that I'll ever manage to get this child to a consult with anyone who knows more about congenital heart disease than I do. I don't know much; I just do the best that I can.

We ordered medicines in September: adult acetaminophen, adult amoeba medicine, antihistamines for both children and adults, cough suppressant (also all ages) and hexachlorophene soap. These are all relatively cheap medicines. We are in luck that the medicines sent by the government are the costly ones.

When I called Nurse Eloyda (in El Pino) to order the meds, she was desperate for medicines for her clinic. We spent about $730, just over half for our clinic and the rest for hers. Now we can all serve our patients better. We are very grateful for Eloyda and for her help.

Our medical work is only one day a week, but it often gives me a lot to think about the rest of the week.

Haves and Have-nots
From: Sister Alegría

We have a treadle sewing machine. Berta often asked us to do sewing projects for her. The timing was particularly bad as I had just made First Profession and we had not yet made all four white (required) blouses for me. In fact, I had only two. In our busy life, I considered getting those blouses made a high priority. It seemed to take forever. The third blouse was finished in March and the fourth in September, 2010.

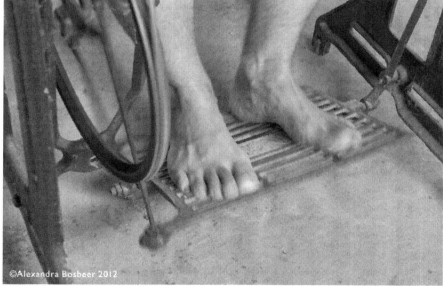

Sister Confianza's feet push the treadle of the sewing machine, 2012

Berta

Berta was very comfortable putting Sister Confianza in a state of conflict of interest. What is my priority at the sewing machine—Sister Alegría's clothing or Berta's clothing?

When cars go past us on the road, not offering us a lift, it is usual that they slow down enough to explain why (too full, only going a tiny distance in our direction). Those who have are under moral obligation to help those who have not. We have a sewing machine.

Berta was only the first neighbor to ask us to sew for her. We now take it as a matter of course. Most of the sewing is altering newly purchased, or hand-me-down used clothing. As owners of a sewing machine we sew for neighbors who do not have one.

An Amigas del Señor Book
From Sister Alegría

We received the first manuscript of <u>Amigas del Señor: Methodist Monastery</u> in September, 2009. We were to return it with any changes in 30 days. We managed to do that by making an extra trip to La Ceiba. We were over busy and deferred our Annual Retreat until October.

We were actually over busy without the manuscript to review. There's an old saying, "If you want something done, ask someone who is busy to do it." It was a joyful task. We laughed as we read of our adventure in our first two years, and enjoyed an occasional use of words that seemed clever. We carefully avoided mentioning it in our updates, since Rosalie, our publisher, had not yet told us a date when it would see the light of day.

A Trip to La Ceiba
From: Sister Confianza   Date: September 30, 2009

We're in La Ceiba today. I am stuffed after a lunch of tripe soup. Many people have raved over it, so I thought I'd try it. I found the meat rather blah, but I enjoyed the broth with cooked *malanga* and *yuca* (like potatoes). I think I'll stick with the armadillo and *guatuza* meat that our neighbor Berta gives us when her husband goes hunting.

Today is Sister Alegría's 62nd birthday! I thank God for her life and the opportunity to live the monastic life with her. I have learned much from her and with her these last three and a half years. Tonight we'll celebrate with a chocolate cake that Allison baked!

96

We came on Saturday to visit our missionary friends, Larry and Allison, in Las Mangas, a small community on the Cangrejal River south of La Ceiba. Last time we visited them was at Easter, 2008, when Sister Alegría had just returned from the US. Larry and Allison got married that June. It is good to see friends and to share with each other all that God is doing in our lives. They are particularly excited to have three Honduran university students living with them, who are part of their young people's discipleship group. Yesterday, Sister Alegría and I went with Larry to see his mountainside property where he is raising corn using a terracing system and growing fruit trees. We're planning to go with Allison tomorrow to see some other mission projects in the area.

We've been without postage stamps for several weeks—there are none to be had in the Department of Colón—so today we bought enough to last over three months. Also today, we were able to pick up our new ID cards, showing that we are legal residents of Honduras. Now we can use them at the bank instead of our passports—much less hassle! It's the little things, sometimes.

The political situation continues to be strange. The deposed president, Mel Zelaya, managed to get back into the country ten days ago and is chilling at the Brazilian embassy. The Organization of American States and other international leaders are involved trying to find a peaceful solution. Most people here and abroad seem to think that electing a new president in the November elections would do it—just put the past behind and move on. Many people see it as a personal problem between Mel and the current president, Micheletti. Probably both sides violated the constitution. We are just thankful that life continues quite normally out where we are. The local concern is whether the rain will come so that the corn can fill out; there were a lot of losses to the bean harvest because of drought.

Who We Are
From: Sister Alegría

These months of September, 2009, to January, 2010, were a time of deep discernment. Berta and her family came into our lives at the same time as Little Sister Magdeleine of Jesus (1898-1989), foundress of the Little Sisters of Jesus. The Little Sisters of Jesus is the Roman Catholic religious order most like ours. We received, from Little Sister Teresita of Jesus, who resides in Mexico, the gift of a Spanish-language book written by a Little Sister of Jesus for the order telling of the first few years of the order. What a precious gift!

Berta

We decided to try out their lifestyle—much less retired in prayer, much more focused on mixing with the poor people of the neighborhood. Berta gave us a workout. We regularly had the opportunity to put aside our scheduled spiritual practices to practice hospitality, times that supposedly were for *lectio divina* ("holy reading") or Spiritual Formation became times of food preparation, sharing, and singing. Even during our first Annual Retreat, we welcomed them and put aside the scheduled program. This gave us the opportunity to really see how well the Little Sisters' lifestyle would work for us. I was amazed that I was able to give heartfelt welcome, even as I lamented the loss of the planned activities. Our scant three-plus years of monastic life was effecting good changes in us.

We put our spiritual practices into the morning hours, so that their afternoon visits coincided with our physical work, which fit with socializing better. Now when we are having retreats, whether short or long, we let our closest neighbors know that we are not available for socializing.

We are clear that we are Amigas del Señor. We are not Protestant Little Sisters of Jesus. We are Amigas del Señor, not Protestant Carmelites, no matter how important Teresa of Avila, Thérèse of Lisieux, and Brother Lawrence are in our thinking. This period of time was crucial in our ongoing discernment of who we are: the Amigas del Señor. We continue our commitment to ecumenical inclusiveness. Our Spiritual Formation months-long "interns" have included Roman Catholic, Baptist, Quaker, and Ethiopian Orthodox.

Overnight Guests
From: Sister Alegría

We never knew when Berta and her children would visit or how long they would stay. She was afraid to be home "alone." Four children but no man meant alone—vulnerable.

The first time they stayed overnight came as a surprise. We had spent a pleasant afternoon together, made and ate dinner, then dusk thickened. She just sat, looking vulnerable and scared. Martín wouldn't be coming home that night.

Oh.

I suggested they stay. They all slept on one bunk; never a complaint. We only had one unoccupied mattress.

When Martín would go to town, he whistled from the road when he returned and they all scrambled to obey his call. Sometimes Berta didn't know whether he would return that day or not. What he told the boss and what he told Berta were not often the same. We never learned what his secrets were.

Forgiving a Grudge
From: Sister Confianza   Date: October 28, 2009

In mid-October, I woke up in the middle of the night with a disturbing realization: there was something from a couple of years ago for which I had not forgiven Sister Alegría. I don't think of myself as one who holds grudges, so this was serious—especially because it was something relatively minor and old!

That week, we were having our first Annual Monastery Retreat, with teachings and readings from Little Sister Magdeleine of Jesus. The Little Sisters of Jesus live as poor among the poor throughout the world, adopting the local lifestyle. They are contemplatives who seek to see Jesus in their neighbor and share God's love through their presence. One of the topics for our retreat that day was fraternal love between the Sisters; it was the perfect opportunity to share with Sister Alegría my situation. I'd spent all morning trying to make sense of the old grudge and figure out how to move on. This is the story:

When Sister Alegría and I moved to Honduras in 2006, one of the things we brought with us was peppercorns, so we had fresh ground pepper in our food for many months. I really like pepper, so when we ran out, I wanted to buy more. However, we couldn't find peppercorns anywhere. Even ground pepper was hard to get: it was only in the bigger cities and when we found it, it had already been sitting on the shelf for a long time. For Sister Alegría, that decided it; the ground pepper lost its flavor too fast to be worth it. But I really wanted pepper (in the US, I was more likely to use it than salt on my food), and I thought to myself, *Well, don't all the other ground spices we have at home lose their flavor as well? And we still keep them on hand.*

Around that time, we were working on issues related to how we witnessed to our call to live in voluntary poverty, that is, our choice to live as poorly as the poor around us do. (It is not involuntary poverty, where one tries to live at the highest standard possible with the little one has.) For example, I had a simple, sturdy toiletry kit. We were doing a lot of traveling in Honduras at the time and Sister Alegría was uncomfortable with using it. It was too fancy and our poor neighbors don't have such a thing; it bespoke a higher lifestyle than we were wanting to live. Since we already had it, I didn't see why we couldn't find a use for it, but eventually I agreed we

99

could get rid of it, even though I didn't fully understand her view. (We only realized much later that it was all that traveling that belied a life of poverty.)

One thing I began to wonder about was our collection of spices. We had all kinds of them, most of which had been brought down or were gifts from the US. They were certainly part of a more upscale lifestyle. There are a limited number of spices available in Honduras, and people buy them in tiny amounts. I thought we should move toward having fewer spices, and certainly only ones we could get here. When I suggested we use up the spices we had, get rid of the yet unopened bottles, and stop buying so many, Sister Alegría said, "No, I don't think that's necessary." Apparently, it didn't bother her. But didn't she see how much it bothered me? And I'd just given in on an issue that had bothered her (the toiletry kit). And anyway, if it was OK to have spices, why not pepper???

That was all two and a half years ago. We never bought more pepper nor got rid of the other spices, though we have been slowly using them up. I have obviously done just fine without pepper and we've both enjoyed the flavorful food. (I hadn't realized at the time how much the spices were helping her to learn to adjust to eating the food here.) So what a shock it was to realize I had never forgiven Sister Alegría about the pepper. As I thought about it, I saw that I'd never spoken frankly to her about it either. I kept all those thoughts in my head, and that grudge in my heart. How could she understand how much I liked pepper or the challenge it was to learn to live without it if I never faced it myself or told her? And how could we come to a shared solution on the spices if we never spoke about it openly? Instead of seeking God's will in the situation together, I did a lot of self-justifying and making excuses to try to get what I wanted. I couldn't even see that, if having fewer spices were the solution (as I thought), Sister Alegría was making progress in that direction by not buying more pepper! I had reason for celebration and instead was resentful.

It is all quite laughable today. Sister Alegría asked me later if I have now forgiven her. I think I have. Now I need to forgive myself for being so selfish and holding it against her. It is a lesson to me about openness: being open and aware of my own feelings and motivations, open in communication, and open to God's will in every situation.

Fear of the Dark
From: Sister Alegría

The first few times that Berta and her children stayed overnight at the Monastery, she and Martín (the older boy) really wanted to make sure the doors and the window shutters were bolted. Our usual practice was to let the temperature decide about windows open or closed. No, for them it was about fear.

We never really explored that fear. Imagine that there are bad guys outside the house who want to hurt or rob us. Does a bolted shutter actually change our risk much? You'll see. Once when they spent the night, Sister Confianza had us all go outside after dark to look at the stars and watch the full moon rise. Timidly, Berta and her children came out and looked, staying close to the back door, and came right back in when we felt done.

The family always participated in Compline (bedtime prayers). One time as we were moving backless benches around to maximize the value of the kerosene lamp, Heidi was thoughtful and then commented: "You don't need to be afraid because you sing to God every night."

Trouble for a Neighbor
From: Sister Alegría   Date: October 28, 2009

Last Wednesday, we visited Berta. They had promised us "new corn" last week. We bought more green bananas than usual. In fact, we bought as many as we could carry. Berta likes them a lot and neither household is harvesting bananas. So we took ten bananas, some lemongrass (for tea) and two small sewing projects that Sister Confianza had done for Berta.

Martín, Berta's partner, was at the house but not working. This is not usual. His face was grave. His uncle had been murdered on Monday. He had lived alone in Hicoteas (the eastern end of the county).

Everyone knows who killed uncle. This is always the case here. There was no motive—just *"por gusto,"* which is to say, because he felt like it, nothing more important than that. Uncle was chopped to death with a machete.

This is the first time in Martín's family that someone has been murdered. It's the kind of thing that happens to other people, to other families. It is often associated with drug use and with alcohol overuse. The very lucrative drug smuggling business sometimes has spectacular murders. Everyone knows who the smugglers are, too.

But a murder in a "salt of the earth" family—no. A hard blow for Martín.

The family discussed what to do. The most obvious action is to kill the perpetrator. The family has no experienced killers. Even if such a reprisal were successful, there might be revenge for that—the start of a whole bloody feud. Martín's mother was afraid of the consequences if that route were taken. She had just lost a brother; that was too much. She didn't want to lose any more loved ones. Out of respect for her fear and her wishes the family decided to do nothing.

You may be wondering about the police. The police do not investigate crimes and they do not pursue suspects. They will arrest someone if it isn't too difficult or too dangerous (especially if you give them some cash—this is strictly gossip, understand). But more to the point, this action would be just as dangerous to the family as trying to kill the murderer themselves. Potential witnesses in court have been killed, as have been those who called the police. Most people are not willing to testify in court; it is too dangerous.

Martín doesn't have a cell phone right now. Someone called his boss, Elías, asking him to drive out to tell Martín (and, I suppose, to bring Martín and the family to town). Elías said that he couldn't do it. Mateo's son came from Limoncito to tell Martín. Mateo took them to Limón that evening.

The burial was on Tuesday. There is no embalming; there is no refrigeration. Even the next day, a certain odor has begun. Berta and a co-sister-in-law cooked mounds of food for the wake.

They walked back to their place on Wednesday morning (yes, all, including the four-year-old). Elías gave Martín $5 (one day's wage). Martín has worked for Elías for six months. He is a tireless worker and the place is being transformed before our eyes.

There are not laws about an employer's responsibility for his/her workers. But everyone knows what those responsibilities are—to help when help is needed.

Martín is dealing with a double blow (or is it triple?). He has lost an uncle to violence; he knows that his family is vulnerable to violence; and when the chips are down, he is on his own, no support from his boss. A tough week for Martín.

Martín and little Martín (eight years old) picked corn and the kids, Martín and I husked it while Sister Confianza helped Berta make *fritos*—fried patties of seasoned ground corn (midway between corn on the cob and fully ripe). Martín sent us home with almost half a bushel of cobs of corn. We will have corn for weeks.

Beth grinds corn at the kitchen counter, 2007

Each day, we sun the not-yet-dry corn. We de-grain what we want to use that day, boil it, wash it, grind it twice, then form and cook our fresh corn tortillas. Delicious. Not a convenience food.

Maybe you would say a little prayer for Martín and Elías. This relationship could use a little divine help.

Berta

The Power of Forgiveness
From: Sister Alegría

We visited a friend during this time, whom I will call Susana. She had recently passed through a severe trial with her husband, whom I will call Samuel.

Samuel had been sexually unfaithful, again. He even had a photo of himself and his girlfriend on his cell phone. That was the last straw. Susana was in misery. Susana decided to fast and pray in the nearby church; so she did. By the fifth day of her fast she was having a lot of trouble physically: headaches and nausea. But she stuck with it, still pleading for guidance.

"If I don't forgive Samuel, I can't get baptized." This came to her mind as clear as a bell. She wanted to be baptized. She decided to forgive Samuel and "to stay." She ended her fast in spiritual peace.

A few days later, there was an evening worship service. Samuel was still keeping up appearances as a good husband; he drove his father-in-law to church. (Father-in-law has no car.) Samuel sat far to the rear of the church.

A friend of Susana whispered to her, "Don't you want to suggest to Samuel that he go to the front and give his life to Jesus?" Susana replied, "No, that's not my task. Maybe it is yours." Sure enough, the friend moves to sit beside Samuel.

"Don't you want to go kneel in prayer at the front of the church and give your life to Jesus?"

"No, I don't want to."

"That's not you speaking, Samuel, that's the devil speaking. Don't you want to go up and give your life to Jesus?"

Samuel did.

Some months later, Susana tells us that Samuel has given up smoking. And, "Look, what a fine figure of a man he is now. Before, he was a skinny little stick. Those vices are bad for the body."

Now, Samuel makes jokes of his anti-church comments before his conversion. Susana and Samuel have both been baptized in the traditional immersion-in-the-river style. They are both overweight pillars of the church. Samuel, who doesn't read, carried his Bible to church with him last time we worshipped there.

Ridiculous
From: Sister Alegría   Date: November 18, 2009

Last month the medicine warehouse in Trujillo burned down—with all the medicine that was ready to be delivered to the public health clinics, including ours! There will be no medicines coming until January (and then only if there is a new warehouse available!—forgive my cynicism).

The Monastery decided to buy medicines. The bank account had $865. We decided to spend $800 on medicines, $50 for cost of living, and leave $15 to keep the account open. We have never actually lived on only $50 for a month, but now seems like a good time to try. We have lots of friends who will give us food when we need it. Some give us food even when we don't need free food.

Monday, we worked at Centro de Salud, giving out our last birth control pills and our last birth control shots. We finished our morning work just after 1 pm. Sister Confianza and I went over to the orphanage for our weekly free lunch. Returned to the clinic to make up the wish list of medicines. I asked the head nurse, Juana Nidia, "Of the more expensive medicines, which is more important: high blood pressure or birth control?"

No hesitation, "Birth control."

We called the Texans (Clines and Herringtons), who are up to their eyeballs in Honduran missions (health care and scholarships to help poor kids go to public school). We all hoped to meet up. They were to be here sometime in November. They have arrived and will be in Tocoa on Friday. That meant that we would be traveling to Tocoa this week.

Arrived home a little past 4 pm and got to work, planning, cooking dinner, bathing, putting laundry to soak. We had picked up mail and decided to defer reading the letters until we return from Tocoa.

Tuesday, we got up and worked. Big breakfast, laundry to wash and leave hanging inside the house, and packing. We'll come home with dirty clothes; we need clean ones to put on. Finally, ready to go. First stop, Berta's house. We had a small pot of cooked beans to give her. They wouldn't keep. And to tell her that we would be gone and will return, God willing, on Saturday. We walk almost a half mile AWAY from our route to visit Berta, but it needed to be done. She gave us two tiny pieces of chicken and some cheese to add to our packed lunch (of toasted corn tortillas and refried beans).

The rain began. We put our rain plastics over the backpacks and put up our umbrellas. About two-thirds of the way, a truck came along. We hailed it for a lift. They stopped. As we were about to climb into the bed of the truck, a woman came out and asked me to see a sick woman. So I did—she was slumped in the front seat. Sixteen years old and had an attack that seemed more like a seizure than a stroke. Sixteen-year-olds can have strokes, but they are pretty rare. She was stable and we decided together that they should take her to the private doctor in Bonito. (They can afford private care, and there was no doctor in the public health clinic today).

Then we climbed into the back of the truck and were dropped off in Limoncito. We visited our friend, Margarita and her daughter, Delmys. They shared sweet juicy oranges. When the bus arrived, we hopped on.

The rest of the trip was uneventful. Our first order of business in Tocoa was to call Eloyda, the nurse who orders medicines for us. Where was the medicine list? Not to be found. We reconstructed the list. We had spent quite a bit of time on it the night before, trimming it down to the money available.

Then we talked about the amount of money available. We didn't remember the exact balance of the bank account. Well, that's easy, look in the bank book. No bank book. It was still home, probably right next to the medicine list. This was not encouraging news.

Next stop, the bank. I took my new residency card and my passport and told my story to the nice young teller. He said that I could make a deposit without the book, but not a withdrawal. I told him that I couldn't get the bankbook—two hours by bus and one hour on foot. I was standing in front of him in my rain-soaked straw sun hat and my mud stained faded blue habit. The withdrawal would be redeposited in a different account with the same bank. Then, of course, there was my earnest tale of woe. He said he would see what he could do.

My national ID card labels me as a "religious." I think that helped my credibility, too.

We waited. I split the time between laughing at ourselves with Sister Confianza (we often don't believe our own lives, why should you?) and praying, *"Venga tu reino, hagase tu voluntad. Thy kingdom come, thy will be done."* After an hour, I was permitted to do my transactions. Thank God.

Then I thought, "Yes, this is how it starts—the church becoming handmaiden to the government." I was so grateful to be a government certified religious, which does give me a benefit of the doubt in many settings. Ah, yes, what would have happened if I were once again an illegal alien? So, we are warned and we keep warning ourselves. I have seen more than enough of the church being handmaiden to the government in my own country. I don't want to be part of it here.

This morning, we called Eloyda, telling her that the money had been deposited and telling her what medicines we wanted. She is confident that there is enough money for all that we asked for. Thank God.

That's the news for today. We'll be in Tocoa until early Saturday morning.

Berta's Wallpaper
From: Sister Alegría

One day in the rainy season, our friend Berta and her four children came to visit us at the Monastery. She asked me if we have any newspapers.

"Yes," I answered, a little confused.

"Will you give me some?"

"Sure." I went to get them.

When I handed them over, she asked, "How did you get them?"

"We bought them."

"Oh."

Berta can't read, so I was really curious what she wanted the newspapers for. I asked.

Our houses are made of wide wooden planks straight up and down. A well-made house, like ours, has narrow strips of wood on the outside covering the cracks between the boards. Her house is not as well made. When there is a windy rainstorm, the water blows through the cracks, getting everything and everybody wet.

Berta made a paste of flour and water and wallpapered the inside of her house where the problem was most grievous. She later reported that it worked well. The little girls were effusive about how attractive their wallpaper was. They especially liked the ads— pictures of "pretty ladies."

How rich and privileged we in the Monastery are! Our walls don't let the rain in (at least not very often or very much). We can afford a newspaper once a month and bus fare to the big town where we can buy one. We can read.

Berta taught me many lessons.

Trees
From: Sister Alegría   Date: December 18, 2009

All of our near neighbors have been actively cutting forest to make pastures for cows (and a little space for crops). This has been going on since we moved here, but the activity really accelerated in the early part of this calendar year.

Berta

By July, we became convinced that we should actively do something about the watershed. We are not activists nor are we community development workers. We are just two nuns trying to live in harmony with nature and our neighbors. We decided that we can plant trees. Our land is forested, some densely, but much in what is called "pine savannah," which means pines and other survivalist trees with large spaces of grass between them. We diverted some of our gardening time and energy to plant trees and will focus the majority of our remaining gardening time and energy on legumes and cover crops. This means giving up, pretty much, short term goals for food production. We planted three types of beans with limited success, one of which provides some food. We treat this food contribution as a fringe benefit, not a primary goal. But we are pretty grateful for it.

We begged cashew seedlings and seeds, for ourselves and for Berta and Martín. Begged lots of guava seeds—same distribution. Both guava and cashew have fabulous characteristics for our purposes. They can grow in very poor soil (which is the kind we have) and they produce fruits. Folks are unlikely to cut down trees that produce fruits. We will not be caring for these trees.

We let mango pits sprout in our mulch-to-fertilizer spot near a *plátano*. We gave them to Berta and Martín to plant. They gave us a lovely avocado. We planted the pit in a seed bag. It grew beautifully, but we weren't able to prepare a proper planting hole for it. We gave it to them to plant at their place. I hope that it does well. We planted a coconut in our backyard. We planted a wide variety of nitrogen-fixing trees.

Our first fruit tree to bear was a lime tree this fall. Seven limes. We're pretty happy with that. Makes very good limeade. We hope for more than seven next year.

Tree Update
From: Sister Alegría

Since 2014, we eat cashew apples in the spring, from the cashew tree that we planted well and cared for. The mangos and guavas at Berta and Martín's have survived. The avocado and cashew did not. Our coconut is growing. The lime tree mysteriously died. None of the leguminous (nitrogen-fixing) trees have done well in our acid clay soil.

Celebrating Advent
From: Sister Confianza   Date: December 18, 2009

The third week of Advent is almost over. I have really been enjoying this season of preparing for the coming of Christ: as a baby in Bethlehem long ago and into my heart today. It is a beautiful thing to have the opportunity every day to once again invite God to be with me and to be my guide. God's incarnation, in the person of Jesus and in each of us, is an amazing reality that we celebrate and practice as we seek to see the Divine in each person we meet.

At the Monastery we have immersed ourselves in the season by using Advent songs to open our thrice daily prayer times. We light candles in a wreath each evening and are using an Advent resource to guide our evening prayers. Yesterday I led us in our monthly retreat, structuring it around the 9th century antiphons that are the basis for the hymn "O Come, O Come Emmanuel." We reflected on the various names for God and Jesus used in the antiphons, like Wisdom, Light, and Cornerstone.

Sister Alegría shows off the Advent wreath, 2013

A couple of weeks ago I was blessed to translate several Advent and Christmas songs into Spanish. Sometimes translations just come to me. They usually require further refining; often it is months before I am ready to share them. At least one of the seven or so from that week ("People, Look East") came together quite easily with some great rhymes, so we're already singing it, which is very exciting. We've found that there are some gaps in the range of themes and theology of the Spanish-language hymns that we have. I have at times translated a song or written lyrics to fill such a gap. Other times I translate songs that I happen to like, and sometimes the words just come with no particular reason at all. I feel that it is a gift from God, and I hope that others may be blessed by it as well.

We're looking forward to celebrating *La Nochebuena* (Christmas Eve) next week with our neighbors. The tradition here is to stay up till midnight to welcome the Christ-child. Hopefully we will get to make and eat tamales together. We've also got a papaya ripening—from our own plant!—to share. Yum!

I hope you experience God's love in your life this Christmas.

Gardening Ups and Downs
From: Sister Confianza   Date: January 27, 2010

<u>Pineapples</u>

We've got a patch of about seventy pineapple plants in our hillside garden. Our acidic clay soil might not be good for much, but everyone agrees it's good for pineapples. They normally take a year and a half to bear. We figured even if we couldn't give them very good care due to limited time and resources (physical strength, manure, etc.) they'd bear eventually. In 2009, we expected a harvest of about thirty fruits. We got five, all in the first part of the year. In August we went to check on the plants; they'd gotten pretty weedy and were looking a little wilty. Many of the plants had brownish leaves in the middle. Upon closer examination, we found that they were rotten, with a hole through the middle to the outside. Some of the plants had begun to put out new side shoots. We wondered what was going on. Was it a bug that had chewed through? We'd seen rhinoceros beetles munching on ripening fruit in the past. So we started asking around.

We talked to one friend who grows pineapples here and he said he'd never seen or heard of such a problem. We contacted the folks at ECHO (www.echonet.org), who train agricultural missionaries primarily for the tropics, and a couple months later, after a long search, they came up with "heart rot"—a fungus. We were devastated. We had lost a whole crop of pineapples, and would have to wait for the sprouts to develop to get more. We didn't even know if we should keep the plants that we had—they might just spread the rot. And, if we replanted the sprouts, it could spread to them too!

One basic rule for healthy crops is "field sanitation" (keeping the weeds down) so in late October we cut the weeds. Our friend Daniel, who has helped us with agriculture stuff in the past, visited in December. He recognized the heart rot as one that had killed a couple of banana starts he had given us earlier in the year and recommended ashes. So, as they become available from our kitchen fire, we've begun putting ashes down on the affected plants. Happily, the plants continue to grow, and just last week we discovered one is turning red in the center, which means it's about to flower. Three of the four pineapple plants by the house (which weren't affected by the heart rot) are also flowering. Just four or five months and we'll have some fruit to eat!

A young pineapple fruit, 2007

Cacaos

On December 23 we spent the day at our neighbors Berta and Martín's place making tamales for Christmas. When we got home in the afternoon, we found a package wrapped in our hammock on the porch. It was a plastic bag labeled "*Adornos Navideños* (Christmas Ornaments)." Inside were all kinds of fruits: oranges, limes, two apples, bananas, and cacao fruits. Apples are only sold in the bigger towns, so we're guessing it was a gift from our friend Juan Donald, the Jesuit priest in Bonito Oriental who comes to say mass in La Fortuna every so often.

Cacao seeds (from which chocolate is derived) lose their vitality very quickly, so we decided to make up some bags with soil to plant some of them. Sister Alegría in particular loves watching plants sprout. Berta showed up the afternoon we were doing that, and her four kids helped out. All 18 seeds have sprouted and are growing nicely in the shade of the acacia. The kids will get to take "theirs" (two each) when they're a bit bigger, and we'll probably give the others away too, as we don't have good land for them. The cacao seeds we didn't plant, we toasted and ground with toasted corn to make chocolate *pinol*. Cooked with milk or water, it is like hot cereal.

Harvest News

The passion fruit vines we planted in 2006 had a nice crop in December and January. They are said to take one to three years before they start bearing. In August, 2008, we harvested maybe a dozen small fruits. Then an insect attacked one of the vines and severed it about four feet above the ground. We gave up our expectations for more fruit. But then it began growing again from below the cut, and this year bore more abundantly! It was as though that insect just gave it a needed pruning. The second vine bore for the first time, and it had fruits as big as tennis balls. The sour pulp inside is good for making a nice drink by adding sugar and water. We gave many of the fruits to friends.

Our papaya plant, growing next to the dry compost toilet where it gets fertilized from the urine runoff, is also bearing. We had our first big fruit from it in August and a second one soon after. We were particularly delighted when we could time the ripening of another papaya for our Christmas Eve celebration with our neighbors by scoring it. This Saturday we picked another one which is currently ripening. There are a bunch of fruits growing close together, so we may have several weeks of papaya feasting. Too bad for us—it's one of our favorites!

2010's first banana harvest was a bunch of about seventy small fruits. It was our first crop of that particular cultivar, and we found that they were quite yummy ripe. We shared many of them with Berta's family, and we've got more banana and plantain plants setting fruit.

Prairie (Confianza) shows off a bunch of bananas in the garden, 2008

This month, we also planted lots of cowpeas in the front yard with the help of the neighbor kids. They're coming up nicely. They should provide good ground cover and even some green beans eventually. It's a very exciting beginning to the year!

Feast of the Kings
From: Sister Alegría   Date: January 27, 2010

We had a party to celebrate Epiphany, the end of the Christmas season (January 6). We invited Berta and her family. It was a cold, rainy day (probably 70-75°F). Martín, the dad, didn't come.

They arrived in the early afternoon, the girls in their pretty party dresses. Sister Confianza served milk that Berta brought and freshly baked gingerbread. It was fabulous and everyone liked it.

It was so cold that everyone was uncomfortable. We went to the dancing circle (west of the house near the west bench). We danced "I woke up this morning with the sun in my heart," then Father Abraham. (All songs are sung in Spanish unless otherwise stated.) Heidi the ten-year-old's red dress flared out when she spun— very festive. We were all warmed up—back to the porch.

113

Honduran newspapers are half the size of US papers. Why is this relevant? Because we needed crowns, of course. This is the feast of the Kings. We were all to be Queens and Kings today.

We made standard newspaper hats (just smaller). If you put it on sideways it looks more crown-like. Our crowns were a good size for the children, but small for adults.

I supervised the two younger ones with pre-folded hats, while Sister Confianza instructed Berta and the two older children in making theirs. When we put them on, we all just laughed (for quite a while). It was hilarious.

Sister Confianza made a "star" using a wad of newspaper on the end of a stick. She wrapped the wad in a sheet of bright yellow tissue paper and tied it with yellow twine. It looked like a giant Tootsie Pop with a triple length stick.

We practiced our kings-following-the-star-bringing-presents-to-baby-Jesus song, hereafter known as the traveling song. When we had it down pretty well, we were ready for the main event: the pageant/worship service.

We opened the worship service (all wearing our crowns, of course) by singing all the Christmas songs that we knew. This is not very many. Honduras does not have a tradition of Christmas carols. The event most celebrated in Christian songs here is the Second Coming.

Then I read the story. Matthew 2:1-12. You know the script.

Ana (six years old) had a sore foot; that meant that she stayed on the porch (palace) as King Herod. With her crown and her lavender dress, she was very regal.

The rest of us went off to our "far country" (the dancing area) and wandered around looking for interesting stars. Sister Confianza climbed on to the bench and waved her star around until we astute astrologers/astronomers noticed it. Then she led us in "This Little Light of Mine." Imagine, if you will, Sister Confianza with a small newspaper hat perched sideways on her head, with her very large "little light." She looked like a whacked-out fairy godmother with a magic wand. No one had ever told me that I should master the skill of singing and laughing at the same time to be a nun. I'll work on it.

We then followed our Star of Bethlehem on a snake dance to the palace, while singing our traveling song. Now Sister Confianza appeared more like a cross between a drum major and a mother duck leading her ducklings. More laughing as we sing.

When we get to the palace, we have to sing, "I Stand at the Door and Knock, Knock, Knock." Martín (eight years old) leads this song; it is sort of his song, because when we did the Luke pageant, he was Joseph and had to sing it trying to get into the inn. Herod was more hospitable. We were allowed in.

The Star and two monarchs removed their crowns to be the high priests and masters of the law. They each wore a rectangle of colored fabric (two purple and one green) on their heads as symbols of their exalted status as holy experts.

I fed King Herod her lines. Sister Confianza led the holy experts in their responses.

We then took a short break. It is Ana's turn to be Mary and Omar, the four-year-old's, to be Joseph. I gave Ana a piggyback ride to the east bench (I mean Bethlehem) with Omar in tow. (They left their crowns at the palace.) I carried a blue shopping bag on this whole trip. This time, I pulled out Baby Jesus (a rolled up towel—you know, one that had once been a habit) wrapped in a "blanket." Mary held him tenderly while Joseph stood by keeping mother and child "safe." Very Honduran; a mere male presence is considered protection. Go figure.

Back to the palace; break is over.

Crowns back on the ex-holy experts and we take off on another snake dance, this one a little longer, south of the house and through the yard east of the house to the prayer bench (or east bench if you prefer)—singing our traveling song again.

We arrive at Bethlehem and ask to be admitted. Yes, we sing "I Stand at the Door" again.

Then we sang all the Christmas songs we knew again, including "Love came down at Christmas." We also sang, "Shalom." Very cosmopolitan to sing in Hebrew, even if there is only one word in the song. It is popular with this crowd and a good song honoring the Prince of Peace.

Now it is time for presents. Out of the blue bag come gold (with red printing) matchboxes for gold. Mary accepts them and wraps them in with baby Jesus. Frankincense—more matchboxes. Myrrh—you guessed it, more matchboxes. They all went into the blanket.

The ground was wet, so our required sleeping was mimed in the traditional head tilted to the side, resting on the hands. We had to sleep so that a heavenly messenger (who looked suspiciously like the star) could warn us away from that Herod guy.

So we went "home" by another way—north of the house. While we were doing this, the star carried Mary and walked with Joseph back to the porch. We finished the worship service/pageant by singing all the Christmas songs we knew, followed by a brief prayer.

The kids played with the matchboxes (and unmade and remade their crowns) for about two hours. We had a raspberry Kool-

Berta

Aid break. Kool-Aid is pronounced here the same as in the US; it is rarely Kool-Aid brand. Omar cracked everyone up when he asked what we made the Kool-Aid from. Only later did I realize that he wanted to know the name of the flavor, as raspberry flavor is rare, here.

We served chicken soup for dinner. We had bought two pounds of chicken, so these were very generous servings by our neighborhood standards. It was plenty, since we were all full of gingerbread.

After dinner, they packed up the matchboxes, the crowns and the left-over gingerbread and went home. It was a very successful party.

Amigas del Señor 2009 Year-End Financial Report
From: Sister Alegría   Date: January 28, 2010

EXPENSES	
Food	$705
Household	325
Alms	2,777
Communication	388
Health	190
Clothing	6
Immigration	1,803
Transportation	87
Library	136
Property Taxes	2
Outstanding Loan	37
Total cost of living	$3,679
Alms	$2,777
TOTAL EXPENSES	$6,456

All categories except Immigration and Outstanding Loan (a new category) went down from last year. The overview of the spiritual practice of money management this year is probably similar to many other households. We spent more than I had hoped and gave less in alms than I had hoped. (Sound familiar?)

Some details:

- Travel: Travel is a new category. It is the bus fare for any overnight trip. It used to be part of household expenses. We travel much less as it becomes ever clearer that this is a contemplative monastery.

- <u>Food and Household Expenses</u>: These expenses were much lower than in the past. One reason is that the land is now providing more fruit and vegetables, expensive items here. Of more significance is our transition more and more into the non-money economy. An important part of how one supports oneself in rural Honduras is the giving and receiving of gifts and favors.

  Economic justice in Honduras means that those who are wealthy pay more and those who are poor pay less. The first time that Don Julio, a wealthy man from La Fortuna, gave us a ride to Bonito, he charged us twice what the bus fare would have been. Now he gives us a free lift anytime that he can, occasionally even going out of his way a little to help us get to Centro de Salud in a timely fashion. (Wealthy, by the way, means that he has a car and a driver.)

  Our friend, Francisco, gave us thirty pounds of corn. This was during the time when we had $50 to live on for a month. We were very grateful. It was also a reminder that poverty itself is part of how a monastery supports itself. Cooking with corn is a lot of work (boil it with *cal* (lime), wash it a few times, grind it in the mill). If we had been living at a higher standard of living (using corn flour), Francisco would not have had a gift for us; corn would have been "beneath" us perhaps. We have had to disappoint friends who would like to give us gifts to raise our standard of living—friends in the US and friends in Honduras. Monastic history has demonstrated clearly that wealth destroys the capacity to "live the life." We are here to live the life.

- <u>Alms</u>: As for last year, the overwhelming majority went to buy medicines. This year, for the first time, we had a medicine need that we could not fill because there was no money on hand. A reminder of what it means to be poor. We worked for weeks having to tell patients that the medicine that would have helped them was not available. Alms were 43% of money spent.

- <u>Communication:</u> For several months Honduran postage stamps were not available. This gave us the impetus to maximize their usefulness. Now almost every envelope to the States carries as much weight as allowed. The enclosed letters are then re-mailed there. We use very few envelopes for those enclosed letters, instead folding them and addressing them on the outside. Envelopes just add extra weight. Several US friends give us stamps and/or stamp and re-mail letters for us. We are very grateful. The stamp shortage has limited our letter sending and saved us money.

Going to email less often has been our plan for this year (2010). Here we are in Bonito, two days in a row. We couldn't finish everything yesterday, so stayed overnight at the Jesuit priests' house. They are very hospitable to us. We'll see if trips less often are feasible.

- <u>Health:</u> Nothing interesting, thank God.
- <u>Clothing:</u> Deceptively small costs. We made five dresses, three blouses and two pairs of pants. All of the fabric and patterns were either purchased in a past year or donated.

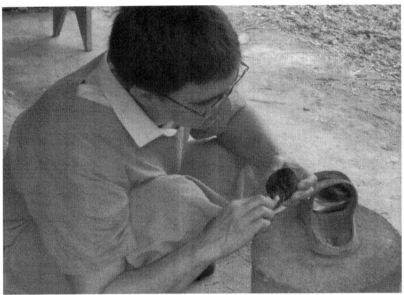

Sister Confianza glues a patch on a flip-flop, 2014

- <u>Immigration:</u> Immigration was an object lesson in the reality that being poor costs a lot of money. Our attorney had failed to file an important report; we had a huge fine to pay. As a result, there was not enough money to pay for residency for five years. We could only pay for one year. (We had put aside 150% of what we thought we would need!) In October, we were ready to pay the rest and were told that we can only do it within a month of our renewal date and that a new round of documents will be needed—not everything, but lots. So our lack of a mountain of cash means that the long-term cost will be more.

As I understand it, most Latin American countries are charging a lot for entrance, exit and residency in their country. This is thought to be in reaction to what is perceived as an unfriendly immigration policy of the United States.

- Library: Library expenses were lower by half. We received as many new books this year as last year, but most were gifts. We were also able to give away books that have less use.
- Property Tax: Stable at $2 per year. This is the result of the early bird discount. If we waited until April to pay, the cost would be $3.
- Outstanding Loan: Our neighbors borrowed money from us when they were having a hard time. Then in September through December they gave us a lot of home-grown food. We considered that food to have repaid about a third of the debt. Their short-term bounty has ended. We consider this money gone.
- Donations: We are grateful for the gifts and donations that we have received this year. We are grateful to Sellwood United Methodist Church for accepting and passing them on to us.

We are also grateful for the gifts in honor of Sister Confianza's Reception into the Novitiate—some to the Monastery directly, some to reduce her educational debt, and some to other organizations. We even received gifts in honor of my First Profession!

School
From: Sister Alegría

School starts in February.

Heidi and little Martín have lost a year of school. Now Ana is ready for kindergarten. Berta is adamant: the children will attend school this year, no matter what.

All year we had been using the side of our water tank as a blackboard. Heidi could still not write the alphabet or demonstrate mastery of one-digit addition/subtraction facts. Little Martín couldn't or wouldn't learn to print his name. Berta was pleased to learn to print her name and to read and write numbers. Heidi specialized in printing word lists. Ana made good progress in printing her name. Omar proudly wrote his initial.

We have seen this in other families, too. The woman seems to have no voice in the couple, until there is an issue really important to her. School attendance is often that issue.

119

Berta

Birth control is a telling issue on power balance. Berta may want more children, but only when these four are larger. This couple makes sure she gets to the clinic. We see other couples in which "her" need to get to the clinic for birth control is not important enough in a given week for the powerful male to help make it happen.

Wasps/Compost
From: Sister Alegría   Date: March 5, 2010

Early in January, we were ready to harvest the compost from the dry compost toilet (think basement to the toilet). Time to fertilize the pineapples, bananas, and fruit trees in the garden.

We innocently approach the door. Wasps are flying all about. The crack above the door is obviously their entry. They get mad. We run. Sister Confianza escapes completely. I receive only one sting.

Well, how are we to get our fertilizer? We are stumped. The next time that Berta visits, she suggests gasoline. Martín has cut down wasp nests and doused the nest with gasoline. It kills them. No, he doesn't burn them. OK, we'll give it a try.

The next Monday, we buy a quart of gasoline from Don Tranquilino (a friend and patient). That is, we try to buy it. He refuses to accept money and laughs merrily when we tell him how we will use it. Oh-oh, he knows something that we don't.

Sister Confianza had a bad reaction once to wasp stings, so I am the wasp woman of the Monastery. I put on long sleeves, pants, boots, work gloves and hat. I take a squirt bottle with gasoline and squirt it into the crack. The next day there are still wasps. I repeat the treatment twice. No apparent change in the wasp population.

We decide to try to open the storage compartment to get at the wasps better. Wasps are not active at night, so, in the full moon, we both dress up in full protective gear and go to open the door. We remove the bar holding it in place easily. The concrete "door" (like a trapdoor, but vertical) won't budge—not at all. We are stumped (still or again)! January is passing and the garden is still not fertilized. January passes. Early in February, our friend and garden mentor, Daniel, visits us. We tell him our troubles. He doesn't even go to look. He recommends Raid. I'm surprised; Daniel is as committed to organic gardening as we are. I'm concerned about putting poison on the fertilizer. He assures me that it will dissipate.

The next Monday we buy Raid. We usually use kerosene as our insecticide for termites. But today we buy Raid.

Wasp woman puts on all her gear and sprays Raid inside the toilet hole and at the entry crack. All the gear was unnecessary. The

120

next day, still a few wasps at the crack. I repeat the treatment twice more.

After a few days in a row of seeing no wasps we decide to examine the door again. We find that it is "cemented" shut by termite trails and nest material. We insert a machete blade, then cut and saw all around the door. Then Sister Confianza just lifts it out, not even needing any help from me.

The sight that greets our eyes: A huge termite nest—the full height of the door (almost two feet); a full grown tarantula sitting on the side of the nest; the wasp nest: five seven-inch fan-shaped empty "combs" of tiny cells hanging from the top of the opening.

Sister Confianza opens the back door to the dry compost toilet, 2013

I flick the tarantula off with the machete. It flies fifteen feet downhill. With some effort, Sister Confianza can get the termite nest out. It follows the tarantula, and tumbles yet further downhill. I cut down the wasp "nest." We can now access the compost fertilizer. Big success!

The last week in February, we take our first load of organic fertilizer to the garden. We fertilize six *plátanos* and more than half of the pineapples. Perhaps this blessing is sweeter because it took so long to arrive.

No More Neighbors
From: Sister Alegría

Berta's last month as our neighbor was surreal. Martín was even less consistent in being home and/or telling Berta when he would return. She and the children spent more and more time at the Monastery, especially on weekends. If she brought any groceries, the amount was token. I would tell her she must bring *yuca* (starchy tuber—fills us up well). By Monday morning when we went to Limón to serve patients and shop, there would be no groceries left. We had eaten everything in the larder. She didn't talk about financial or other stress. She just brought us her kids to feed.

Then they left.

Our grocery bill plummeted.

A Full Water Tank
From: Sister Confianza   Date: March 5, 2010

At the end of December, 2008, we cleaned the water tank, then were disappointed to get less rain than expected in January, so it never filled to overflowing. You've read how in February the outflow valve got broken off, and a wooden plug was put in to stop the flow, though it was still dripping extensively. The tank had emptied to only about 100 gallons, and it was a heck of a way to begin the dry season!

We worried for some time about what to do about the broken pipe, but in the end left it as it was. We kept a bucket to collect water from the drip which lessened over time as, we assume, the plug swelled up. I wondered to myself, *How would we get the plug out and make a new one when we needed to empty the tank and wash it again?*

From February through June we went to the creek to rinse our laundry and bathe in order to conserve water. We also found ourselves cooking less corn for tortillas since it uses so much water for boiling and washing. That was sometimes an agonizing choice, since corn is the cheapest staple food. We ate a lot of *pinol.* In July, the rains finally came—only a month later than expected!—and we began doing our laundry and bathing using the tubs at the house. Yet the tank never refilled all the way.

Finally it was November, the beginning of the true rainy season, and we decided it was time to take our chances, drain the tank, and scrub it out. It had been over ten months since the last cleaning, and our reading about water tanks was that they should be washed every three months. We'd already decided to do it only twice a year since we'd found that the water was pure enough for drinking even without pasteurizing.

On a drizzly Wednesday in early November, we opened the taps to let the water out; because of the wooden plug, we couldn't do a fast drain from the back. We filled our tubs with water to have some for the next couple of days. Once it got down to several inches of water inside, I went in through the trap door on top. Using a hammer, I was able to pound the plug out the bottom so the last of the water could drain away after I'd scrubbed the walls and floor. The part I felt least sure about was finding a new plug, so I was grateful when we easily found another stick that fit in the hole. Then we waited for rain.

We didn't have to wait long, for it started raining in earnest that evening. In fact, it was such a big storm that the pounding on the roof kept me awake much of the night. The wind was so strong it blew open the window shutter near the head of my bed—twice!—because I hadn't latched it properly. I admit, I got rather grumpy when I found that my pillow was wet from the rain that came in.

The next morning, when we went out to have prayers on the porch, I could hear the tell-tale drizzle of water running out of the overflow spout. Eight hundred gallons of water collected in one night! Praise the Lord for small miracles! All my concerns about whether our plug would hold or we'd even get enough rain dissipated. In fact, the plug was dripping less than the other one had when it was first put in.

We figure the tank will be good for another year before cleaning it again. And in mid-February a heavy rain topped it off, just in time for the upcoming dry season. Barring any calamities (which, I've noticed, always come our way) we are set with water for the next few months. Thank you, God!

Berta

Sisters Alegría and Confianza sing during Lauds, 2012

5
Musical Interlude

"Make a joyful noise unto the Lord. Sing to the Lord a new song."
—the Psalmist

A Singing People
From: Sister Alegría

We are a singing people. It is our Methodist heritage. John Wesley is generally considered the founder of Methodism, but his younger brother, Charles, was the great hymn writer (e.g., Hark, the Herald Angels Sing).

Here are John Wesley's instructions for singing from Select Hymns, 1761.

1. Learn these tunes before you learn any others; afterwards learn as many as you please.
2. Sing them exactly as they are printed here, without altering or mending them at all; and if you have learned to sing them otherwise, unlearn it as soon as you can.
3. Sing all. See that you join the congregation as frequently as you can. Let not a slight degree of weakness or weariness hinder you. If it is a cross to you, take it up and you will find a blessing.
4. Sing lustily and with good courage. Beware of singing as if you were half-dead or half-asleep; but lift up your voice with strength. Be no more afraid of your voice now, nor more ashamed of its being heard, than when you sang the songs of Satan.
5. Sing modestly. Do not bawl so as to be heard above or distinct from the rest of the congregation, that you may not destroy the harmony, but strive to unite your voices together so as to make one clear and melodious sound.
6. Sing in time. Whatever time is sung, be sure to keep with it. Do not run before and do not stay behind it; but attend

125

closely to the leading voices and move therewith as exactly as you can and take care not to sing too slow. This drawling way naturally steals on all who are lazy; and it is high time to drive it out from among us and sing all our tunes just as quick as we did at first.

7. Above all, sing spiritually. Have an eye to God in every word you sing. Aim at pleasing Him more than yourself, or any other creature. In order to attend strictly to the sense of what you sing, and see that your heart is not carried away with the sound, but offered to God continually; so shall your singing be such as the Lord will approve here, and reward when he cometh in the clouds of heaven.

I love it! Do you not feel entertained and instructed?

When I first met Sister Confianza, (then known as Prairie Cutting), in June, 2005, I became very optimistic about music in the Monastery. She actually majored in music at university!

In the first two years of monastic life, Sister Confianza translated a few songs. If I saw her working at the table, I would pay just enough attention to learn if she were working on music or on something else. If it were music, I made sure not to interrupt her.

Her parents came to attend her Reception into the Novitiate. I gave copies of the translated music to April, her Mom. I asked her not to talk about the music with Sister Confianza. "This is a monastery. We are about spiritual growth—not about ego-building." April demonstrated her gratitude for the gift of music copies and obeyed my warning.

A year and a half later, we spent a half-day retreat writing about music, writing about our own translation/composing. I only had one translation. Didn't take me long to write about that. Then we shared what we had written. What was I screening for? Ego. It seemed to me that the balance of ego and ego-free work was acceptable.

Humbled and grateful for her collaboration, I lifted the embargo on music conversation from April. The shelter of a monastery is a nice safe place to begin song writing, translating, composing. This is an area of our monastic life that we have done very well.

At the beginning of 2010, we formed the Music Committee, which meets no more than once a month.

A new song is debuted at a meeting of the committee, sung by the presenter. No comments are made.

Next meeting, the hard work begins. Translation: use the dictionaries: direct Bible quotes: look them up. Discuss the theology: Is this a message we as a Monastery want to promote?

After a while, provisional approval.

The next meeting, if still in agreement, we give final approval.

Once a song has been approved, it must be shared. Maybe we sing it at a church. Maybe we put it on Flickr. Maybe we email it to someone who might appreciate it.

Musical Theology
From: Sister Confianza

It is a thoroughly Methodist teaching that through hymns, we learn theology. Melodies have a way of sticking in one's head, and words set to music are remembered more easily. If you were raised in a church that sang hymns and other songs, you probably learned more about how God works and who God is through the music than from the Bible readings or sermons. At the Monastery, we are quite aware of this. We want songs that teach our values.

One Sunday during our first months in Honduras, Beth asked me to pick the hymns for our morning worship service.

"What's the theme?" I asked. "What readings are you using?"

She seemed surprised at my questions.

"I'd like to choose songs that go with them," I explained. Ever since then, this has been our tradition: to use songs in worship that reinforce or pick up on themes from the scriptures or other readings. Of course, certain passages—particularly in the Old Testament—make points we are not interested in promoting (like vengeance or violence). In that case, we might choose a song that teaches just the opposite!

We include two to three songs in each of our daily prayer times and four or five in Sunday's programmed worship.

Here, then, for your edification and your singing pleasure, are a few songs that have come from the Monastery over the years. Some are translations of songs by others, some are original. Most have tunes we've sung elsewhere. Many are adaptations of scripture. Several are rounds—simple songs that can be sung over and over, with voices coming in at different times, making for fun and interesting harmony.

En la Casa de Dios

Letra: Las Amigas del Señor, 2012 (Psalms 27:4,8; 65:4; 84:1-4; 122:1; 134:1; 135:1; Isaías 38:20)

Música: William Moore, 1825
HOLY MANNA

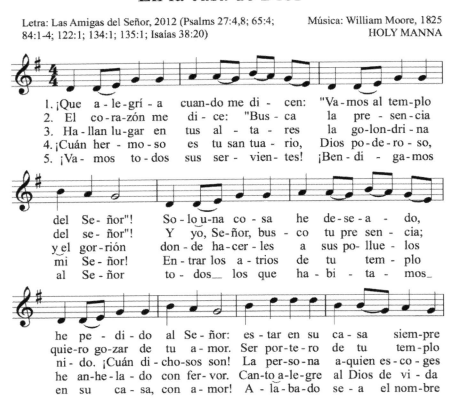

1. ¡Que a-le-grí-a cuan-do me di - cen: "Va-mos al tem-plo
2. El co-ra-zón me di - ce: "Bus - ca la pre - sen-cia
3. Ha - llan lu-gar en tus al - ta - res la go-lon-dri - na
4. ¡Cuán her - mo - so es tu san tua - rio, Dios po-de-ro - so,
5. ¡Va - mos to - dos sus ser - vien - tes! ¡Ben - di - ga-mos

del Se - ñor"! So - lo u-na co - sa he de-se-a - do,
del se - ñor"! Y yo, Se-ñor, bus - co tu pre sen - cia;
y el gor-rión don - de ha-cer - les a sus po- llue - los
mi Se - ñor! En-trar los a - trios de tu tem - plo
al Se - ñor to - dos_ los que ha - bi - ta - mos_

he pe - di - do al Se - ñor: es - tar en su ca - sa siem-pre
quie-ro go-zar de tu a - mor. Ser por-te-ro de tu tem-plo
ni - do. ¡Cuán di - cho-sos son! La per-so-na a-quien es - co - ges
he an-he-la - do con fer- vor. Can-to a-le-gre al Dios de vi - da
en su ca - sa, con a - mor! A - la-ba-do se - a el nom-bre

En la casa de Dios — In the House of God

As I delved into reading the Psalms, I noticed numerous references to persons who lived in the House of God, the Temple, and the desire for and joy of being so close to God's presence. Sister Alegría and I experience that joy living in God's House, the Monastery. I made a list of relevant verses in 2007, thinking it would be neat to have a song with that theme. In 2012, during our Holy Week Retreat, it came together. The first line in Spanish, from the Bible translation we use regularly *(Versión Popular),* fit a familiar jaunty tune. The other lines followed quickly. I chose the order of the verses to give a feel of the desire for God's house, getting to enter it, and finally fulfilling the dream of living there. The song went through the Music Committee process in just a few sessions; the slowest decision to come was the title!

pa - ra po - der lo a - do - rar to - dos los dí - as
yo pre - fie - ro a la mal - dad. Es - tar un dí - a
a vi - vir cer - ca de ti y la lle - vas
con to - do el co - ra - zón. Los que vi - ven
del rey nues-tor y sal - va - dor. To - dos los dí - as

de mi vi - da y su her-mo-su - ra con - tem - plar.
en tus a - trios que mil a - fue - ra va - le más.
a tu ca - sa siem - pre va a ser fe - líz.
en tu ca - sa te a - la - ban; fe - li - ces son.
de nues-tra vi - da can - ta - re - mos al Se - ñor.

Amigas del Señor Monastery, 2015

In the House of God

Words: Las Amigas del Señor (Psalms 27:4,8; 65:4; 84:1-4; 122:1; 134:1; 135:1; Isaiah: 38:20; 54:5)

Music: William Moore, 1825
HOLY MANNA

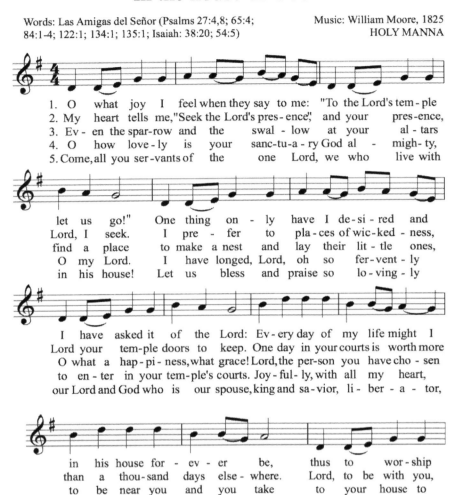

1. O what joy I feel when they say to me: "To the Lord's tem - ple let us go!" One thing on - ly have I de - si - red and I have asked it of the Lord: Ev - ery day of my life might I in his house for - ev - er be, thus to wor - ship

2. My heart tells me, "Seek the Lord's pres - ence", and your pres-ence, Lord, I seek. I pre - fer to pla - ces of wic - ked - ness, Lord your tem - ple doors to keep. One day in your courts is worth more than a thou - sand days else - where. Lord, to be with you,

3. Ev - en the spar-row and the swal - low at your al - tars find a place to make a nest and lay their lit - tle ones, O what a hap - pi - ness, what grace! Lord, the per-son you have cho - sen to be near you and you take to your house to

4. O how love - ly is your sanc-tu-a - ry God al - migh - ty, O my Lord. I have longed, Lord, oh so fer-vent - ly to en - ter in your tem-ple's courts. Joy - ful - ly, with all my heart, to the God of life I sing. Hap - py are those who

5. Come, all you ser-vants of the one Lord, we who live with in his house! Let us bless and praise so lo - ving - ly our Lord and God who is our spouse, king and sa - vior, li - ber - a - tor, ev - er new and still the same! Eve - ry day of

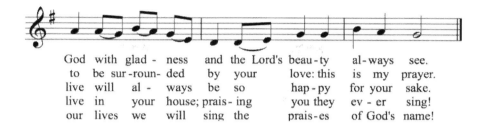

God with glad - ness and the Lord's beau-ty al-ways see.
to be sur -roun- ded by your love: this is my prayer.
live will al - ways be so hap - py for your sake.
live in your house; prais- ing you they ev - er sing!
our lives we will sing the prais-es of God's name!

Trabajamos y oramos — Work and Pray

"Pray and work" is a motto of the Benedictines and a traditional monastic combination. Prayer is our job and our tasks can be prayer. Manual labor is considered particularly good as meditative work. This song is a round that is a great way to pray while doing non-strenuous tasks like forming tortillas or sorting beans. A new voice can come in at each measure.

Music © 1976 April Hall. Used with permission.

Trabajamos y oramos
Work and pray

Letra/words: Las Amigas del Señor, 2013 *Música*/music: April Hall, 1976
GOD OF GRACE

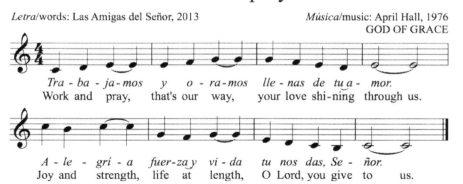

Tra - ba - ja-mos y o - ra-mos lle - nas de tu a - mor.
Work and pray, that's our way, your love shi-ning through us.

A - le - grí - a fuer-za y vi - da tu nos das, Se - ñor.
Joy and strength, life at length, O Lord, you give to us.

131

Por los días seis — Six Days

Taking a sabbath day each week is one of the ten commandments, so we do it. No business, no purchases, no work except cooking. The directions in Exodus 20 and Deuteronomy 5 are clear: do your work in six days and then neither you, your servants (or people you pay), nor your animals will need to work on the Sabbath. Following Christian tradition since the fourth century, at Amigas del Señor we take our day of rest on Sunday, the Lord's Day.

This round, to the familiar tune of "Row, row, row your boat," is great to sing on the other days of the week—especially on Saturday, when we know the day of rest really will come soon!

Por los días seis
Six days

Letra/words: Las Amigas del Señor, 2014
(Ex. 20:9-10a; Deut. 5:13-14a)

Música/music: Traditional
ROW, ROW, ROW YOUR BOAT

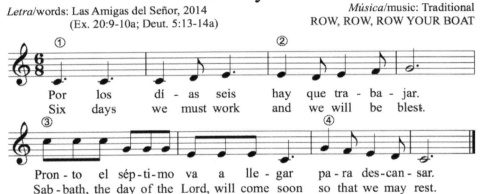

Por los dí - as seis hay que tra - ba - jar.
Six days we must work and we will be blest.

Pron - to el sép - ti - mo va a lle - gar pa - ra des - can - sar.
Sab - bath, the day of the Lord, will come soon so that we may rest.

God Used a Donkey

Donkeys appear in a number of Bible stories and the pictorial tradition of the pregnant Mary riding one, so we decided to hail this beast of burden in a song. We are committed to speaking and worshiping in Spanish; this and other songs were first written in that language, and later translated to English to share with a wider audience.

GOD USED A DONKEY (Dios usó un burro)
words: Las Amigas del Señor, trans. by Las Amigas del Señor, 2011
(Numbers 22:27-28, Luke 2:4-7, Mark 11:7-11)
music: Edwin O. Excell, 1897 'BLESSINGS'

1. Ba-laam's don-key stopped and stood still in the road
2. On the way to Beth-le-hem a don-key mild
3. Je-sus went, o-bey-ing the voice from a-bove,

when to it ap-peared an an-gel of the Lord.
went with Jo-seph and Ma-ry, who was with child.
to Je-ru-sa-lem to give his life with love,

Ba-laam, he got an-gry and he raised his rod,
Then the don-key lent its man-ger as a bed
car-ried by a don-key that was—oh!—so proud

So the don-key spoke to him the word of God.
where Je-sus, the In-fant God, could lay his head.
when it heard the shouts of "Glo-ry!" from the crowd.

A-ny wil-ling crea-ture God will use

if it's grea-dy and does not re-fuse.

Lord, I pray that I be wil-ling, too,

like the hum-ble don-key that said "Yes!" to you.

133

Por el maíz — For Health and Strength — *Por pan y fuerza*

"For Health and Strength" is a table grace and round that I grew up with. Early on I translated it to Spanish. However, in Honduras the staple food is tortillas, not bread. At the Monastery, we eat *maíz y frijoles* (corn and beans) like other *campesinos*, so we adapted the grace. Other substitutions can be made depending on the meal being served, e.g. *"arroz"* (rice) instead of *"maíz,"* or *"huevitos"* (little eggs) for *"frijoles."*

Por el maíz
For Health and Strength
Por pan y fuerza

Words/*Letra*: Traditional, trans. and adapt. by
tradicional, trad. y adap. por Las Amigas del Señor, 2007

Music/*Música*: Traditional round
Ronda tradicional
FOR HEALTH AND STRENGTH

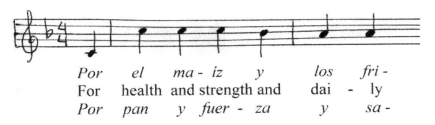

Por el ma - íz y los fri -
For health and strength and dai - ly
Por pan y fuer - za y sa -

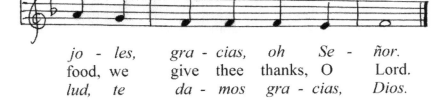

jo - les, gra - cias, oh Se - ñor.
food, we give thee thanks, O Lord.
lud, te da - mos gra - cias, Dios.

Permanecen — And Now Abide

God is love and love is the basis of Christian life. Wanting a song about love in Spanish, I looked up I Corinthians 13:13 in the Reina-Valera Spanish translation (akin to the King James Bible in English). The words practically fit themselves to the tune of a round that Sister Alegría and I both knew in English, also about love. Later, we put the words of the same verse in English to the tune as well.

Permanecen
And Now Abide

Words/*Letra:* Las Amigas del Señor   Music/*Música:* Unknown/*Desconocido*
(1 Cor 13:13), 2012, 2016

Per - ma - ne - cen la fe, la es - pe -
And now a - bide faith, hope, and

ran -za, y el a - mor. El ma - yor de
love, these three; and the great - est

es - tos tres es el a - mor.
of these is love, love, love.

Buscando a Dios

Sister Alegría began reading Teresa of Avila's books in the early 90s when she quit work and started focusing on her spiritual life. Saint Teresa's contemplative life and writings have continued to be a strong influence at Amigas del Señor. She wrote many poems, often for special occasions like Christmas or the Profession of a Sister. Once, I was using the poem *"Buscando a Dios"* ("Seeking God") for *lectiodivina,* and a melody began to come. A year later, I shared the new song at Sister Alegría's First Profession. The words are God telling us how beautiful our soul is, and that we should look there to find Him. A singable English translation has not yet come.

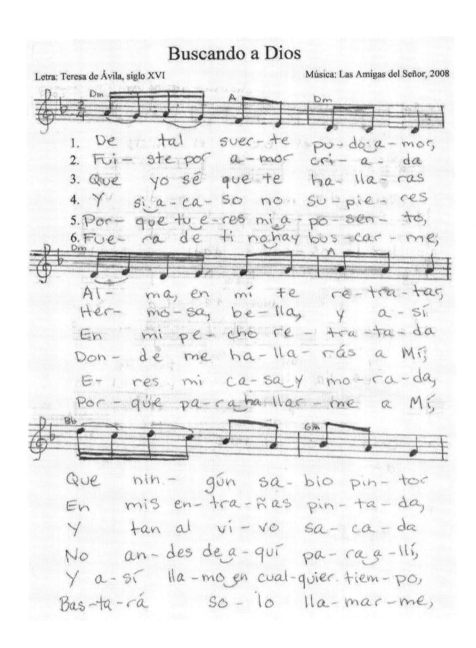

Buscando a Dios

Letra: Teresa de Ávila, siglo XVI   Música: Las Amigas del Señor, 2008

1. De tal suec-te pu-do a-mos,
2. Fui-ste por a-mor cri-a-da
3. Que yo sé que te ha-lla-ras
4. Y si a-ca-so no su-pie-res
5. Por-que tu e-res mi a-po-sen-to,
6. Fue-ra de ti no hay bus-car-me,

Al-ma, en mí te re-tra-tas;
Her-mo-sa, be-lla, y a-sí
En mi pe-cho re-tra-ta-da
Don-de me ha-lla-rás a Mí;
E-res mi ca-sa y mo-ra-da,
Por-que pa-ra ha-llar-me a Mí,

Que nin-gún sa-bio pin-tor
En mis en-tra-ñas pin-ta-da,
Y tan al vi-vo sa-ca-da
No an-des de a-quí pa-ra a-llí,
Y a-sí lla-mo en cual-quier tiem-po,
Bas-ta-rá so-lo lla-mar-me,

Su - pie- ra con tal pri - mor
Si te per- die- res, mi a - ma - da,
Que si te ves te hol - ga - ras
Si-no, si ha - llar- me qui - sie - res
Si ha-llo en tu pen- sa - mien - to
Que a ti i - ré sin tar- dar- me

Tal i - - ma- gen es - tam- par.
Al - ma, bus- car- te
Vién- do te tan bien pin - ta- da.
A Mí bus- car me
Es- tar la puer- ta ce- rra- da.
Y a Mí bus- car- me

has en MÍ.
has en ti.
has en ti.

"Alma, buscarte
has en Mí,
Y a Mí buscarme
has en ti."

Working by candlelight, 2012

Shepherds Watch Their Flocks by Night

"En la nochelospastores" is a Spanish *villancico*, or Christmas carol, from the <u>*Mil Voces*</u> hymnal. We used the second verse in the 2010 Epiphany pageant as the "kings-following-the-star" song. Like all of the songs that come out of the Monastery, no individual is credited for the words, translations, or music. The Music Committee process, with final acceptance at the Meeting for Worship with Attention to Business, means that the songs are claimed by the Monastery as a whole, and therefore credited to Las Amigas del Señor.

Estoy a la puerta — I Stand at the Door and Knock

Sister Alegría learned this song as a child, taught it to me, and translated it to Spanish for our use. Revelation 3:22 is Jesus speaking to the lukewarm church at Laodicea. "Just let me in!" he says to them—and to each of our reticent hearts.

We have found that motion songs are a favorite for everyone here, not just little kids. They go like this:

- Start out standing in place and sing, "I stand at the door and—".
- On "knock, knock, knock," mime knocking on a door with one fist.
- Repeat.
- Cup right hand behind ear and lean in that direction to sing "If anyone hears my voice."
- The second time, use the left side.
- Place hands flat together like in prayer for "and will," then separate hands a few inches further on each "open" until arms are wide for "the door."
- Step through imaginary door on "I will come in."

Sisters Confianza and Alegría share a laugh, 2012

140

Estoy a la puerta
I Stand at the Door and Knock

words/letra: unknown/desconocido
trans. by/trad. de Las Amigas del Señor, 2009

music/música: unknown/desconocido
I STAND AT THE DOOR

Es - toy a la puer - ta: toc, toc, toc. Es -
I stand at the door and knock, knock, knock. I

toy a la puer - ta: toc, toc, toc. Si al-gui-en me o -
stand at the door and knock, knock, knock. If a-ny-one hears my

ye, si al-gui-en me o - ye, y la puer-ta a-bri -
voice, if a-ny-one hears my voice, and will o-pen, o-pen,

a - bri - rá, ¡yo en - tra - ré!
o - pen the door, I will come in!

No tengasmiedo — Be Not Afraid

I was interested in having a song about Mary of Nazareth's call to become the mother of Jesus. I jotted down some ideas in my music notebook early in 2007, and in 2013, I received this tune and lyrics. Aren't we all called to let God work through us for the benefit of the world? It can be a scary prospect, but Mary and Elizabeth's examples give us courage.

No tengas miedo

Letra: Las Amigas del Señor (Luc 1. 26-54), 2014

Música: Las Amigas del Señor, 2014
FEARLESS

1. «No ten-gas mie-do», el án-gel di-jo
2. «No ten-gas mie-do, pues el es- pr̄-ri-
3. «No ten-gas mie-do», I - sa-bel di-jo
4. »No ten-go mie-do», Ma-r̄-a di-jo
5. «No ten-gas mie-do», nos di-ce el Se-ñor

a Ma-r̄-a. «Por-que e-res ben-de-ci-
tu de Dios____ te cu-bri-r̄ y el po-
a Ma-r̄-a. «Por-que e-res ben-de-ci-
al Se-ñor.____ «Yo soy fe-liz y me
a su pue-blo. «Por-que e-res ben-de-ci-

da por Dios. Vas a te - ner
der de Dios te lle-na-r̄,
da por Dios y has te - ni-do
lla-ma-rán siem-pre di - cho-sa
do por mi. Voy a u - sar-te

un hi-jo: el Dios de la li - be-ra-
Tu vas a dar a luz el hi - jo de
la gran va-len-t̄-a a de-cir "S̄" a
por-que gran-des co-sas Dios hi-zo en
a lle-var a ca-bo en el mun-do mi

142

ción ». «¿Y co-mo pue-de ser?
Dios ». « En - ton-ces con-fia-ré.
Dios ». «Yo a- la-bo al Se-ñor,
mi. A los po-bres es-co-gió,
plan ». «A - yú-da-nos, Se-ñor

sin hom-bre, soy mu-jer.» Le pre-gun-
Tu pa- la-bra a-cep-ta-ré. La es-cla-
mi Dios y Sal - va-dor, por-que Dios
Y a los ri-cos des-pi-dió. A su pue-
a con-fiar en tu a-mor. Con la va-

ta Ma-rí - a a Ga-bri-el.
va del Se - ñor siem-pre se-ré ».
me ha mi - ra - do con a-mor.
blo mi-se-rí - cor-dia mos-tró ».
len-tí - a de Ma-rí - a no

última vez

ten-dre-mos mie-do.»

Be Not Afraid

Words: Las Amigas del Señor (Luke 1. 36-54), 2014

Music: Las Amigas del Señor, 2014
FEARLESS

1. "Be not a - fraid," the an-gel Gab-riel said
2. "Be not a - fraid! The Ho-ly Spi-rit will
3. "Be not a - fraid," E - li-za-beth said
4. "I'm not a - fraid," said Ma-ry to the Lord,
5. "Be not a - fraid," God says to us, now,

to Ma-ry, "For you are blest by the
come on you and then God's pow'r will rest
to Ma-ry, "For you are blest by the
her God. "I'm filled with hap - pi - ness
his peo-ple. "For you are blest by me,

Lord, your God. You're going to have
up - on you. You will give birth
Lord, my God. You had the cou-rage
and joy. They'll call me bles - sed,
your Lord God, and I will use you

the God of li - be - ra - tion as your own
to the ho - ly child who is called Son of
to say "Yes" to God, to be - lieve and o -
for Al - migh - ty God has done great things in
to ful - fil my plan in the world that I

144

son." "And how can this be?
God." "I will trust you and o - bey,
bey!" "My soul prai-ses the Lord,
me: the im- po-ver- ished he chose
love." "Please help us now, O Lord,

For I am on - ly me," the vir-
be - cause I am God's slave. May it be
my Sa-vior and my God, for God
and the rich, a - way he drove. His mer-
to trust ful- ly in your love. With the coun-

gin Ma- ry asks. "I just don't see..."
with me ex - act - ly as you say."
has looked up - on me in his love.
cy to his peo — ple he shows."
age shown by Ma - ry we will prove:

last time

We're not a - fraid.

145

Dios es quien nos hizo — God's the One Who Made Us

Psalm 100 is Sister Alegría's favorite. Many songs are based on it, but few emphasize verse two, that we humans are not self-made, but rather creations of God. This round celebrates exactly that fact. The English version deviates slightly from the Biblical text for the sake of rhyme.

Dios es quien nos hizo
God's the One Who Made Us

Letra/words: Las Amigas del Señor, 2013
(*Salmo*/Psalm 100:1,3)

Música/music: Australian round
KOOKABURRA

① Dios es quien nos hi - zo, no no - so - tros
God's the one who made us, we did not.

② a no - so - tros mis - mos; su - yos so - mos.
God's the one who saves us; we're his flock.

③ ¡Can - tad a - le - gres, can - tad a - le - gres
Sing all cre - a - tion! Sing with e - la - tion

④ to - tos al Se - ñor!
to the Lord, your God!

6

Health Crisis

"Breathe on me, Breath of God."—Edwin Hatch

Pollen

From: Sister Alegría   Date: March 29, 2010

The *chaparrón* is what I call the "ugly tree." Its virtues are that it resists forest fire very well (bouncing back fast) and it will grow where no other tree will. When it blooms, the aroma is lovely—and heavy with pollen. It blooms in March. In spite of taking regular allergy meds, my nose and throat got worse and worse.

Last week, we didn't go to work on Monday or Tuesday because of rain. On Wednesday, we went. After work, we were resting casually at Sor Leonarda's place (where we were to eat lunch), when suddenly I couldn't breathe and had spasmodic coughing. Laryngospasm (vocal cord spasm). I had never seen it in a patient nor had it myself, but it was easy to recognize. I begin the "home remedy," calm, slow inspiration. Expirations take care of themselves. The episode is instantly accompanied by a frantic desperation for air; calm is not so easy.

Sister Confianza: "What do I do?"

Me: "Get Karen." (Barely audible.)

She: "What do I say?"

Me: "I can't breathe." (No more audible.)

And she is off. We are about 100 yards from the clinic.

One teenage girl comes to stand at each side of me, one hand on my shoulder, the other holding my hand. And I breathe. Kids gather around to watch (remember that we are in a household of 50 children). The big girls shoo them away. And I breathe.

The episode is definitely improving, when Sister Confianza and Dr. Karen show up, sweating and out of breath. She had seen this once in her hospital training.

Health Crisis

Soon, Connie, the young nurse, arrives with the IV medicine (high dose hydrocortisone). Karen puts it into one of my veins. Then she scolds me for working when I am sick; I should rest. Scolding is an ordinary part of most Honduran health care. It must not be taken too seriously.

Soon, breathing is normal. We rest a bit, the big girls go back to their homework, we eat our lunch, we go back to the clinic for the medicines to take home, and we do our town errands. We're not walking especially fast. We get two lifts home, having to walk less than a mile. All is well.

Voice rest, antihistamines, soothing drinks, oral steroids, rest (at least as much as I can stand). We use up the steroids, but I am not back to normal—still lots of mucous, cough and frog voice. That's why we are here in Bonito today. We are here to buy "high test" medicines to suppress the allergy symptoms. We were completely successful in finding them and I have taken the first doses.

Since it is Holy Week, Centro de Salud is closed, we are not expected to work.

Sister Confianza is our designated speaker. She is also our designated singer. I play the alto recorder in worship when the song is easy enough.

Supposedly good characteristics for monastics are things like humility, courage, compassion, hope, faith, devotion. But in this monastery, it seems as though flexibility is the most necessary characteristic.

The ugly tree seems to be almost done blooming. We have the medicines. We feel strong. But this has certainly been a trial for us. Please hold us in your prayers.

Denial
From: Sister Alegría

Within a week or two, I realized that I had fallen into the "if I can just be at home, I'll be alright" trap. Well, I wasn't all right. Does the term "denial" come to mind?

Easter Miracles
From: Sister Confianza   Date: April 13, 2010

I used to think that my life had a lot of interesting coincidences in it, but since moving to Honduras four years ago I have come to believe that it is God's hand working to arrange everything just so. Sometimes I can't figure out why things happen in a certain way, but other times the benefits are obvious. Easter Monday was one of those days where it was easy to see the material blessings— little "miracles"—from God.

From Thursday to Saturday of Holy Week, Sister Alegría and I had a three-day retreat of continuous spiritual practices. We expanded our three daily worship services/prayer times with extra psalms, hymns and gospel readings (following the traditional events of that week) and we also did a variety of other prayer practices including *lectio divina*, silent worship, prayer of gaze, and Taizé music. It was very good and very intense, and by Sunday we were pretty tired.

Sisters Alegría and Confianza at prayer time, 2012

We had planned a special program for Easter Sunday, but before we began, our sometime neighbor Berta showed up with her four kids. They had moved back to Limón shortly after our Epiphany celebration and enrolled the three older kids in school, which began in February. Martín has continued to come out regularly to work on Elías' property and the whole family had been back out one week in March. Martín had said they'd be out again for Holy Week, and we had wanted to invite them over for Easter, but they weren't at the house when we went over on Tuesday. Now, here they were and we had the chance to celebrate together after all—without the stress of planning ahead!

One traditional Easter food here is *miel de papaya*—unripe papaya stewed in brown sugar syrup. Well, we have green papayas growing, and Berta knows the recipe, so she cooked up that dish for us all. She had brought over a couple liters of fresh milk as well as *yampá* (a potato-like food) which made great additions to the meal. We told the story, using a picture book, of Jesus' death and resurrection to remind ourselves what we were celebrating that day.

After our guests left in mid-afternoon, Sister Alegría and I again noticed how tired we were. On both Tuesday and Saturday, she had had an episode of coughing and difficulty breathing. I had done all the reading and singing during our retreat (though she could play recorder) because her voice was still hoarse. I was concerned about her health, and we decided that true rest was in order for recuperation. We could go in to work on Monday (and we needed to buy groceries) but only if a car came along to give us a ride; we didn't want to overdo the physical stress. The rest of the week: rest.

On Monday morning we walked down our path to the *desvío* and waited. Sister Alegría was restless to go, but it didn't seem wise to me to try walking, so I sang a Taizé song called "Stay With Me" until a pickup came along. It was filled with guys from La Fortuna going down to cut weeds along the roadside. They gave us a ride to the main road. From there, it seemed to me we might as well walk the half mile to Rosa and Chito's where we could wait for a ride to Limón. (And yes, it was I and not we making the decisions to wait or walk that morning. With Sister Alegría being sick, I've had to be Sister Guardian and take the lead on many decisions about what we do, as well as be caregiver.) We'd hardly gone 100 feet when along came the bus that takes school kids to Limoncito. It was on its way back to Limón and the driver, Miguel (nurse Wornita's husband), gave us a lift the whole way in. Two rides—two miracles—and counting.

There weren't all that many patients at Centro de Salud, which was good; we figured Sister Alegría was limited in how long she could give consults. But, since the only other trained worker there was the young nurse Connie, Sister Alegría felt obligated to see most of the patients, particularly since there were some serious cases (including a baby with pneumonia).

During the morning, Sor Leonarda stopped by with a crate of medicines from the most recent medical team from the US that had been to Limón at Clínica Carolina. After we finished with the patients about noon, Sister Alegría rested on a couch in back and we went through the box together. There were a number of useful medicines for Centro de Salud, but also a lot of expired ones. Most of those had to be tossed, but two could still be used—not to give to patients, but for us personally.

One was Tylenol Sinus. I get a lot of sinus headaches and have had sinus infections in the last year and a half. We have sometimes been able to buy decongestant, but it cost 25 cents per dose, so I would only take it when the headaches were really bad and made me tired. When I saw the bag with hundreds of pills I felt a rush of gratitude and relief just from the idea that I could take a dose whenever I notice the symptoms and not have to suffer so much! The other medicine was Benadryl, which Sister Alegría has been taking for her cough and allergies recently. Even though both medicines have officially expired, the active ingredients aren't things that go bad quickly, so we've now got a year's supply of two very useful medicines. We're feeling pretty poor these days, and it seemed to me they were literally sent from God. Miracle number three.

After work and lunch at Sor's we went to visit Samuel, the mechanic. We had left parts from our food mill with him a couple weeks earlier to see if he could fix them. The handle, which turns the grinding mechanism, kept popping off. We could jerry-rig it with a piece of cloth (tip from Berta), but it seemed that the bolt holding the handle on was getting stripped. We still had thirty pounds of corn, but what good is that if we can't grind it to eat?

When we arrived at his shop, Samuel had bad news: he hadn't been able to find a replacement bolt that fit. Disappointed, we began to pack up our parts. Suddenly Samuel said, "Wait! I have an idea. Let me see it again." He took a hammer and pounded the bolt, flattening it just slightly so that it was now in effect bigger around. When he screwed it in, it held: Miracle number four. We could eat our corn and didn't have to purchase and carry extra grains that day.

Next we went for mail, taking our time walking across town to the home of Hernán, the postmaster. It meant walking over a mile, but it seemed worth it to get our mail, since it had been a couple weeks. A few weeks before that, we had used up the last of our stamps. Every week we'd ask Hernán if he would find some for us. The usual response was that there were none in the whole Department of Colón. Because that has been the case since we moved here, we usually buy stamps in La Ceiba, but the year before when we'd run out once, Hernán was able to come up with some. We prayed for the same miracle.

On Monday, it occurred. Hernán had enough stamps for ten big letters, so we paid him and were able to send off a couple letters we had ready to go. Moreover, in one of the letters we received that day, there were US stamps. Those are useful when we fill a big envelope with letters to go to the States, or have the luck to run across some gringos in Honduras who are willing to carry letters back for us. Communication and connection are important to us, so it is a relief to be "back in business." Miracle number five.

Finally it was time to leave town. We bought our groceries and waited for a ride out of Limón, as is our custom. It wasn't long before a double cab pickup stopped for us. We had chatted with Adán a couple of years ago at Chito's place and he gave us advice about raising chickens. On Monday, he gave us a ride and continued the conversation about chickens. (He really recommends them. You know, hens to throw food to and a rooster to crow in the morning...) Adán was on his way home to Francia, but he felt sorry for us having to walk home alone. He was concerned about "bad guys," and so he went completely out of his way to drive us all the way to our path in the *desvío*! That was a huge favor and we were very appreciative. It's like God planted that concern in his mind so we wouldn't have to walk home. Six miracles in one day and I'm sure there are many more I haven't counted.

Once again, I overflow with gratitude, wonder and praise for the way God takes care of us and provides for all our needs. I've come to fully expect God's blessings, and every week find myself eager to see what God has in store for us on Monday and every day.

Health and Disease
From: Sister Alegría   Date: April 13, 2010

Sister Confianza and I are in La Ceiba. As you remember, I had laryngospasm and cough. We treated it as though allergy were the cause of the whole problem. We did a reasonably strong treatment and it helped very little.

When you have a guaranteed accurate diagnosis and a reasonable treatment doesn't help, you go to a stronger treatment. But I did not have a guaranteed accurate diagnosis; I suspected that there was a little something besides the allergy going on. The stronger treatment would have been medicine that could have some pretty negative side effects, especially in someone over 60. As a pediatrician, I was certainly NOT ready to try that.

We worked in Centro de Salud on Easter Monday, but *Doctora* Karen didn't, so I didn't get a general physician consult.

I had a suspicion that there was something abnormal in my throat, maybe even something structural. I really wanted an ENT (ear, nose and throat) doctor to take a look. The closest one(s) is in La Ceiba.

On Thursday evening, we decided that we had waited long enough (or perhaps a little too long).

Friday am, we get up early and walk our path to the *desvío*. Then I sit down to rest and we wait about 20 minutes. Along comes Don Julio in his car. We climb into the back and we are off. (We know, of course, that God sent Don Julio that day, perhaps in response to your prayers.) After about 45 minutes, the women riding in the cab arrive at their destination and we move into the cab. He takes us right to the bus station in Tocoa. A bus is just pulling out for Ceiba; we catch it.

Arrive Ceiba about noon. Get off at the bank (about four blocks before the bus station). Withdraw 4,000 Lempiras (for medical expenses). That's $211. Walked (oh, so slowly) to the bus terminal.

Sister Confianza calls Doctora Karen, to tell her that we won't be working on Monday and to ask for names of ENT doctors. Doctora Karen's phone doesn't work. Sister Confianza calls Eloyda (the El Pino nurse). She tells us the location at which ENT doctors work. No names, no telephone numbers, nothing more—and it is clear that she thinks she has met our need.

We go to the pharmacy next door to ask for advice. The salesgirl says that the doctor isn't in; she is at her office at the corner. So we walk to the corner.

There is a CLOSED sign on the door. But the door and the wall are glass. We can see a man sitting in the tiny waiting room. Now we are really at a loss. We just stand there a while considering our options. I'm sure that we look just how we feel.

Then the man gets up, opens the door, invites us in, and asks how he can help us. He asks if we are part of a mission, saying that he asks because of our clothes. He just returned from a mission to Bolivia. He is a physician and gives us his card. One of his family names is the same as that of the *doctora*.

He knows all four of the ENT doctors in town, gives us their names, their work schedules, and tells us that three of them have offices in Medicentro. That's the place to go. He tells us to take a taxi and what to pay the taxi. I am so grateful that the tears come as I thank him.

We don't take taxis. They are too expensive. On this day, we take a taxi.

The third ENT office that we check actually expects the doctor to be in this afternoon, but too late for us to get to El Pino in a timely manner. He already has two patients waiting. Then she says, "Have you come from far?" We are road dusty, road weary and wearing our backpacks. We have no secrets. She takes my name to register me as the first patient for Saturday morning.

153

It is very nice to see our friends in El Pino. They make us welcome. Early Saturday morning, we go to the city to see the doctor.

Dr. Pintor is all we could have hoped for. Explains everything, does a thorough ENT exam. Thorough exams are decidedly rare in Honduran medicine.

The underlying problem is acid reflux. The acid burns the throat, the vocal cords, turns on bronchospasm and vocal cord spasm. He tells us about his own case. Right now, the active problem is severe asthma.

We had packed a backpack with essentials in case he would admit me to the hospital. As he sits down to write the prescriptions, he comments that a lot of doctors would admit me to the hospital, give oxygen, etc., etc. But he is confident that outpatient care will do fine.

By now he has learned a little about our life style. He laughs at our comment that we have to fry food almost every day in order for me to keep my body weight up. In his middle class patients this is hardly the story. He actually laughs a lot as we discuss our life style. He gives us a list of dietary limitations.

Eloyda can loan us the clinic nebulizer. He gives me samples of the H2 blocker and writes the prescriptions for the needed medicines. One of the medicines is chamomile tea—not the pallid stuff you get, rather a rich dark tea made with the entire plant, usually sweetened. He waxes eloquent on the virtues of chamomile. He sounds like a commercial. We should return on Monday for a follow-up appointment. Then he refuses to charge us—professional courtesy. He says, "Nowhere in the world do doctors charge other doctors." I don't tell him that those days have passed in the US.

I start the medicines immediately and gradually feel better and better. Some nasty side-effects (jitteriness), which I accept gladly as the price of improvement. Our friends in El Pino feed us and visit us and pray for us.

Monday morning, back to the city. We take a stool sample—to be tested for H. pylori (the "ulcer" bacteria). Results to be done by noon.

We do more price shopping for the long term medicine that is needed. We visit the immigration office (which is very close) to confirm what will be needed in June.

By 1 pm, we are awaiting our appointment. The stool test is negative.

He is pleased with my progress and writes another whole list of prescriptions. This is routine in Honduran medicine. We understand what each one will do and thank him. We had a serious conversation about the dietary limitations and bring it up. He laughs again and says that sheet is not for us; we eat a very healthy diet. The only limitation needs to be citrus fruits.

Then we go to the pharmacy and start pricing medicines. We don't have enough money to buy them all. This is also routine, even for people who live far more comfortably than we do. We decide which ones are the most important and buy them. Less important, buy some, but not the recommended amount, the very least important, we don't even price.

Back to El Pino, again very tired. Each day I feel better. But we wanted to email you to let you know what was going on. Today I am feeling much better. I slept well last night, better than I have in weeks. We don't have to go to the city today, more rest.

We might go home as early as Friday. But I need to be able to walk the 1.5 miles from the bus to the Monastery. I wouldn't be able to do that yet today. We'll see.

Our Angel
From: Sister Alegría

I didn't have to walk the 1.5 miles after all. Eagle-eye Sister Confianza spotted Don Julio's car in Limoncito when we passed through. She also, as Sister Guardian, had assessed me as incapable of doing the walk. When we got off the bus, we went to the nearest shady spot; in a few minutes, our angel, Don Julio, picked us up. We are also now convinced that the distance is more like two miles.

Velorio
From: Sister Alegría   Date: April 15, 2010

Sunday night (April 11), I was well enough to attend the evening worship service. Sister Blanca preached. She is a good preacher and was full of vigor. Sister Confianza told me later that Blanca made a lot of good points that I would have appreciated if I hadn't been nodding off.

Blanca's son, José (age 37, but looks 28), was eager to speak with me after worship. I met José ten years ago when he volunteered in the little clinic in El Pino. He wanted to become a nurse. Now he has achieved his dream and is happy to tell me that he is working in a private clinic.

Yesterday, at noon, we heard that Blanca's son, Marcos, age 34, had died.

155

Marcos had worked at the Dole pineapple plantation earning starvation wages. (Up close and personal, Dole is not very pretty.) He did things like gather and sell firewood to help provide for his wife and five children. They live in destitution.

Yesterday, Marcos and his 14-year-old son went to pick *sapotes* (fruit) to sell. Marcos climbed the tall tree. His son reports that Marcos suffered a sudden charley horse and fell. He landed on his head, which split open from mid-forehead at the hairline straight back. It opened up "like a squash." He died instantly.

His body was taken to *Colonia Metodista*, where the church has a low-cost mortgage, low-cost house-building project. The Honduran dream definitely includes home ownership. Several small houses close together were used to accommodate the wake. Marcos has six surviving brothers, four surviving sisters, both parents, five children and a wife pregnant with twins. It was a big wake. It was a clear and balmy night, most of the folks were outside all of the time. Whole families attend, children are not left out.

We walked half a mile to participate. This was our first Honduran wake. We had barely arrived when José took us under his wing. He told me that he had sewn up his brother's head; since he is a nurse, he could do that. He directed us to the (incredibly cheap) coffin, with the obligate glass window over the face. Marcos was a handsome man. His head looked intact, with a white cloth, turban-like, covering his crown. His nostrils have white cotton plugs, as is traditional.

Poor José. But he was able to give that last gift to his dear brother.

Then José took us to Blanca (in a different house). She told us about when she had lost another child, at age three years—of black measles. That was bad, but this was worse. We prayed for her, doing traditional laying on of hands combined with ordinary hugs. Then she asked us to do the same for her daughter, who had just given birth two weeks ago. So, we did. Both women seemed to derive comfort from our prayers. I gave Blanca my hanky. Most Hondurans don't carry hankies. Fortunately, mine was clean; I had just put a fresh one in my pocket.

Two young sisters of the church went around offering little cups of coffee and small breads. The church is taking care of the wake. One serves the nicest food one can afford for a wake. Many people stay all night.

The burial was this morning. It was a mile's walk away and we decided not to attend. The body is not embalmed and must be buried within 24 hours. There would have been a bad smell already even though the night was cool (84 degrees or cooler).

We left money with Sister Reina, a leader in the church, to pass on to the widow. Most folks will do the same.

This experience put in perspective our petty little troubles. I am well on the mend. We will return to the Monastery tomorrow.

Sexual Minorities
From: Sister Alegría

I have a special love for José. He is a celibate, fairly obviously gay man. He has suffered a lot of persecution, even within the church. He always seeks me out. Unconditional acceptance is mighty rare for sexual minorities here in Honduras. We, as vowed celibates, have voluntarily joined the group of sexual minorities.

In the Wesleyan (Methodist) tradition, theological truths are based on the quadrilateral: Holy Scripture, Tradition, Reason, and Experience. When we read the Bible, we notice that it used all the latest up-to-date scientific data. For example, there is a giant upside-down bowl defining the sky with water, lots of it, above that bowl; and the earth is immovable, on pillars. When we look at modern science, we don't think we have to throw out all the precious teachings of the Holy Bible because its up-to-date science is no longer up to date. Likewise, with homosexuality and other sexual and gender variations, we choose to go with modern science, without diminishing our respect for the Bible.

Another Incredible Monday: April 26
From: Sister Confianza   Date: June 1, 2010

We'd spent ten days without leaving the Monastery, resting and recovering after our trip to La Ceiba. Now it was Monday, time to go in to the clinic and to buy groceries. Sister Alegría was not well enough to do the long walk, so we knew we could only go in if someone gave us a ride. God would have to provide or we'd stay home.

We went to the end of our path and waited. This morning's ride was from a youngish man from La Fortuna we hadn't met before. He had a fancy enclosed vehicle with air conditioning and drove extremely fast on the *desvío*, but we hardly noticed the bumps. He gave us a ride all the way to Limón.

A US medical team was in town, so there were few patients at Centro de Salud. That meant Sister Alegría didn't have to work too hard. We were also able to give her a couple of nebulizations to help treat the asthma.

One thing we were really hoping for was mail, since it had been a while, and Sister Alegría thought there might be something from my mom. She shouldn't walk to the postmaster's, however. Happily, Sor Leonarda allowed a couple of adolescent girls to accompany me while Sister Alegría relaxed at Sor's place. Sure enough, there was a package from my mom as well as numerous other letters.

After lunch, Sister Alegría was having a lot of side effects (jitteriness, etc.) from the asthma medication, and I had a bad sinus headache. Sor expressed concern about us getting home, but Sister Alegría said, "Sister Confianza is confident we'll get a ride, so we're OK."

All I'd said was, "We're not walking," but she'd taken it as foreknowledge of a ride! So, we went ahead and bought groceries, filling our packs.

We heard a rumor that Don Chepe from La Fortuna was in town. Often he returns with a truck full of people and goods for his small store. It was late, and I was a bit concerned, then we went to Andres' store and saw Chepe's merchandise waiting on the counter. We waited. Soon, Chepe arrived, and he had plenty of space. Sister Alegría and I stood in the bed of the truck, wind in our faces, hanging on to the tall metal frame with our knees bent to sway with the vehicle as he drove us all the way to our path. Quite a contrast to the smooth morning ride!

When we were leaving the house in the morning, I had the horrible realization as I closed the padlock that the keys were not in my pocket—they were still inside the house! It's my fear each time we leave the house and return home that I've lost the keys, but this was the first time it ever happened here. What would we do? I was strangely comforted by the fact that we'd been robbed twice: the thieves demonstrated that the house can be opened without keys. When we got home in the afternoon, we knew our task: to break in.

Upon arriving, however, we faced a shocker: A board that we'd left leaning on the water tank had fallen over while we were gone, breaking off the PVC pipe and spigot. The tank was empty and the dry season had just begun in earnest! But first things first.

The keys had been left on a shelf right inside the door, so we pushed the door, bending the latch just enough to open it a crack. We took the piece of wire from the bathroom door latch and slipped it through the crack to try to reach the keys. My thought was to knock them off the shelf, then pull them through the crack at the bottom of the door. We took turns at it for some time without much success.

We couldn't see at all what we were doing, just heard the scratching of the wire on the wall.

When we got tired, we took a break for afternoon prayers. Then back to the puzzle. Soon, I heard the jingle of the keys. I wiggled the wire a bit more and realized the keyring had hooked right on to the wire! I carefully brought it up and out a space at the top of the door. Finally we could open the house—and without having ruined the lock, latch or door! I praised God, because I knew it wasn't MY ingenuity that made it happen.

The Sisters wash laundry in the stream, 2012

Now to the tank. The water level had already gotten pretty low, because we'd kept using it for washing clothes and all our other needs in recent weeks. (Sister Alegría had been in no position to hike down to the creek and back.) Now I was doubly grateful for that decision: if we'd begun conserving the water by going to the creek, what good would it have done? We would have been more tired and all the water we saved would have been lost anyway! Now, we didn't have to face the question of when or how much to conserve water—it was decided for us. This week, there'd be no trying to get "extras" done, or even things like gardening work. We'd just do what was needed to get by: go to the creek every day to bathe, wash clothes, and carry water back up for drinking and kitchen use; gather firewood; and cook our meals. We'd take all the time necessary to do the basics and rest as needed.

What amazed me was my lack of being upset about losing all the water. I didn't curse God or bad luck for bringing this upon us, I just laughed at the absurdity of the whole thing! Sometimes I call God the Big Joker in the Sky.

Wishing showers of blessings (or blessings of showers?) for you.

Annual Immunization Campaign
From: Sister Alegría

On Friday, April 30, we went with the health care team to La Fortuna as part of the annual immunization campaign. We took several plastic gallon jugs along to carry home clean drinking water— no trip to the stream that day. (The jugs are empty liquid medicine jugs.) Doctora Karen was there, too. When I asked her about going to Plan de Flores, she responded that she didn't want me there in the heat. I should rest. So I did.

Prayer, Air, Water, Food, Rest
From: Sister Alegría   Date: June 3, 2010

These things: prayer, air, water, food, and rest, are the essentials of life here in the Monastery. My illness has really been a graphic lesson of what is necessary and what is not.

Air: The asthma has cost us a lot. In order to breathe adequately, I had to walk very slowly. And breathing took so much energy that I tired quickly.

Water: You have already heard about this year's water tank disaster. Until the rain started two weeks later we walked to the stream six days a week to bathe, wash laundry and carry water back up to the house. Sister Confianza carried the majority of the water. We climbed the hill slowly, resting often so I could breathe. Usually that was the only real action I could do in a day. By the way, we now have a plug in the tank and lots of water.

After the rain came, we stopped going to the stream. I started improving rapidly with the breathing. Now I am nearly normal. We ran out of medicines, so that slowed things down.

Food: We have to eat. Sister Confianza did the cooking. I did little puttery things to help, like peel and cut up green bananas to boil. We went together to get wood for cooking. When we got down to nothing, God provided in wonderful ways. One day, a dead tree seemed to just appear to Sister Confianza along the path to the garden—just one example.

Dinner: corn tortillas, beans, and scrambled eggs with katuk, 2013

Rest: We took a lot. Non-essential work didn't get done. We both got enough rest, thank God.

Prayer: Prayer is the main work of the monastery. Since my voice barely worked for a month, Sister Confianza did ALL of the speaking parts in our three daily worship services (yes, even what would have been responsive reading). She sang solo for all the songs. I played recorder. Since I am not yet an accomplished recorder player, the results were variable. But our prayers continued.

We put our fasting practice on hold. Last week we did a modified fast, but this week, no fast at all.

Our *lectio divina* (prayerful reading) stayed on schedule.

Spiritual Formation daily activities continued. Ironically, we were just finishing a book on healing prayer. Very humbling.

Another spiritual formation activity is reading and doing the exercises in A Course of Miracles. We continued with it, too.

Our twice-a-week music time had one singer and one recorder player. Occasionally, Sister Confianza also played recorder. But with all of the hard work being hers, sometimes her wrists weren't up for recorder playing.

What we couldn't do and missed a lot was shared reading. One reads aloud; we stop often to make comments and share ideas. It is a method to invite another person into our conversation. Lately, our guests have been Teresa of Avila (the "big" Teresa) and Little Sister Magdeleine of Jesus. We find these readings helpful in monastic formation and in community formation. Sometimes one reads while the other works. Well, we only had one person with a voice and she did most of the work. Shared reading had to be put aside. That was hard. It is an important part of our curriculum and it is what we are used to. Just like anyone else, we find the familiar, the usual, to be a comfort in times of trial.

Our dancing prayers are still on hold. I miss them.

In the last two weeks, things have moved rapidly back towards normal. We are again doing gardening and sewing. We are doing shared reading. I sing a little. I even gave the Sunday morning sermon: Elisha and the oil miracle for the widow. It is a good reminder. Just like that widow, I seem to need my miracles sort of "reality-based." God could just "beam" us to Centro de Salud. But that would scare me, so God sends a car to give us a lift. God could make a tree grow overnight in our front yard that would bear all kinds of food—even precooked and ready to serve. But that would scare me, too, so God sends a friend and neighbor to give us permission to harvest *yuca* from his field.

We're in La Ceiba/El Pino right now. We went to the bank and the pharmacy. I am now taking, again, the two most important medicines.

By the way, the (hired) driver of the car that gave us a lift to Centro de Salud one recent Monday was my patient. He is 64 years old and described symptoms very similar to my recent problem of reflux with resulting asthma. Thanks to what I had learned from the specialist, I was able to ask the right questions and interpret the physical exam to make the diagnosis and treat him. We only have second choice medicines, but I am very optimistic. He drinks a lot of caffeine; stopping that will make a big difference. One never knows, does one?

Politics

From: Sister Alegría   Date: June 3, 2010

We have been bemused about Honduran politics since the coup. We live far from the center of political power, but we listen to the people.

Whenever I ask someone their opinion about the government or politics, they get the same look on their face—distaste, perhaps. The same word comes up—*feo*. It literally means "ugly," but in this context, dirty or slimy might be a better translation.

There is no question but that Mel Zelaya was a properly elected president. That's about the only thing that is obvious.

Many people were optimistic that the presidential election would resolve problems. It did not.

When Pepe Lobo Sosa was inaugurated President in January, this year, a blanket pardon was issued to all who were involved with the "activities" of June 28, 2009. Soon, attempts were made to bring Mel Zelaya back to Honduras to stand trial.

Who did what that was illegal depends on your political stance and interpretation of the Honduran constitution. We don't forget that the winners write history.

There are more soldiers and police officers (with big guns in hand) visible than in recent years. It is not rare to have a bus stopped. Sometimes only the men are asked to step outside and sometimes everyone. This happened on our way to Ceiba this week. It is not at all clear what for. It seems to me that it is just an ordinary reminder that the government has arms and soldiers to "protect" the people and the State. There have been unexplained deaths. The big newspapers seem to be in the "wealth and power" category (with the coup movers).

The most common attitude is that this election did not clean up the mess; the current government is semi-legitimate (if that much); there is no process to fix things up. Everyone wants to avoid bloodshed, especially their own.

The Honduran government has murdered dissenters in the past. It seems to be a proven technique for keeping power in the hands of a few.

That's the way it looks from here.

Our own politics: We came to Ceiba to renew our residency status. More problems. We'll try again next month.

My Current Political Analysis of the 2009 Coup
From: Sister Alegría

Since any Honduran can ask for a Constitutional Assembly poll, it was legal for Mel as President to do so. The constitutional assembly would have been approved had the poll been held. There were and are lots of dissatisfied Hondurans and Mel was ready to use dirty tricks to make it pass. The rich and powerful surmised both and had to stop that, so they did.

The winners write the history. Micheletti is now one of the ex-Presidents of Honduras. He was President for about six months. All about ego.

The Liberal Party split: some loyal to Mel forming the *Libre* (Free) Party, some loyal to the party name. The National Party is now the only major political party.

Mel was charged with trying to overthrow the government. He was pardoned when it became obvious that the current Honduran president (2009-2013) had no respect in the Western Hemisphere. Mel and his wife are active in Honduran politics.

Honduran Patriotism
From: Sister Confianza   Date: June 24, 2010

Hondurans are proud to be Hondurans. They love their country even if they don't like its politics or government. One way they are able to express their patriotism and unite across their differences is through soccer, the national sport. Playing soccer (called *fútbol*) is the pass-time of many boys and some girls. Every town and village has a team. There is also a national soccer league which many people like to follow. But the epitome of all is the national Select team.

The 2010 World Cup of Soccer is occurring in South Africa as I write. It's been known for many months that Honduras would be participating. What a great source of pride. The World Cup occurs every four years, and the last time Honduras played in it was in 1982—over a generation ago. You can imagine the excitement everyone feels, and it's contagious. I've never been very interested in sports, but I sure feel happy for Honduras.

Sister Alegría and I first began to notice the buzz from advertisements by some of the big companies in the country, like cell phone networks and the national lottery. They were promoting drawings to win all-expenses paid trips to South Africa to watch

Honduras play in the first round. Some big employers had trip packages for employees, and I even heard about a municipality offering one. Can you imagine? In this poor country, only a very few would have the material resources to make such a trip. Now it was being offered (by lottery) to citizens of a lower economic level.

On Monday in Limón, Sister Alegría and I had the opportunity to see part of Honduras' second game. They had already lost to Chile and now faced Spain. The president declared it a national holiday; government offices were closed and kids got out of school early. (The local nurse did decide to open the public health clinic, so we worked as usual.) We saw people around town wearing blue and white shirts (the national colors) and even hand painted ones that said "*Viva Honduras.*" On TV they showed the Honduran fans in South Africa cheering wildly, waving flags and sporting blue-and-white clown wigs. Even the ads all had soccer and Honduran pride themes.

There was lots of cheering by the viewers, but we noticed that it was all for defensive plays, blocking the opponent's goals. Honduras lost 2-0, to everyone's disappointment. One man told us that Spain was strong and well prepared, so there was never a chance. Another person (a local soccer coach) clarified that Honduras, being a poor country, doesn't have money to maintain a professional team full time or get expert training the way some richer countries do. But we all recognize what a great privilege it is to play in the World Cup at all: something that Hondurans can be proud of for many years to come. Friday is Honduras' third and final game, against Switzerland.

This morning, Sister Alegría and I went to the Immigration Office in La Ceiba and renewed our legal residency for four more years. We, too, are proud of Honduras' appearance at the World Cup, and we are also excited that the USA team has made it into the second round, even if we don't agree with that government's military policies.

Health Care
From: Sister Alegría   Date: June 25, 2010

Two weeks ago, Doctora Karen gave me a consult because I wasn't getting well fast enough. She recommended a Chest X-ray, EKG and internist consult. We came to the city to obey those instructions.

Chest X-Ray ($12): normal, but a quality that would never be accepted in the US.

Consult with our charming ENT doctor. His physical exam and experience tells him that the slow recovery of the throat is within the normal range. I should just keep on with the good compliance on reflux treatment. No worries, no reason to suspect yet another problem in the throat. He (like I) thinks that the breathing is not heart, but lungs, likely asthma. He sent me to the only pulmonologist on the north coast. His office is four blocks away.

Dr. Pintor walked down to the X-Ray department and had the tech hand me the chest X-ray to hand carry to the pulmonologist. The pulmonologist is fully convinced that it is just asthma, with a strong allergic component. He encouraged me to continue with the allergy and asthma treatment that Dr. Pintor prescribed. He also recommended SingulAir for two to three months and directed us to a pharmacy that offers two-for-one as a start-up promotion. He is not at all concerned about my exposure (several times) to the young woman with disseminated tuberculosis. (Consult: $32, with the old age discount. Note: This is high.)

We went to said pharmacy. This expensive medicine is not included in the promotion. Two dollars per day, just for this medicine. I am already taking medicines that cost $2 per day!

This made us think.

Last week, Doctora Karen asked if our church would please buy medicines for Centro de Salud. We had just received the shipment for three months and many basic medicines were not included at all, others had token amounts. We made a list of what is needed/wanted.

I wrote out two lists. The first list was what I thought we should have. It cost twice what we could spend. The second list pared down the first to what we could afford, remembering Dra. Karen's priorities. I reduced most medicines by a small amount, but had to reduce birth control by two thirds. Ouch.

Three months of birth control costs $2.50 for one woman. That means that the $60 that we would spend for partial treatment for one woman (me) costs the same as 72 months of birth control for our poor neighbors. Our patients for the most part are poor and don't want to have a baby every year. This may look like a conflict of interest, eh?

While I have been sick and recuperating slowly, I was supposed to rest a lot. We had to consider the balance of one person's health (mine) versus the health of many (those we serve at Centro de Salud). We decided that we would go on Mondays only when we could get a lift right at our path. One day, we served 60 patients (in 6 hours), getting door-to-door rides. My work in the clinic is not very physical. We chose the health of many and it cost us almost nothing.

We have bought the most important medicines for reflux and for asthma. We have enough for a month and a half. We will not buy the expensive SingulAir. We will buy the birth control that we had planned.

I feel normal now if I don't get too active. Better all the time, but not yet normal activities. Our spiritual practices continue, perhaps more deeply than usual.

Of course, we always appreciate your prayers. I don't want you to think that we are dealing with life and death stuff for me.

Mortality
From: Sister Alegría

True. It wasn't life and death, but it brought up the question of my mortality. What will/would Sister Confianza do if/when I leave for Heaven. Deep, productive conversations.

Monday, June 21
From: Sister Alegría   Date: June 25, 2010

We knew that our plan for the week was to work in Centro de Salud on Monday and then to go to La Ceiba for health care and immigration requirements. As we discussed the various options of details, I didn't like any of them. So we decided to keep alert to what God seemed to be telling us about our schedule.

By 6 am, we are at the end of our path waiting for a ride. None comes. Time passes, but no cars. Finally, a young man on horseback, leading another saddled horse, stops to chat. I ask if a car is coming down from La Fortuna today; he says no. He is on his way to the highway to meet his sister who will arrive by bus. They will return on horseback, of course.

He offers us a lift. We each climb on a horse and he walks. *Gracias a Dios*, there are real saddles with proper stirrups, even. We go to the highway. This is one and a half miles of up and down—a huge gift from our new friend.

Soon a bus comes along—a bus that doesn't usually go into Limón, but today it does. We arrive at Centro de Salud at 9:30, an hour and a half later than we were expected. There are only two nurses serving all of the patients so we get right to work, finishing about noon.

Juana Nidia, the RN, confirms that we are welcome to stay at her house. It is a long walk from her place to the bus in the morning.

We're still not sure. She asks if we're coming; I don't know, so I say, "God hasn't told me yet." She finds this an acceptable answer.

We go to Sor's place for lunch. We decide that we will stay; the afternoon offers good rest time and we could even read our mail. Accordingly, Sister Confianza and a teenager called *"Flaquita* (Skinny)"* go off to get the mail.

Less than a block on their way, they are flagged down by a woman who asks Sister Confianza about me and says that she has a sick person who needs attention. Sister Confianza is not a nurse; she is reluctant. Then the woman says, "I don't know when my baby is going to die." Reluctance overcome, Sister Confianza follows the woman into her house, where there is a tiny, suffering baby lying on the bed—looks as though he has suffered terrible burns. Sister doesn't need to be a nurse or doctor to see that this child needs immediate health care. They all troop back to Sor's place.

In the back porch, surrounded by about 18 children, one to twelve years of age, I give sort of a consult. Mom doesn't breast feed and the baby is obviously badly malnourished. The burned look is because he hasn't been bathed in a long time (weeks). I tell the mom that he needs to go to the hospital today and that we'll take him. She goes home to get some clothes while I keep the baby. I do not trust this Mom; I will not let this baby out of my personal custody until we're at the hospital.

Each of us, immediately upon seeing this child, understands what our travel plans are supposed to be.

We walk in the direction of where we hope to get a lift. Mom's friend says, "Where's the car?" She is imagining that we have a car and a driver. I tell her that we have no car and that we travel by hitchhiking, that's how we'll get to Tocoa.

And so we walk. Soon a truck stops and takes us to Francia. Another truck comes along quickly to give us another lift—all the way to the gate of the hospital. Later I learned that he drove five miles past his destination to get us to the hospital. The drivers/owners of both vehicles understand that they are providing ambulance service to save a baby's life.

The emergency room staff take care of us immediately (I am still holding the baby). A nurse first puts in an IV and draws blood for tests. She sends the mom to register the baby. Mom is scared silly. She's never been in the hospital before and she is a racial minority. Sister Confianza goes with her to the registration desk.

Smooth pediatric nurse; I am constantly in awe of good pediatric nurses. The young doctor is equally helpful. She and I examine the baby together. This is the first real exam I have done. The baby is swollen all over. He is four months old and only weighs

8.4 pounds, much of that water weight.   Severe protein/calorie malnutrition (kwashiorkor).

We can evaluate him better after a bath. The nurse bathes him. All the charcoal-looking flakes come off, leaving only the raw red spot on his cheek and raw, swollen genitalia. He has not been burned. He doesn't seem infected. His basic needs have simply been neglected.

We talk openly about malnutrition and admission is arranged. Mom looks with pleasure on the clean cloths brought with which to swaddle the child.

The hospital has formula, but no bottle. Mom has a bottle, but no formula—a match made in Heaven. Mom is so pleased as she bustles about preparing the bottle of formula for her son.

Mom is required to stay in the hospital and care for the baby. The doctor predicts a one week stay. Mom will receive all of her meals (but no bed in which to sleep). While we're still together in the emergency room, another Garifuna woman comes in to chat with the Mom—oh, good, solidarity.

We give the mom 100 lempiras, twice the cost of the bus fare back to Limón. We had all been in the ER for just over an hour.

We leave the mom and child in the hospital. Mom's name is Adolfa and baby's is Deiber. Please pray for them. Mom has a lot to learn and a lot to overcome when she returns back to Limón. "Good people" have a hard time forgiving this kind of thing.

We decide to go to our friends in Ceibita, a suburb of Tocoa. The last bus of the day has already left. We take a taxi—same price as the bus ride for the two of us from Limón to Tocoa would have been. We arrive at dark and are made welcome.

The pastor is out of town, but, of course, the parsonage is open to us anyway. As we settle in, we bathe, eat a little something, and do evening prayers. We realize that we missed afternoon prayers. Well, at least Sister Confianza did. I spent two hours holding Baby Jesus in my arms.

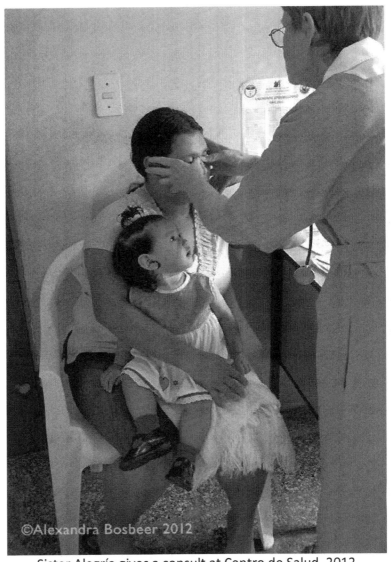

Sister Alegría gives a consult at Centro de Salud, 2012

7
Growing Spiritually

"Your faith is tested by trials, like gold is tested by fire."
—First letter attributed to Peter

On Strike
From: Sister Alegría   Date: August 10, 2010

    I wrote the following in a flurry on Tuesday, July 13, 2010. Just imagine yourself sitting on one of our backless wooden benches in the Monastery listening with Sister Confianza as I read aloud my ranting:

    Yesterday, I went on strike.
    When we arrived at Centro de Salud there were a lot of patients waiting and the nurses were checking them in. My exam room had been transformed. The broken-legged exam table had been replaced by a strong one and draped with a sheet. The cot also had a clean sheet. All of the books, folders, and stacks of paper were gone. There was a tall file cabinet, and stacks of stuff on a high shelf on the wall. A new freezer (Danish make) expressly manufactured for hot places. The desk was cleared except for a few mostly useful items.
    Lovely. I was delighted. I cut my papers on which to write prescriptions, got out the form for my daily tally of patients (name, sex, age, neighborhood, diagnosis, etc.). I got a chart and called the first family in to start giving consults.
    That's when the trouble started. When I was ready to listen to the child's chest, there was no stethoscope to be found. My good Eli Lilly pediatric stethoscope had disappeared months earlier. I had brought my adult Eli Lilly stethoscope and used it as well as I could. Now IT was gone, too.

I walked all through the clinic, pharmacy, exam rooms, reception area—nothing. Then I did it all again. Nothing.

I was very frustrated. I was still on walking restrictions and here I was using up all my walking energy looking futilely for my stethoscope. I went into the back room where Juana Nidia was reviewing a chart and I sat down (I thought to rest).

"Juana Nidia."

"Yes, *doctora*."

"I'm on strike."

"Why is that?"

I explained that I need a decent stethoscope to examine patients and I can't find one. These others won't do.

She calmly accepted this data and continued attending to the chart. She walked out looking for Connie and returned. A patient came in and she chatted with her a little, sent her to be weighed, walked out again. After her third time of walking out, I was wondering how long this strike was going to last. A family was waiting for me in my exam room and at least 30 other patients were in the waiting room and the porch. I sat. (It occurred to me that this was a sit-down strike—no placards, no picketing, just peaceful sitting.)

Wornita came in. She brought a new junky stethoscope. A recent visiting medical team had brought them. We get gifts of stethoscopes and blood pressure cuffs. They fall into two categories: hand-me-downs, almost worn out when we receive them (Think about it, why was that clinic getting rid of the equipment?), and very poor quality equipment. Some of this poor quality stuff bears respectable brand names, but is obviously the bargain basement cheapest line. For example, "It's a poor country; the patients will be skinny, we can save three inches on the cuff and two inches of Velcro!"

So the cuff pops loose often while I'm taking a patient's blood pressure. This is with a new Welch-Allen cuff!! It was given to us by an international helping organization. This equipment gets a lot of use and wears out fast. No one ever throws this junk away. It might be the only thing available at some point. If I can measure a blood pressure one time out of five attempts instead of not being able to attempt it at all, I'd better keep that option.

The stethoscopes are of a quality acceptable for taking blood pressure, but not for listening to hearts and lungs. It's hard being at the bottom of the trickle down economy.

I (tearfully) explained the stethoscope situation to Wornita. If we don't have a decent stethoscope we might as

172

well have the health promoters do consults (They're the ones who go out into the community teaching clean water and mosquito control stuff).

And so I sat.

Wornita disappeared and in three minutes flat she returned with BOTH of my good stethoscopes. One earpiece on the pediatric stethoscope was gone, but the adult one was fine. I took them and went back to work. My strike had lasted fifteen minutes. I should have gone on strike months ago.

I am not called to be successful, I am called to be faithful.

What is it to be faithful? What is it to be a Prima Donna? What is it to be a fraud?

To do the best I can in a bad situation with inadequate equipment—sounds like faithful. Refusing to work when I don't get what I want—sounds like spoiled little rich girl, the Prima Donna. When is a pediatric consult not a pediatric consult? What does it mean when a pediatrician without a decent stethoscope says, "I can't hear a heart murmur"? It certainly doesn't mean that there is no heart murmur. When is a pediatrician working without adequate equipment defrauding her patients? They think they've received a real pediatric consult, not a part or most of one. How is that keeping faith with my patients?

What is it to be faithful?

That's all from July 13. I am calmer and have some distance by now. The pediatric stethoscope has disappeared again.

Harvesting *Yuca*
From: Sister Confianza   Date: September 8, 2010

For several months now, Sister Alegría and I have been blessed with free *yuca* (aka cassava or manioc) from Mateo's field just over a quarter of a mile from the Monastery. It's an effort to go get— it takes time and energy—but we've decided that what it saves on our grocery bill and adds to the variety in our diet is worth it. Plus it is locally grown food, versus the processed and shipped in corn flour, wheat flour, and rice that we purchase.

We generally go twice a week, on Wednesday and Friday or Saturday, making it our physical work of the day. Since until very recently walking and other activity has been hard on Sister Alegría's asthma, it has meant we've had to choose carefully how to use the limited capacity we've had. We've done a lot less of the gardening at the Monastery than we would have liked, but there is also a sense that harvesting food, even though we didn't plant it, is still gardening—and it adds to our experience! Besides, we enjoy eating it!

Come along on a typical outing:

We made enough food the evening before for there to be leftovers, so after Lauds (morning prayers) at dawn, we eat a cold breakfast of beans and toasted tortillas. Sister Alegría sharpens the machete with the hand file, while I prepare us each a half-liter bottle of water which I place, along with a pair of work gloves, in a sack. We put on our pants, work boots, sunscreen, and wide-brimmed hats and set off.

The path to the road has a bit of a climb, so we take it slow with frequent rests so Sister Alegría won't get out of breath. We continue slowly north along the road until we reach the *yuca* field. Mateo and his family cleared the hillside of trees and brush about a year ago by slashing and burning, then planted the *yuca* sets—pieces of woody stem about one inch in diameter and a foot long. The field has never been cleaned, so it is overgrown with woody weeds and vines.

Sister Alegría and I climb under the barbed wire fence and find a nice-sized *yuca* plant nearby. The stalk is woody and branching, about seven feet high with green palmate leaves. I use the machete to cut down the weeds around the plant, and cut off the stalk to about a foot high. The base of the stalk is almost three inches in diameter—the bigger it is, the more likely it will have bigger and more tubers.

Next, Sister Alegría and I take turns digging around the base. We use the machete blade to lift the soil. This particular plant has nice brown soil around it. Some days we get one that is in heavy clay, which is harder to dig and the tubers don't grow as well. Sometimes they are impeded by rocks or roots from other plants. This is no ideal *yuca* field—it grows much better in sand. One major advantage of *yuca* as a crop, however, is that it doesn't require fertile soil.

One of the tubers we uncover, which radiate out from the stalk, is very large. When we finally get it out of the soil, it is about two feet long and four inches in diameter—the largest one we've ever harvested. (Some varieties get even bigger.) There are also a few smaller tubers the size of large carrots. We put them in our sack and take drinks of water before leaving. It is a hot morning, which is why we came so early.

On the road, we meet the man who is the caretaker at our neighbor Elias' property. He is returning on the mule from delivering the day's milk to the main road. We greet him, and he offers to carry the sack to our path. We are very grateful; the climb is steep.

However, we ask him to leave it at a certain spot on the way—we will want our water and have plans to get firewood.

Along the side of the road are two small standing dead trees. I cut them down with the machete (it's a real multipurpose tool!) and we break off the smaller branches. This has been one of the biggest blessings in going for *yuca*: We have been able to carry firewood back with us almost every time, and thus not had to take a day specifically to go for firewood.

Sister Confianza hauls firewood, 2013

We continue our stop-and-go walk back to the house. I carry the trunks on my shoulder and the machete in my hand and Sister Alegría carries the sack of *yuca* and picks wild berries—little sweet green and purple ones that also add to our diet diversity. We arrive tired and hot. After drinking plenty of water and changing back into our habits, we rest by doing our daily meditation.

At lunchtime, Sister Alegría prepares the *yuca* for cooking. (This is one of the "sweet" varieties that can be eaten after simply boiling. There are also "bitter" varieties that require extensive processing to remove toxins. That's what the Garifuna people make *cassave* from and also where tapioca comes from.) First she scrubs the tubers clean. They have a thin, papery brown skin, below which is a

175

pinkish, thick peel. She removes it by slicing down the side and using the knife and her fingers to peel it off. Then she cuts the tubers into four-inch lengths, puts them in the pot, and covers them with water.

I build the fire and make tortillas. (It's been my job to tend the fire since Sister Alegría got sick; we've wanted to keep her far from the smoke.) By the time the beans have come to a boil and I've finished making tortillas, the *yuca* is also cooked—the pieces soften and start to split apart. For lunch and dinner we eat it boiled with salt. It is white, pure starch and very filling—something like dry potatoes with twice the calories. In the morning we'll break up the cooked pieces then salt and deep fry them like French fries—by far our favorite way to eat *yuca*. Enjoy!

What's in a Name
From: Sister Alegría   Date: September 8, 2010

On Thursday, August 26, I renewed my Profession for another year. It was a Grace-filled, worshipful and celebrative day. It also felt like a coming of age of the Monastery.

As a young monastery we have had to (and continue to) learn some things the hard way. Experience is a good teacher, but not gentle. Our special "milestone" days have been entering the Postulancy, Reception into the Novitiate and First Profession. They have all been celebrative, but until this Renewal of Profession, they all had a fair amount of stress and overwork (which varied from minor inconvenience to almost overwhelming).

We seem to have learned how to do it. Renewal of Profession is a celebration of Community, a celebration of commitment and a celebration of having a Sister with one more year of monastic experience. So we celebrated! After Unprogrammed Worship (Quaker-style), we did a liturgical dedication service. We are a singing people; we sang 11 songs in all. Some of that is to make up for all the lost musical opportunities when I was sick. It was a lovely service.

We had a special meal for dinner—cooking as a community. We ate rice with chaya greens, flour tortillas, sour orange syrup (think honey) and scrambled eggs with onions. (Both eggs and onions are luxury foods.) And we relaxed a lot.

Renewal of my Profession included the first anniversary of my name of Alegría. I had had no idea that it would be such a blessing. *Alegría* means joy.

I had not taken very seriously the question of taking a new name as a religious. I liked my given name. It was chosen carefully by my parents who loved me before I was born. How could it get any better than that?

Then I entered monastic spiritual formation. Brother Lawrence reminds us that we "give all for all," demonstrating with his life. Was I willing to give all to God? I have no trouble giving God my osteoarthritis or my enjoyment of wearing bright colors. But my name? Spiritual formation taught me that my lovely psychological comfort with my name had nothing to do with spiritual growth. Monastic spiritual life is not about being a well-adjusted, well balanced middle-class American. It is about being focused on God. Think of Teresa of Avila, Brother Lawrence, Francis of Assisi, Gandhi and Teresa of Calcutta. None sought a "well-balanced" life.

I decided to give up my good name. Ah, yes, back to basic principles: spiritual growth is about giving up something good for something better. But I had no idea if it would be something better. I found out.

The first "outside" person that I told my new name to was Rosa. She said, "That's perfect. You're always smiling." Now that is affirmation. Hearing my name for the first time, almost every person smiles and says, "How pretty." Some even chuckle.

But the best is reading the Bible. It is full of Alegría. Psalm 100 (my favorite) has my name three times in the first two verses in our most used translation, _Versión Popular_. Regularly, you are exhorted to praise God, sing and shout with Alegría (with me!). I hope that you will.

So much for which to be grateful in August.

By the way, on Saturday, August 28, I proclaimed myself well—still a little out of shape, but well. We walked three miles on Monday. Sure, I got tired. Now that we don't NEED door-to-door lifts, God has stopped sending them. If we received no lifts on a Monday, we would walk nine miles. We've never done that.

Well?
From: Sister Alegría

Sister Confianza didn't contradict my self-proclaimed wellness, but she obviously didn't believe it and continued to try to spare me aerobic work.

Dengue

From: Sister Confianza

Date: October 8, 2010
(written Sunday, October 3)

The most prominent thing in our life in September (besides deciding to make my First Profession), was me having dengue fever. It was a classic case, except that the onset was gradual. I started with a terrible sinus-like headache on Sunday, September 12. It hurt especially above the eyes. On Monday at the clinic, I found that when I bent over my head throbbed. When I eventually told Sister Alegría that I wasn't feeling well, I was almost in tears. She prescribed Tylenol Cold. For a few days I was tired, my body ached and I didn't have much appetite.

Finally on Thursday Sister Alegría said, "Maybe we need to take you to the doctor." Then she looked at my eyes and said, "It looks like you have a virus. You must have dengue fever." She had seen a lot of patients with dengue recently. In fact, the whole country is on alert for it. We had thought of ourselves as relatively safe, since the dengue-carrying mosquitoes can't travel far, and the Monastery is remote from other people. However, the two of us go to the population center of Limón every week.

Since dengue is a virus, there is no medicine to cure it; you just have to wait it out for two to three weeks. I spent the next few days pretty much in bed. Sister Alegría says when I wasn't sleeping, I was suffering. I could hardly eat and had very little strength. Sister Alegría was all of a sudden in the kitchen cooking for the first time since her illness began in April, as well as doing all the other physical work! I managed to attend our daily worships, but didn't stand up for songs, and my voice was weak when I read. We did very few other shared spiritual practices. Sister Alegría read to herself a lot. I couldn't read aloud nor concentrate to listen.

On Saturday, we had to go to the creek to wash clothes. All I could do was get myself down there and back (a steep 1/8 mile each way), walking slowly and resting on the way. Sister Alegría did all the washing as I sat on the bank. We had guests on Sunday—new neighbors, a mom and her kids. Sister Alegría had a lovely lunch with them. I was excused. We didn't go to Limón on Monday. *Gracias a Dios,* we had plenty of groceries.

I started to get better. I slept less and began to eat a bit more. I could do a little more scrubbing each time we did laundry. My hands and voice were trembly, but regaining strength.

On Monday, September 27, we did go to Limón. We waited for a ride to go in. Sister Alegría thought I shouldn't do any work at Centro de Salud that day, though I thought I could do some, if I could mostly be sitting. That turned out to be a good thing. Nurse Wornita's daughter was very sick with diabetes, and Wornita had to take her to the hospital. That left just Sister Alegría, Dr. Karen, and me to run the clinic—no nurses to give shots or anything! Dr. Karen jumped right in checking in patients. I just dispensed medicines from my chair in the pharmacy. Hernán, the mailman, even came by, so we didn't have to do any major walking in town.

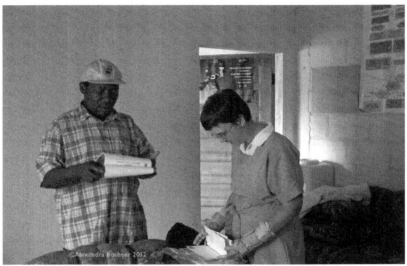

Hernán, the postmaster, delivers the Sisters' mail to Centro de Salud, 2012

We did have to walk most of the *desvío* home and arrived in the dark, but God gave us the strength.

I have continued to improve all week. I can't say I am completely healthy yet, but I am in the range of normal. I lost eight pounds during the illness. Thankfully I had that much to lose.

The biggest blessing was that on Friday the 24th it began to rain. We've been able to do our laundry at the house since then. A week later, the tank was full to overflowing. I think that's the first time that's happened this calendar year—but certainly since April when it went empty! (Have you noticed that the only times we've had to go to the creek for washing this year was when one of us was very sick? What's that about, God?)

Sister Confianza to Make First Profession

From: Sister Confianza   Date: October 8, 2010

Amigas del Señor Monastery
is pleased to announce that
Sister Confianza
will make her First Profession on
Thursday, November 25, 2010

*____*____*____*____*

Please keep us in your prayers during this time of preparation and celebration.

I am very excited to be at this juncture in my monastic life. For the last 18 months I have been immersed in the Novice experience—accepting the role of beginner, the one who has much to learn. It wasn't that easy to do—I am the older sister in my family, a smart person who was taught to believe in and rely on myself. I thought I knew it all—or at least, ought to know it all. Coming to the Monastery showed me that I had much to learn.

My only knowledge of monastic life and nuns before coming to Honduras in 2006 came from the Sound of Music and a few other stereotypical images. I had not done much reading or personal work in the area of spirituality. Nor had I ever lived in a tropical country! Obviously, I had much to learn, but it took time for me to become receptive.

When I became a Novice in May, 2009, I was ready to take that beginner role, to stop pretending I knew how everything ought to go, and to accept that I have something to learn from others. I was ready to ask questions and receive answers and follow others' guidance. I was ready to put down the burden of the one who knows all and can do all without anyone's help. I was ready to enter into a community that would support me on my journey.

My Novitiate has not always been an easy journey. I have questioned myself and my decision to join. I have questioned whether I could live the values of the Monastery. I have had to face who I am and where I come from and what is the appropriate relationship to have with my parents, family, and friends in the US. I have struggled through physical illness and pain. I have experienced the challenges of life as a poor person in the Third World—the challenges of getting drinking water and of taking care of a sick Sister far from good health care and medicine. But through it all, I know that God has been with me and I have had moments of joy and peace and consolation. I have known true community and celebration and seen love between Sisters and neighbors. I have sung out with joy and eaten delicious food. And I have prayed. Every day, I pray for God's blessings and guidance, that I might follow God's will and know God's love. And every day, I see those things manifest in my life.

When it came time to consider whether I am ready to make my First Profession, I was cautious. I wanted to make sure I was listening to God's voice and not just my own ideas. Though I had felt clear at the time I entered the Novitiate, after my Reception I sank into a period of doubt and questioning—questions that would have been better faced before that step. I didn't want to make the same mistake this time.

We convened a Clearness Committee at the beginning of September. The one question that came to my mind was whether I have a lifetime call to be a nun. I pondered this, but had no clarity. My life experience had been moving to a new location every few years growing up as my parents changed jobs. I can't imagine an entire life spent in one place doing one thing. I am sure God calls some people to do that, but I also know that God calls other people to do different things—to get off their duff, do something new, go somewhere else. How could I make a commitment to do one thing my whole life if God might want me to do something else?

As my clearness process continued, I realized a couple of things: First of all, making my First Profession is not a lifetime commitment—it's a one-year promise to live the life of a nun. In a way, I was asking myself the wrong question! I don't need to know at this point whether I have a lifetime call. At this Monastery, it is understood that women may come with short-term calls. It is a call to be a nun now, fully, but recognizing that God does call people to change direction in life. Therefore, a Sister who joins makes her First Profession for one year, and after that continues to make commitments of one or several years. She is a full Sister, fully committed to this life at this time. If and when she hears God's call to be doing something else, she can listen and have the support of this spiritual community as she discerns what God wants from her. She may hear the call to make a lifetime commitment. But if she is called to go somewhere else, then at the end of her committed time she is free to do that, having fulfilled her commitment to this life. She would not be breaking vows, nor negating that she had a monastic vocation for the time she was there. It was one part of her spiritual journey.

I can see that these are my own concerns—the questions of being wrong about my call, making mistakes in my life that are irreversible, keeping my word. I want the assurance that I am doing the right thing and following God. Learning to trust in the discernment process of the Monastery has been a major part of this for me. As a monastery, listening to each other and to God, we discern the decisions we ought to make, the steps we ought to take. One thing that has upheld me in the last few years as a Postulant and Novice is the fact that as a Monastery we discerned that I have a monastic call. Even if there was some question about whether it was a call to this particular monastery, I could trust that we had discerned God's basic call for me and not keep questioning it.

The second thing I realized is that at this monastery, we don't have a vow of stability. At this point our order has only one monastery in one specific location in the world, but it may not always be that way. God may well call a Sister to a new ministry or a new location that wouldn't have her leave the order. Instead, if it were discerned that this is a call for the whole monastery, the Sister could be sent with its blessing—commissioned to go do this new ministry as a sister of Amigas del Señor. To me, this leaves open the possibility of God's call within a call. It opens my imagination to the hopes and possibilities that the future might hold. Secure in God's hands, sure of the monastic vocation that has been discerned, the sister goes (I go?) forward in joy, following God's call with the joyous blessing of her Sisters, into a future that only God knows. And God assures us of victory.

These thoughts and imaginations helped me come to clarity that yes, I should profess as a Sister of Amigas del Señor, and that now is the time. I have learned much as a beginner, a novice, and now can take the role of one of the "big Sisters" and accept my place as one with experience and responsibility. I can look toward the future, knowing that this year, this is what I'm doing and where I'm supposed to be. I can keep my ear open to God's call for me—maybe to stay here as a nun, maybe to do something else, part or not of the Monastery. I can trust in God to guide me, take care of me, and surprise me with joyful as well as painful experiences. I don't know what God has in store for me, but I go forward with hope, expectation, excitement and trust, at this time of my First Profession.

Sister Confianza's Spiritual Crisis

From: Sister Confianza   Date: November 22, 2010
                                         (written November 7, 2010)

October was a challenging month for me. I had to face myself as I am, with no pretenses, and learn to let go.

Just as I was getting over dengue, my wrists got sore: my tendonitis was flaring. I followed *Doctora* Karen's recommendations and stopped doing activities that would aggravate it. That meant no using the ax or machete, no washing laundry, no sorting corn and beans, and no grinding toasted corn. It also meant much less writing.

I felt bad because Sister Alegría was stuck doing all the work. Usually I do a good portion of it—especially the more strenuous activities like splitting and carrying wood. It turned out I could still carry firewood and cook (except for using the knife). I learned to form tortillas left-handed, but most of the time, asked Sister Alegría to press out the *masa* on the circles cut from plastic bags. Any activity I could do I did in order to facilitate Sister Alegría's work: filling and moving buckets with water, sweeping, hanging clothes. One thing that helped was being reminded by Teresa of Avila in our Second Annual Monastery Retreat that, as a contemplative, my main job is to pray. When I didn't have physical work to do, I could think of God and know that I was doing my part.

Even so, I saw Sister Alegría with the burden and wished that I could do more. All I noticed were the things that I couldn't do, and I felt useless. It was upsetting and sometimes I cried. I realized I was in the middle of a spiritual crisis—a time of testing or a refining fire—and what I needed was to go through it. I was having to face that who I am is not based on what I can do. I was having to learn to depend on God and others for everything.

I knew God was allowing me this experience to teach me, and I had hope of coming through a better person, but I wanted it to get over quickly so I could stop suffering!

After three weeks of pain and anguish, I began to wonder if I would have to become completely useless—to literally not do ANYTHING—in order to fully learn my lesson.

Early on Saturday morning, October 30, I wrote the following in my journal:

> Let go. Of everything. All goals, all ambition, the idea that I can do anything myself. Even write. Today, I try with my left hand. I have to let go of my ideas of what I want and what I think needs to be done. I need to let God take care of me. I have to give up being useful and doing my share! I

183

want to let God give me his gifts and to accept them freely—
not prove myself. Oh, Lord, help me. Free me. Open my
mind and take away my fears. Let me be grateful for what I
have and for who I am, for your unconditional love. Let me
know grace. Transform me and make me new. Amen.

At the same time, Sister Alegría wrote this in her journal:

> Weekly Review last night. Another jam-packed week.
> Hermana Confianza's continued facing of God *mano a mano.*
> After Review we talked more about this scary time for
> her. I recognize that we did a few things this week that
> bought psychological relief/comfort and material gain for the
> Monastery at the cost of her spiritual progress—carrying
> home the scrap lumber and the large amount of cooking wood,
> making the hammock chair. But God saved us from ourselves
> in the sewing. She worked on the blouse at the cost of
> worsening her wrist.
> So today we will consciously collaborate with God in
> the stripping naked of our precious Sister.

Apparently, all I needed was the permission that she gave me
to go through with it: if I had to stop doing anything at all, it was
OK. She'd be OK. We'd be OK. She was on my side. As she said to
me that morning, I am the person with the most to gain by coming
through this crisis successfully and she is the one with the second
most to gain. By that afternoon, I was feeling positive again. I
regained my hope and trust in God to take care of me (and us!). He
would provide for our needs.

Sister Alegría wrote in her journal that afternoon:

> Hermana Confianza was calm and comfortable. She
> just seemed to accept her status as a one-armed lefty. You
> truly are a God of miracles! I'm impressed.

Since then my wrists still ache and Sister Alegría is tired
from all the work, though her arms have gotten stronger and her
asthma has improved. But the basics are getting done: the laundry
is washed and there is food on the table. When Sister Alegría didn't
have the strength to cut trees on Wednesday, God showed us fallen
branches and dead saplings that I could snap off and carry home for
firewood. Other goals or hopes we leave aside. We have positive
attitudes and I am looking forward to my eight-day, end-of-Novitiate
silent retreat beginning on Thursday, November 11. It may be my

chance to truly let go and be dependent on God and my Sister: She will be taking over the cooking and I will only do other tasks when asked. My focus will be prayer and spiritual practice. I thank God for supportive community.

Please keep us in your prayers!

Monday, November 8
From: Sister Alegría   Date: November 29, 2010

We're in Tocoa for a few days. You were expecting something from us early in November and were wondering what happened. Well, I'll tell you.

Monday, November 8. We had a plan. We would go to Limón, work in Centro de Salud, have lunch at Sor Leonarda's place, get our mail, and hitch a ride to Bonito. We'd go to the bank for the cash that would now be available, check a little email, stay overnight at the house of our friends, the Jesuit priests, spend time doing errands and internet. As always, we recognize that a nun proposes and God disposes. It is actually rather rare that our Mondays unfold as expected.

It had rained all night. This meant that the road would be bad and there would be no cars coming down from La Fortuna. After Lauds at 4:30 and breakfast, we took off in light rain walking to the highway. The rain got heavier. We now realized that there would be few patients at Centro de Salud and considered skipping the Limón part of the plan.

The first car to come along was our friend, Luís, the municipal chauffeur, headed for Bonito. That decided our destination. He dropped us off at the internet. It was still early and the bank wouldn't be open yet.

No internet. They will not have internet again. Big blow. We get a bus to Tocoa. We notice that we won't get to see our friends, Juan Donald and Gus, but we look forward to seeing the sisters at the church in Ceibita (Tocoa).

The bus guy comes to collect the fare. I reach into my pocket—it is empty!

Flashback: Before breakfast, Hermana Confianza had checked with me that I had the banking materials in my hidden pocket. "Yes," I patted it. Later we realized that I was still wearing yesterday's dirty dress (it had been a cold night and I had worn it for an extra layer for warmth). So I changed dresses, forgetting to move the cash ($16—300 lempiras) and banking materials to the clean one!

Back to the bus: Normally, I carry the large bills and Hermana Confianza carries the small bills. She pays the bus fare ($2.50) with small bills.

Obviously, our first stop is the bank. We have done a withdrawal once before without the bank book, so we are confident.

It is still cold and our clothing is wet. Not warmer inside the bank, but as we wait, we notice that we are drying out.

Need to replace the bank book. There will be a fee of $2.50. I don't have $2.50, but I can pay it after I make my withdrawal. This is fine. Go to the lady who can do that. She does. We wait half an hour for her email data to come from La Ceiba. (Fascinating. First Tocoa gets a stop light; now the bank is actually "connected" to Ceiba. The 21st Century has arrived in Tocoa, Colón.)

She hands me the bank book and the bill. More waiting in line. We imagine splurging for hot food for lunch—maybe a hearty Honduran soup.

Get back to the teller. The bankbook doesn't have the balance printed in it. He goes to fetch the data and returns with a very serious look on his face. The check hasn't cleared the bank yet. There were three bank holidays in October. The usual 30 days is extended. The money will not be available until November 11.

I say, "You have to help us. We have no money for food and not even bus fare to get home."

He leaves again, this time to the head office. The serious look on his face persists. We have 94 cents available to withdraw—nothing more. A tear comes to my eye. "I don't know how to beg alms. I've never done it."

He says, "It will be all right." It is nice to hear an echo of Julian of Norwich when one really needs it.

I withdraw the 94 cents (18 lempiras). He rips up the bill for the new bankbook.

We take seats. Hermana Confianza digs out all the cash and counts it: $4.10. The bus fare is $5. But the bus guys know us. We are hopeful.

Our friends, Ingrid and Angel, have a plastics store on our route to the bus station. Ingrid is looking especially cute in her cold weather cap (ideal for northern winters). We haven't seen them in almost a year. Nice chat. We tell the story of our day. Ingrid says, "Would it help if I loaned you a dollar?" Yes, it would. We go into the store and Angel forks over the money without question (four 5 lempira bills). We chat and joke some more. Angel is peeling oranges and gives us each one to eat on our way.

I'm not supposed to eat citrus, so I eat 1/4 orange and Sister Confianza eats the rest. The bus guy greets Sister Confianza with "La Fortuna," our destination. It is nice to be known.

The bus guy comes to collect. He charges $4, an unrequested discount. What lack of faith. In order to believe that God will take care of us, we needed double favors. I wonder when we will learn.

We each eat a tortilla (left over from breakfast) when we get to our road. When we stop for afternoon prayers, our friend, Javier, comes along on horseback. We invite him to join us. He accepts and dismounts; he stands at a distance, observing closely. Javier is not a churchy guy.

As we walk on, he has his horse walk slowly so we can all chat. I tell him about our day. When I get to the part about begging alms, I add, "Who would believe a gringo begging alms?"

His face is more expressive even than his words. "It would be unbelievable."

I ask him if he has ever begged alms. "By the Grace of God, I have never had to."

"Then you can't teach me."

Soon it is time to part ways and we Sisters walk the rest of the way home. As we are making a big dinner, Sister Confianza remembers that once she had forgotten her bus pass in St. Paul and had to beg quarters from other passengers. So we do have some experience upon which to build if/when we need it.

We notice that we didn't do any of the tasks that we had planned. It sounds like a day filled with frustration, but it wasn't. It seemed to flow from one moment of Grace to the next. We had much for which to be grateful as we entered Compline and the Grand Silence.

A Word about Prayer
From: Sister Alegría

Bedtime prayer is called *Completas* or Compline, that which completes the day. Before it, day; after it, night, The Grand Silence. Our Compline has three hymns, two psalms and a reading from the Old Testament, book after book, chapter after chapter.

No matter what Order it is a part of, every Christian monastery prays the Lord's Prayer at least once a day. The traditional monastic teaching on that emphasizes "forgive us our debts as we forgive our debtors," (also translated as offenses, sins, and trespasses). The point is that each nun or monk reminds her/himself that (s)he is required to forgive if (s)he hopes to be

187

forgiven. It's a good time to just do the forgiving and a good time to notice what you yourself did this day that requires forgiveness. It is a given that in a monastery there will be plenty of opportunities to practice forgiveness.

Compline by candlelight, 2012

El Padre Nuestro (the Our Father, or Lord's Prayer) has become part of me. When things are tense, I pray over and over, *"Venga to reino, hagase tu voluntad* (Thy kingdom come, thy will be done)". This is also a vow. If you pray that God's reign come and God's will be done, you are promising to do your part. So do your part.

Living in poverty by Honduran standards has sensitized me to the line "Give us this day our daily bread." Jesus' followers were poor; their daily bread was not a given. They prayed that there would be food to eat each day. We do too.

First Profession
From: Sister Confianza   Date: December 1, 2010

I had a very nice end-of-Novitiate/pre-Profession retreat November 11-18. My focus was The Song of Songs and Teresa of Avila's meditations on it. One of the ways of reading the love poetry is as a conversation between the soul and God/Christ. It is a traditional monastic idea to consider Christ as one's True Spouse. I feel I'm just a beginner at learning to love God with my whole heart, soul, mind and strength, but it is certainly my ideal.

The following is a compilation of verses from the Song of Songs that speak to me. The citations are in parentheses, from the New Revised Standard Version. Different editions of the Bible label the changes of speaker differently, which gave me the liberty to adopt my own labels.

Selections from the Song of Songs (NRSV)

Chorus: What is your beloved more than another beloved, O fairest among women? (5:9a)

Bride: My beloved is [...] distinguished among ten thousand. (5:10)

Groom: You are altogether beautiful, my love; there is no flaw in you. (4:7)

Bride: His speech is most sweet, and he is altogether desirable. This is my beloved, and this is my friend. (5:16)

Groom: I am a rose of Sharon, a lily of the valleys, (2:1) a garden fountain, a well of living water and flowing streams. (4:15a)

Bride: Many waters cannot quench love, neither can floods drown it. (8:7a)

Groom: Set me as a seal upon your heart, as a seal upon your arm; for love is strong as death. (8:6a)

Bride: When I found him whom my soul loves, I held him and would not let him go. (3:4b) My beloved is mine and I am his! (2:16a)

Groom: Arise, my love, my fair one, and come away. (2:10b)

Bride: He brought me to his banqueting house, and his intention toward me was love. (2:4)

Groom: How sweet is your love, my sister, my bride! How much better is your love than wine! (4:10a)

Chorus: Eat, friends, drink, and be drunk with love. (5:1c)

The day after my retreat ended, we decided to go to Bonito. Our money was now available from the bank. We spent around $100 on fabric, medicine, and food. We splurged on vegetables and fruit; for a couple of months we have not had a balanced diet. On Saturday, we made a beef and vegetable stew in honor of my profession, and ate well for most of the week.

The day of my First Profession, November 25, was lovely and relaxing. We had Unprogrammed Worship, then the Profession ceremony and worship, in which I received my white blouse. We read together for fun and did other prayer practices. We even ate a

Snickers bar! The next day we were able to plant an avocado seedling in honor of my Profession. It was the first time such an occasion has fallen at a good time of year to plant a tree.

Thanks for all of the nice thoughts and prayers you have sent my way. I hope you had a happy Thanksgiving.

Being OK with What Is
From: Sister Confianza

"You are wasting your lives," Sister Alegría's mom once wrote to her. Sister Alegría assured me that parental disapproval and even rejection is common among those entering religious life. When Sor Leonarda announced that she was joining a congregation of Sisters, her mother responded, *"¡Puedes olvidarte que soy tu madre!* You can forget I'm your mother!"* (She reclaimed her, though, when Sor made Perpetual Profession six years later.)

When we convened the first session of my Clearness Committee on August 31, 2010, I faced the fact that I dearly wanted my parents' approval of my monastic vocation. I was hurting from all their questioning over the previous fifteen months. In the letters they wrote to me, my mom and dad each expressed their concerns: "Why don't you call us by phone? Must you live so far away and so isolated? What about your safety? I wish you had institutional support. I'm uncomfortable with you relying solely on donations. I want to see you use your talents and the advantages we have given you." I wanted them to accept my chosen life as it is, and support me as they had in my various life decisions up until joining the Novitiate in May, 2009. I wished I could convince them that our monastic lifestyle was good and that everything would turn out OK.

I wasn't completely secure in my own call, but their non-acceptance made me want to prove it to them. I suppose this was my adolescent "acting out" that I hadn't done as a teenager. A part of me said, "If they don't want me to do it, then I'll show them I can." That, in turn, provoked a fear of failure. If for some reason I didn't live out this commitment, then I would end up going home with my tail between my legs, and they would have been proven right. Looking back I see my pride. At the time, I just felt stuck. I needed to get out of this unhelpful cycle in order to hear what God—not my parents or my pride—was saying.

I wrote to God in my journal:

During the brief period of Unprogrammed Worship before the Clearness Committee, I felt overwhelmed by You.

My heart ached from stress but at the same time felt ready to burst with your love. I thought, "What would I do (or how would I be) if I truly followed God and trusted in him?" And I answered, "*Derramaría amor por todos lados.* I would pour out love all over." I wouldn't worry about so many things. I wouldn't judge myself or others. I would smile at everyone and love everyone without being afraid of anything or anyone. I would live happy in your hands.

I realized that my life couldn't depend on my parents' approval. I had to be OK with things as they were. I needed to accept my parents as they were and where they were. I began to see that all their concerns came out of their love for me and their desire for my safety and wellbeing (as well as their interest in closer communication with their beloved daughter). So I chose to stop clinging to my desire for their acceptance, and trust that God would continue to work in them as he was working in me, confident in God's final victory.

A burden was greatly lifted. The pain went away and I could move on with my life unencumbered by that need for approval or the fear of failure. To my great joy, my mom sent me a letter and a card for my First Profession, affirming my discernment and decision to continue at Amigas del Señor. Now that I wasn't attached to the outcome, I received what I'd wanted all along. My long-distance relationship with my parents has only grown and matured since then, as we all learn to live with what is and take joy in one another's lives.

The Sisters read letters on the porch, 2009

Path to the Monastery, 2008

8
Living the Life

"Sempiterna brota la esperanza. Hope springs eternal."—Unknown

Rosalie Grafe
From: Sister Alegría

I met Rosalie Grafe (with her brand new master's degree in publishing) in 2008 when I visited Portland. I was convinced that if Rosalie didn't accept us, we shouldn't try another publisher. She did accept us. She and two volunteers reviewed our updates of January, 2006, to July, 2008, selecting what they thought should be in the book. Then we waited.

As you've read, in September, 2009, we reviewed the manuscript. Then we waited.

Rosalie's volunteers dropped out; she took over all of the editing to get it out for December, 2010.

Amigas del Señor, the Book
From: Sisters Alegría and Confianza   Date: November 30, 2010

That's right! Thanks to the diligent work of Rosalie Grafe at Quaker Abbey Press, the story of the founding and first 2.5 years of the Monastery as told in our email letters home is now available in book form. We can hardly wait to see it.

Please purchase and read the book, titled Amigas del Señor: Methodist Monastery. Give it to friends for Christmas, for birthdays, or just because it is Tuesday. If you know a courageous, strong-willed woman who seems ready to give all for God, give her a copy. Send this announcement to your friends so that they can buy it for themselves or their friends. Post this at your church or in its

193

newsletter. Suggest the book as reading for your book club or women's group.

All profits from the book go to the Amigas del Señor alms fund which is used primarily to purchase medicines for local health clinics serving the poor in Honduras.

Baby Jesus (Starving Baby Follow-up)
From: Sister Alegría   Date: December 2, 2010

Deiber (with his mother, Adolfa) was in the hospital for two weeks at the end of June. They tried to give him a transfusion (routine care here for starving babies), but couldn't keep an IV in. He was sent home without it. He could take only one ounce of formula at a time. But he ate every hour. They came home with a free supply of formula powder.

He didn't gain weight for a month. All the nutrition he took in was needed to remake the damaged tissues. I put him on iron drops for his anemia. I saw him often.

Sor Leonarda gave Adolfa bus fare to go to Tocoa to the feeding clinic where she received free formula.

Now Deiber takes solid food, smiles brilliantly and has a normal weight and body habitus for age. Mom uses one word, repeatedly for him: "*Tremendo.*" She is so proud and grateful.

Thanks   for   including   them   in   your   prayers.

Sister health follow-up:
I am still taking medicine daily, but not much. I am well and have never been stronger.

Sister Confianza has regained the weight she lost with dengue. Her wrists are still a problem, limiting her activities, but the angst is gone. When we were robbed two years ago, her high-quality prescription splints were stolen. No problem, her wrists were fine at the time. When she had a small flare, we constructed new splints, using a cut up shampoo bottle, used fabric for padding, and Velcro straps. They seemed to do fine. This recent flare has not been so responsive to treatment. We were able to find one adequate right wrist splint yesterday here in Tocoa. There were no excellent splints, nor any for the left wrist. We are hopeful.

Stethoscope update:
    Both of my stethoscopes are available. When I am done on Mondays, I close the door to my exam room, then I put the adult stethoscope on a high shelf between folders. I stand on a chair to do that. The pediatric stethoscope I put in the second-to-the-top drawer of the file cabinet. Ssshh. Don't tell anyone my hiding places or they'll disappear again.

Blessed Christmas

From: Sisters Alegría and Confianza   Date: December 2, 2010

    Enjoy this poem. You'll hear from us again next year.

Love Came Down At Christmas	*El amor nos vino*
by	translated by
Christina Rosetti, 1885	Las Amigas del Senor, 2010

Love came down at Christmas,
Love all lovely, Love divine;
Love was born at Christmas:
Star and angels gave the sign

   El amor nos vino
   en la Navidad, dando claridad,
   bello y divino.
   Anunció el cielo que él nació.

Worship we the Godhead,
Love incarnate, Love divine;
Worship we our Jesus,
but wherewith for sacred sign?

   A Dios adoremos,
   encarnado, humanado.
   A Jesús cantemos,
   al amor divino que nació.

Love shall be our token;
love be yours and love be mine;
love to God and neighbor,
love for plea and gift and sign.

   Tuyo es el amor,
   y es el mío: don divino.
   A Dios demos amor,
   y a nuestro projimo.

Christmas Story

From: Sisters Alegría and Confianza   Date: January 12, 2011

    This little story is a gift that we received during our December day-long retreat. We both liked it and we hope that you do, too.

    She was very young, carrying a ragged bundle. As she walked along the street, things happened.

The newspaper vendor insisted that she was dressed in blue silk and the child in green velvet. His face shone as he told about his sudden decision to give up a lawsuit that he had filed two years ago and had caused him much bitterness.

The businessman was certain that she was his sister and quickly searched in his store for a suitable gift for the baby—his own flesh and blood: clothing to warm the baby on that chill day.

The food vendor insisted on giving the young woman a full meal, encouraging her to have more and more, while she, the vendor, had the privilege of holding the radiant child.

Two little girls, on their way to the grocery store for their mother, stopped to admire the baby. When they arrived at the store, they noticed that the few coins they had been carrying had been multiplied ten-fold. The family would eat well this day.

An old woman, on her way to the clinic to get medicine for her painful kidney stones, stopped to bless the baby. As she touched the child, her pain disappeared. She decided to visit an old almost-forgotten friend instead of continuing on to the clinic.

The fruit vendor, discouraged, was sorting out the rotten from the still sellable fruit, when his attention was captured by the child. He chose the largest and best fruit to give to the young woman and child. Returning, serene, to his fruit stand, he noted that all of the fruits were now in perfect condition. Wonderment.

Where did she come from? Where did she go? Whose is the child? Hers? Who is the father? Where do they live? None of these questions matter.

How can I meet them again? That is the question in every heart.

Fin.

Instrumental Music
From: Sister Alegría

Playing a musical instrument, especially learning to play, is a rich spiritual practice. I played cornet from 5th grade through high school, then put it aside. At 45, I got it out again, even bought a silver trumpet. I played in a few church ensembles (Sellwood UMC and Rose City Park UMC) and, briefly, in Mt. Hood Community Orchestra. Trumpet playing was a good prayer practice for me. I especially liked playing favorite hymns. It was deep to sing the words in my head as I played. From 1992 until the early years of this century, I played a lot.

As it became clear that I was called to material poverty in monastic living, I realized that I needed to give up the trumpet. It was hard. I started soprano recorder on my own, then switched to alto recorder (harder, but nicer sound). Then I moved to Amigas del Señor.

We play recorders. It is not about practicing for the sake of performance. It is playing as prayer. It is worship.

People who set their hearts on spiritual growth are often frustrated. "So I meditate 20 minutes every morning; I don't see myself being any better." Fill in any spiritual practice that interests you; the feeling is the same. Often, others can see the changes, but the practitioner, the aspiring saint, notes the ongoing failures, the seeming stagnation.

If you play recorder (at whatever low level) and you do it every day or even twice a week, you'll gradually become a more accomplished player. You can hear the progress. This is a spiritual practice with built-in encouragement. Your progress as a musician is evident; that strengthens your faith that your other spiritual practices are also bearing fruit.

Sister Confianza majored in music at university. Her instrument was clarinet. The recorder is very similar to the clarinet, just a whole lot easier. What was challenging for me was boringly easy for her.

Playing recorder is one of the founding practices of the Monastery. Over and over again, we would reaffirm the practice in Meeting for Worship with Attention to Business, play for a month or two, then nothing. It wasn't working.

Frustration. Failure. Incomprehension.

In December, 2010, I decided to get to the bottom of it. Why? Why was our instrumental music program failing to get off the ground? I reviewed minutes of our meetings and my own journals. Then I asked probing questions of us both. What is it that keeps us from fulfilling this simple obligation? That's when Sister Confianza admitted that she didn't like playing music with me because I am such a poor musician.

I felt personally attacked, and one of the basic spiritual practices of the Monastery was attacked. Inclusiveness, a basic Christian concept, was under attack. Sister Confianza and others in her family have been active in the movement to include fully in the church persons who are sexual minorities. Inclusiveness is important to her. That value didn't make playing recorder with me into a desirable activity.

I cried, I wailed, I slammed wooden window shutters—hard. I was amazed at how satisfying that activity was. I said horrible things to my Sister.

Privately, I reviewed every compliment I could remember on the topic of music. But they were all long ago and far away.

Then I looked hard at my own responsibility. I had not decided her refusals, but I had let her refusals decide my behavior. For five years, I had been irregular, unfaithful in this spiritual practice. I had to face my own irresponsibility and unfaithfulness. Ouch! More pain. I decided to play recorder daily without regard to her attitude or participation.

She played every day with me without comment.

Sister Alegría plays the soprano recorder, 2013

We've read, a few times, Robert Ellsberg's <u>All Saints</u>. Lots of foundresses in it. It was very encouraging for us in this neophyte monastery. Ellsberg often demonstrated that we were right on schedule, e.g., receiving lots of outside criticism and lack of understanding. All these women who founded religious orders seemed pretty saintly. All we had for a foundress was me. The first five years of our monastic life we were both painfully aware of every apparent weakness I had. (Note: When I read this section aloud to Sister Confianza, she spoke sadly, "It makes me sad to hear that."

Me: "But that was my reality."

She: "Yes, that was my reality, too." Still a sad voice.)

It was our reality, a part of our reality that was painful and that we do not celebrate. But it was not our entire reality. It is not about us. It is about God, who cares little for what we foolish humans call strengths and weaknesses. God can use a "weakness" as easily as a "strength." We do not lose sight of that fact.

Ellsberg introduced us to Little Sister Magdeleine of Jesus, the foundress (1938) of the Little Sisters of Jesus. She confessed honestly in her letters that being a foundress is hard. She speaks my mind.

This was a hard time. We were each lonely in our individual ways. By October, 2011, the worst was over. We now play recorders on schedule. Occasionally, Sister Confianza gives me a compliment about music. She notices when I don't believe her. Healing is slow. Why do I choose to include it? Because it was a secret. Secrets are poison to spiritual growth.

Year-end financial report for 2010
From: Sister Alegría   Date: January 12, 2011

Another calendar year whisked past.

```
EXPENSES
Provisions              $454
Household expenses       251
Communication            203
Health                   580
Clothing                  65
Immigration              165
Transportation            83
Library                    0
Property tax               3
Total cost of living  $1,804

Alms                  $2,279
TOTAL EXPENSES        $4,083

INCOME (donations)    $3,488
```

Our 2010 financial facts include two that particularly please me. First, our year's expenses were more than $2,000 LOWER than in 2009. Second, for the first time we actually succeeded in spending more on alms than on our own living expenses. Alms were 56% of outflow.

You may wonder why we send financial reports to people, most whom do not contribute in any way. Right now we have no direct accountability to any outside person or organization. Thus we write our financial reports, accountable to everyone.

The expenditures in most categories decreased from 2009. I'll just mention a few details.

- Food: Our cost of food dropped a lot. We harvested more from our land. We also received more gifts/donations of food from local friends/supporters. The many months without gardening work being done means that we don't expect to repeat the record this year.
- Clothing: This year we began repairing flip-flops with pieces of old boots and epoxy to extend their useful life. We find that the cost of epoxy is lower than replacing flip-flops so often.
- Alms: Although the percentage went up the absolute amount went down. There simply wasn't money available when the need was felt.

  We bought more birth control pills and injections than ever before. The public health center never has enough. Some of our patients can buy them, but most cannot. If the clinic is out, they go without. There is a huge demand for birth control. Women do not want to have as many babies as their mothers did (8 to 14!). They also want to space their pregnancies.

  We spent $688 on birth control this year. This supplied 275 women with three months each of birth control. We still ran out. Birth control is our priority in health care.

  We also gave a small amount to help out Marcos' widow and children.
- Health: Our health costs were very high this year, as you already know. We bought some expensive "modern" medicines and chose not to buy others. We also received a lot of free medicines. At Centro de Salud we may not dispense outdated medicines, but we can bring them home. We received free (outdated) ibuprofen. Sister Confianza does not recommend liquid ibuprofen as a taste treat, but she took it when it was available.

After I got back to normal function, we looked back at my illness and the decision to forego the most expensive medicines. I estimated that I would have come back to good function at least two months faster with it. The economic result of that would have been increased garden production (from October, 2010, through all of 2011). We pay Third World food prices, but First World medicine prices (for the newest medicines). It would not have paid for itself. We made the same decision about those medicines that any other household in our economic class would have made. Economically speaking, it was the right decision.

- Library: No expenditures. You'll remember that I labeled this as the area of temptation with regard to poverty. We received the loan of several good books (it is good to have friends who are missionaries), and some very useful donated books.

New Dress Fabric
From: Sister Confianza

In July, 2010, we decided it was time to find a new blue fabric for our habits. Before founding Amigas del Señor, Beth and her friend and sometimes travel companion, Jyl Myers, designed the habit dress. Jyl had found a simple denim dress at Goodwill, with a square neck and a wide tie around the waist. They made a pattern from it and sewed one dress which Beth began wearing occasionally. Beth bought several bolts of sixty-inch-wide light blue denim (it takes two yards to make one dress), and had it shipped to Honduras.

Trying to live in poverty, Sister Alegría and I used our habits till they wore out. Unfortunately, we discovered that they faded almost faster than they wore through. We had to retire some of my dresses when certain provocative areas faded so much they stood out from the rest. When we made new dresses, the contrast to the old ones was so dramatic we couldn't pretend they were uniform, though we wore them regardless. Then one day, a friend referred to us as having gray dresses. That was the last straw. We wear blue habits!

It was time to get new cloth—a type we could buy here in Honduras. We found a nice medium-blue woven fabric and over the next few months made ourselves new habit dresses, finishing in January, 2011. We have found that they fade only slightly, so we feel we are always within the range of a uniform blue. The one downside is that it is a cotton-polyester blend, so can't be composted when it wears out.

Anniversary
From: Sister Alegría   Date: January 26, 2011

Amigas del Señor celebrates its Fifth Anniversary on Tuesday, February 1. We'll have special services and special food and we'll rest a little more than on a usual Tuesday. Say a prayer for us. We'll pray for you, too. Five years. My, my.

We came to Bonito today to buy medicines. We don't actually buy them here; we deposit the money in Eloyda's bank account so that she can buy them. Obviously, donations have arrived.

We hadn't planned on coming this week, but on Monday we learned that we won't be getting more medicines in Centro de Salud for almost a month and we don't know how much will arrive. We are out of anti-allergy meds for kids, anti-bacterial soap for skin infections, iron pills, folic acid pills, amoxicillin in capsules (the only antibiotic that we use for bladder infections in pregnant women, i.e., essential), trimethoprim/sulfa in tablets, our most useful high blood pressure medicine and more. So, we called Eloyda and she got right on it. Hopefully the medicines will arrive yet this week and we'll be back to normal service level. There was a little money to buy medicines for Eloyda's clinic, too.

Water Tank Update
From: Sister Confianza   Date: February 16, 2011

Some of you have followed the stories and mishaps of our water tank, and pray that we are well-supplied. Thanks for your concern! Here's what happened in recent months:

You may remember that in April, the spigot broke off the tank. We used a plug fashioned from a stick of wood for seven months. Our hope was to be able to fix the spigot. We bought a little PVC connector piece that would work to re-attach it, but we wanted to wait to do the repair until we knew the rain would refill the tank. It didn't happen quickly; the real rainy season doesn't start till November.

Finally it seemed the time was right. We purchased some PVC glue, filed the connector piece to fit into the pipe in the tank, and one day at the end of November pulled the plug and drained the tank. I climbed inside it to do the yearly scrubbing of the walls and floor, and removed the wooden drain plug at the back. We glued the connector piece into the tank and the spigot into it, and let it set for

24 hours. Next we needed a new plug for the back drain. The trick is to get a piece of wood that's perfectly round to fit into the tube. What to do? There was a dead but still green *nance* tree nearby that might have a branch of the appropriate circumference, but it would be a big job to cut down the tree. Sister Alegría and I were at a loss.

As I was cooking, I saw among some scraps of firewood in the kitchen a straight stick of just the right diameter. Sure enough, it fit! We wrapped a plastic bag around it to plug any leaks around the edges and stuck it in. Then it rained. By mid-January, the tank was filled to overflowing. We've been using the water ever since, and hope for the usual mid-February storm to fill it up again before the dry season.

We think that in 2010 we actually went to the creek less often than in previous years—just two weeks in April and again in September. I don't think it's because we've had more rainwater at the house, but rather that we've learned to live with a little more faith that God will provide: We only went down when it truly seemed necessary. (Ironically, each time was when one of us was quite sick!) We understand now why poor people build their houses next to the stream, even though there is less breeze and more mosquitoes. Water is life. We had a rich person's perspective when we decided to build the rain-collection tank for water. It cost as much as the main house! Ah, well. Live and learn.

The Tiny Lizard Society
From Sister Alegría   Date: February, 23, 2011

Teresa of Avila is one of my mentors. She warns against spiritual leaders (guides, directors) who teach us to be toads or to catch tiny lizards (i.e., who do not encourage us to be all we can and should be)! We are not on earth nor are we invited into the Reign of God to be toads or to catch tiny lizards! We are to be slayers of dragons!

You, dear reader, live in a culture that is a Tiny Lizard Society! It would have you learn to catch tiny lizards. What's wrong with catching tiny lizards? Not much. What's good about catching tiny lizards? Not much. So don't endure teaching about how to catch tiny lizards—it distracts you from the Real Stuff.

The people who live in the US are the richest population in the world. It is ordinary to have, to use, to store (hoard) many times one's fair share of world resources as though there are not billions of hungry, thirsty, homeless and naked in the world.

John the Baptizer says, "The one who has two coats should give one coat to the person who has none." Straightforward—keep only your fair share. No lizards, large or small in this teaching—maybe a dragon to slay.

If one has six coats—oh, what to do? The Tiny Lizard Society would enter into debate about which ONE coat to give away, to whom to give it, and how to give it.

The Medium Lizard Society might debate whether or not the person with six coats ought not give three away. Half for you, half for others. Sounds rather reasonable. Oh, yes, very reasonable, generous even.

So let us return to the Tiny Lizard Society: The one with six coats should give one to someone with none. So far, so good.

The one with five coats should give one to someone who has none. (A little better)

The one with four coats should give one to someone who has none. Now we are up to the Medium Lizard Society, good progress.

The one with three coats should give one to someone who has none. (You can see where we're going.)

The one with two coats should give one to a person who has none, just like John the Baptizer said in the first place.

Skip Tiny Lizard Society. Skip Medium Lizard Society. Go for the Real Stuff. Dear reader, how many coats are in your closet?

One Way to Make a Living
From: Sister Alegría   Date: February 28, 2011

One day recently:

We're riding in the back of a pickup truck towards Bonito. The truck stops to pick up more hitchhikers—a man, a woman and a 10-12 year-old girl. They are standing at the side of the road, not especially close to any house or any woods. They have six large bundles of firewood. The pieces are each about three feet long and the bundles are almost 1.5 feet in diameter. It is wet since rain fell last night.

The firewood is heavy. The adults work together to put the first three bundles in the truck. Then the man carries the others on his shoulder and tips them onto the first three. It is obviously hard. All three scramble over the top and sit on the firewood and the truck moves on.

Me: "Do you sell firewood?"

Her: "No, we make tortillas." (Ah, the firewood is to cook the tortillas.)

Sister Confianza later learns that they do all of their traveling by hitchhiking. They wanted to go to Bonito yesterday, but no lift came along.

I am amazed. It is rare that we ride in a truck with as much empty space in the bed as on this day. It is hard to imagine hitchhiking with six large bundles of firewood.

We get to the center of town and the man quickly unloads all of the wood. Then we get out—it would have been very difficult to climb over it.

We thank and bless the driver and go our separate ways.

I think about them. What a way to earn a living!

Military/Medicines

From: Sister Alegría   Date: March 2, 2011

It is said that 70% of all paranoid people have someone out to get them. I'm feeling like I'm one of those. Actually, we who live in Honduras are in that 70%.

Let me share my upset with you and you can decide for yourself.

For several months the medicines provided to public health clinics have been sadly inadequate (more than usual). In the last four months, even the hospitals are dramatically short of medicines.

Dra. Karen talks about the country being very poor. A couple of years ago, I had said, rather flippantly, that the government was practically bankrupt. She smiled condescendingly and said that it was not.

Times have changed. The coup of 2009 and the US financial troubles have made the country even poorer than it was two years ago. Dra. Karen is not defending the financial status of the government any more.

Two weeks ago, we read in the papers that the government has prioritized health and education. For over a year, there are articles (usually on the front page) about the army being used to help decrease crime in the streets. This week's paper had more of that. You know the story: "See how much the army is helping to make you safe from the bad guys."

Yesterday, we talked to Eloyda at the El Pino clinic. She has little medicine. Some came as a donation from Gloria Borgman's medical mission team as they returned from the Mosquito Coast. The rest is a donation from the Air Force. The Air Force!!!

Well, the armed forces are going around donating medicines to the public health clinics and hospitals. (Some of the medicine

205

labels are in English.) The armed forces are doing medical mission trips to remote places.

This is the source of my paranoia. Money for health care is now funneled through the military. The health care system is to be grateful to the military and dependent upon the military. The citizens, too, of course.

This seems to be a strategy to militarize the country. It is not even subtle, but it can be very effective.

That is the way it seems to me today.

By the way, we were able to fund some medicines for Eloyda's clinic. The only liquid medicines were antibiotics—nothing else (and you know how I feel about our kids). AND there was no birth control. She'll be able to rectify that for at least a little while.

Eloyda with a freshly stocked pharmacy, 2016

Why do We Wear Habits?

From: Sister Confianza   Date: March 23, 2011

In recent months, we've been doing a flurry of sewing: making dresses from a new blue fabric that is more fade-resistant than the denim we were using, and making white blouses for me, now that I am a Professed Sister. We're so excited to finally be in uniform almost all the time!

You may wonder why this is important. The short answer is, "Because the world needs to see that there are nuns." A longer answer is below, which shows how habits fit the five traditional Quaker testimonies: Simplicity, Peace, Equality, Community and Integrity. The article first appeared in the March, 2011 newsletter of the Multnomah Monthly Meeting of Friends, with whom we spiritually share in a "Covenant of Caring."

Friendly Habits: The Quaker Testimonies of Amigas del Señor
From: The Sisters of Amigas del Señor   Date: March, 2011

Each person in the world lives her or his values. The lived values may not be the spoken values, but the life lived speaks the truth. Nuns, of course, are no different. Like yours, our physical habits represent our spiritual habits.

Habits of Simplicity
We wear uniforms, called habits, because we wear them habitually. We each have three jumper/dresses and four blouses. No energy is spent concerning fashion. No time is spent wondering what is appropriate to wear. No self-analysis is done about what we "feel like" wearing. We just get up in the morning and put on our clothes. We are always dressed for any occasion.

For wood cutting and garden work, we wear (with the same blouses) pants and rubber boots for protection. For everything else we wear habits and flip-flops.

We make our own clothing using a treadle sewing machine.

Habits of Peace
Material poverty is our Peace Testimony. Our physical habits reflect our spiritual habit of accepting, using, and keeping only our fair share of the world's material and energy resources, because social and economic justice are integral to peace.

Habits of Equality
At Amigas del Señor, we all wear the same clothing, the same colors, the same basic design. When seen from afar, we all look alike. We have no "stars," no prima donnas. We are all sisters, together.

Equality applies not just within the Monastery, but also in relationship to others. We do not dress up more to spend time with an "important" person, nor do we dress down to spend time with a "lesser" person. All are equal and all are treated, as well as we can, with love and respect.

Habits of Community

Our habits remind us visually every day that we are a community, that we are Sisters one to another. Each day as I put on my habit, I am choosing to be part of this monastic community today.

We also have our place in the neighborhood; our habits identify us as belonging with one another and to God. We are the local nuns; "*las hermanitas* (the little sisters)" we are called.

Habits of Integrity

Wearing a habit helps us to remember that we are each all of a piece, that our lives are integrated. Each part of my life fits into the whole. There is not a frivolous persona to be put aside for the sober persona. There is no intellectual persona to be put aside for the manual worker persona. There is no persona at all. I am just who I am at each moment of the day in whatever company with whatever activity. I am your sister. I am God's daughter.

The Challenges and Blessings of Poverty
From: Sister Confianza   Date: April 13, 2011

In January, Sister Alegría and I began digging *yuca* regularly again, after several months of not doing it. We had stopped at the end of August when the digging got too difficult and the tubers too small. The intervening months gave them time to fill out. Getting *yuca* twice a week cuts in half our purchase of grains. The price of beans skyrocketed during the winter from 18 Lempiras ($1) to 28 Lempiras ($1.50) per pound. We decided to try out buying chicken, eggs, and cheese for a complete protein to go with our *yuca* (which has none, unlike grains). Grocery costs stayed about the same during that time, but what a delicious diet we had! *Yuca* cooked in chicken broth is pretty wonderful! Now the price of beans has gone back down, so we're back to eating corn and beans. (We get some chicken each Monday in the lunch Sor Leonarda provides for us.)

In February, a new family moved to Elías' nearby property. The middle-aged couple (who have two teenage boys who work alongside their father) showed up at the Monastery one day seeking a medical consult for the wife, Santos Emérita. Sister Alegría diagnosed an infection, and we brought home medicine for her the next Monday. Emérita came over Tuesday morning and Sister Alegría administered the penicillin shot. (Sister Alegría tells me it's the most painful shot there is, but Emérita didn't even flinch!) The next day, Emérita brought us some fresh milk from the cows they were milking.

Since the family didn't have any *yuca* at Elías' place, we started taking them several pounds of *yuca* when we went to dig it. Most of the time they would give us a liter or two of milk and/or some *cuajada* (fresh cheese). What a windfall for our diet and for our budget! The milk products meant fewer beans, as well as nutritional and gastronomic variety: cups of warm milk, cream sauce over boiled *yuca, pinol*. Yum!

Though each household gained in food variety, it's not like we had a trade or bartering system going. Each time we took them *yuca*, it was a gift (we didn't tell them ahead that we'd bring it over) and each time they gave us something it was a gift freely given. (Once they apologized for only having milk to give us, nothing else, but we were always delighted.) This is how poor people get by: giving and receiving favors outside of the cash economy.

One Sunday toward the end of March, I bumped my left foot on the door jamb. It hurt a lot and left a scrape and a bruise. I continued normal activities that week: going to town on Monday and for *yuca* two other mornings. That Wednesday we went to Bonito. I wore two thin socks on my injured foot to protect it a bit, but by the end of the day it hurt a lot; I walked barefoot much of the way home to avoid the rubbing of my flip-flop on the wound.

Instead of getting better, my foot got worse. By Saturday, we could see that it was infected—the wound was now gaping, swollen, and red, and the skin around it felt warm. I spent Sunday with my aching foot elevated in the hammock, trying not to feel miserable. On Monday, we were due to go to Centro de Salud. We knew I couldn't walk the whole way, so we prayed for a ride and God provided.

It's handy having a doctor in the house, but even so we noticed what different decisions we make in our life here compared to what we might have done in the States. I really identified with our poor neighbors who often wait as long as possible before seeking medical care—you never know if the problem will resolve itself. In my more sedentary life in the US, my foot would likely never have gotten infected in the first place. Life is just plain dirtier here. I was walking around barefoot and digging *yuca* in socks and boots during that week; dirt got in the wound. I washed it every day, but we don't have any Band-Aid's. Then, we didn't go in to see a doctor as soon as we realized that it was infected. Centro de Salud is closed on the weekend, so if we had thought it necessary we would have had to go to Bonito for care. Instead, I began soaking it in hot water with antibacterial soap and putting on antibiotic ointment, which we happened to have left from a past medical case. On Monday morning, we saw that the swelling had actually gone down from the day before—my body was healing itself, which is not something Sister Alegría had seen much before in her medical practice! If we had not had the commitment to be at Centro de Salud anyway on Monday, we would have waited it out at home.

Sister Alegría prescribed erythromycin tablets for the infection and one of the nurses professionally cleaned and bandaged my wound. (I was grateful to be spared that painful penicillin shot, since the infection had actually improved some!) I still worked in the pharmacy that day, though without flipflops. We didn't go pick up mail since that would have added a mile of walking, but just got our groceries on the way out of town. Again, God provided a ride for us all the way home.

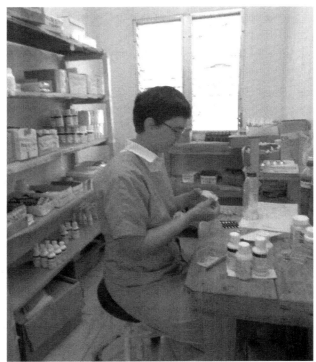

Sister Confianza in the pharmacy at Centro de Salud, 2014

The long day was hard on my foot (so much for the improvement we'd seen in the morning!). The rest of the week we treated it with care. We didn't go for *yuca* or do any other long walks. I continued to go barefoot around the house and yard (the soles of my feet really toughened up) and I put my foot up when I could. By the end of the week it was much improved—the swelling was down and the skin beginning to close in and heal.

Around here, standard medical advice for recuperation includes long periods of "total" rest—a different attitude than in the US where the goal is to keep doing one's regular activities as much as possible. We understand now that the life is so active, rest really is needed. A "quiet" day still involves work like hand washing clothes and cooking over the wood fire!

On Wednesday of the week of my recuperation, Emérita showed up with some milk and *cuajada* for us. When we hadn't brought them *yuca* on Tuesday, as had become our routine, she wondered what had happened. How thoughtful! We were glad to have a big sweet potato from our garden to give them. I truly felt like part of a larger community where neighbors care about and for each other.

The next week, we went for *yuca* on Wednesday (having let my foot recoup on Tuesday after another busy Monday with fewer rides) and took some to the neighbors. During our friendly conversation, Emérita informed us that they would be moving at the end of the week! This was the last time we'd be getting milk from them. What a disappointment! Not so much about the milk (our physical work would actually be less by not digging so much *yuca* and trekking to the neighbors), but to be losing new friends. The owner Elías doesn't pay as much as the caretakers think is fair for their work. It's the same problem we've seen over several years that has kept folks from staying long at that place. (Since Berta's family, who were there ten months, some four or five families and individuals have been through there in the last year.) We consider Elías our neighbor, too, though he lives in Limón. We have heard some of his life stories—both good and bad experiences. We mourn the difficulties he and his workers have had. Please say a prayer for him today, and for all the poor folks who don't earn enough to live on and don't have access to medical care.

Physical and Spiritual Injury
From: Sister Confianza

My foot injury occurred during a worship service gone sour. Like most Sundays, I had planned the program to include four scriptures: a Psalm, an Old Testament passage, a selection from an Epistle, and a Gospel reading. We were going through the Gospel According to Matthew, and this week's portion was from the Sermon on the Mount: "You have heard it said, 'Do not murder,' but I tell you, do not even get angry."

I announced the theme at the opening of the service, held in the porch as usual. As we read together Psalm 133, "How good it is for kindred to live in harmony," Sister Alegría began to tear up. I thought she was moved by the sentiment, but as the program progressed, she revealed that she was offended by the theme. It seemed to her that I had chosen the topic as a commentary on her anger related to the state of the Monastery's instrumental music program and the pain I'd inflicted on her.

She gave me the choice to continue the service or just stop right then. I chose to continue, going inside to get something (perhaps a hanky for her) and stubbing my foot as I came back out. Sister Alegría stayed through the program, but the next day on our walk to Limón she told me she wished that she hadn't.

I felt terrible. I'd had no intention to hurt her, but my insensitivity struck again. In not considering how the theme spoke to her reality, I thoughtlessly chose the scriptures and went on with the service, even though she was in pain.

It seemed to me that my foot injury was an outward manifestation of the interior trauma we were experiencing, and we both had hoped that my physical recovery paralleled inner healing as well. Unfortunately, the process of unlearning and relearning is often slow. Our wariness and discomfort in playing recorders together persisted. Though I felt I was making progress in letting go of past prejudice and judgment, and growing in compassion, sensitivity, and openness, the change was slower than we both hoped.

Holy Week
From: Sister Confianza

In 2011, Sister Alegría and I had a particularly lovely Holy Week. We celebrate Jesus' triumphal entry into Jerusalem on Palm Sunday. This year, Sister Alegría cuts an armful of greens from the giant grasses that grow on the hillside. We spread the three-foot long, three-inch wide leaves on the porch, just as Jesus' disciples had laid branches and coats on the road where he passed that day. I use the machete to lop off a couple of leafy branches from a wild tree near the house; our young coconut palms do not have any suitable branches. We have a festive procession singing *"El Rey de gloria viene"* ("The King of Glory Comes") as we wave the branches and march around the yard before settling in the porch for the mid-morning worship service.

When I was choosing scriptures for the program, I discovered that Jesus' famous ride on a donkey—such a lowly steed for someone acclaimed king—was not a brand-new idea. Just as many of his teachings can be found in the Hebrew Scriptures, so this act: The great King David had his son Solomon ride on David's mule to be anointed his successor (I Kings 1:32-35). Our Palm Sunday worship on April 17 focuses on this and other Bible stories about donkeys.

Instead of a sermon, most Sundays we share reflections on the day's Bible passages and today is no different. We have a most interesting discussion about Balaam's ass, who spoke to the disobedient prophet after being impeded by an angel that Balaam didn't—or wouldn't—see (Numbers 22: 21-35). We close by singing our upbeat song *"Dios usó un burro"* ("God Used a Donkey"), asking God to help us be as ready to serve him as were those humble beasts.

Sister Alegría and I spent the rest of Holy Week a little differently than sometimes, focusing on resurrection and being prepared to receive new life. With the hot weather—*Semana Santa* is officially *verano* (summer) here—we went down to the creek several days to bathe and wash laundry. Besides saving water, it was our nod to the regional custom of going to the beach or river to swim/bathe during Holy Week.

Every day, we read from Hannah Hurnard's <u>Hinds' Feet On High Places</u> (*Pies de ciervas en los lugares altos*) in Spanish, sitting on rocks with our feet in the refreshing waters of the stream. The book is an allegory of the spiritual life. It tells the story of *Miedosa* (Much-Afraid), a young woman who learns to trust in God as she serves the Shepherd King. She journeys through strange lands in order to reach the Kingdom of Love. Since that first reading, <u>Hinds' Feet</u> has become a perennial favorite for Sister Alegría and me. We read it together almost every year, and particularly appreciate the author's presentation—explicit in her introduction—of the celibate life as a valid choice for Christians.

On Wednesday, we went to Limoncito to visit friends. We took the shortcut from above the county dump that follows a path through several properties right down to the Limoncito River bridge. The first house we pass is where Xiomara lives, a woman we'd recently met at Centro de Salud. Her oldest daughter just graduated from sixth grade and they had asked if we had any resources for a scholarship for her to attend junior high. Today, she shows us her diploma, which hangs on the wall of their two-room house, which is smaller than ours for a family of six.

Sister Alegría reads from *Pies de ciervas* in the stream, 2016

Sister Alegría and I go on our way and at the bridge come across a big truck selling fruits and vegetables. We buy some, including a beautiful cantaloupe that looks like it should be ripe on Easter Sunday. We have a nice visit with Margarita and family. They, and some other friends, give us more goodies: *sapote* fruit, plantains, *rosquillas* (crunchy rings of baked ground corn and cheese), and even some frozen chicken. It was a bit overwhelming! Mateo kindly offered to drive us home in the afternoon, which was a great gift since Sister Alegría was suffering a bit from asthma and we were both tired from the physical work of the previous couple of days.

This year's three-day Holy Week Retreat began with a Love Feast on Thursday morning. Sister Alegría and I had imagined a nice simple meal. Well, with all the gifts of special and perishable foods, the menu changed. We ate a delicious chicken soup with flour tortillas and *sapote*.

Friday we fasted as we commemorated Jesus' crucifixion—a reminder that we must die to self before being resurrected.

We were pleased that some of the vegetables and fruits saved well enough to eat on Easter Sunday. We found ourselves wondering if it was really appropriate to have so many special foods that week. After all, they are expensive, and we try to live poor. We realized, however, that High Holy Days are called "Feast Days" for a reason: they give balance to our life with its weekly fast days and everyday simple fare. At the Monastery, we continue to serve special foods on special occasions.

Immunization Campaign
From: Sister Alegría   Date: May 11, 2011

We are a contemplative monastery, but during the annual immunization campaign, we live the life of "active" sisters.

On the first day, Monday, April 25, the auxiliary nurses went out on foot immunizing in neighborhoods in Limón, while Juana Nidia, Sister Confianza and I staffed the clinic. We served about 40 patients (plus immunizations).

I had made a list of medicines and quantities for our traveling pharmacy. Hermana Confianza began packing it. I have never been satisfied with the nurses packing the mobile pharmacy. Whole classes of medicines get left out. Hermana Confianza has a gift for packing and she is the acting pharmacist, so she would know where to find everything.

About 1 pm, when we had seen all of the patients, we went to Sor's for lunch, then returned to get really serious about the packing.

It was a long day, but not stressful. We got home well after dark. For the first time ever we went to bed without dinner because we were so tired and it was so late. We ate a lot on Tuesday.

Friday, April 29, we went to Villa Nueva (New Town), far east of us, a neighborhood that in the past did not have a road, only a trail; the nurses had gone on horseback south from Plan de Flores. The Monastery used donation money to pay for Chito to take the team. $69. It goes up every year. Gas now costs $5.03 a gallon. The

$69 paid for gas, Chito, his two young helpers and the rattletrap truck for the day.

Chito in his pickup truck outside Centro de Salud, 2016

The helpers opened and closed cattle gates, chased cattle out of the way, jacked up the car when it got hung up on a rock, changed a tire, and every 10-15 minutes added water to the radiator that leaks.

It was quite the road—rough one lane with blind hairpin curves. At every blind curve there was a precipice on one side and a shear wall on the other. It was a new road to Chito, too. It was less impressive on the way home.

We used the one-room school with the approval of the young teacher (Margarita and Mateo's son). The nurses immunized all 11 kids on the list. Cooper gave rabies shots to all 20 dogs. I gave 34 consults.

Of the 34 consults, 12 people were anemic as I judged by paleness of conjunctiva and mucosa in the mouth and diet history. Only one had been noticed by mother to be pale. (2016 note: This knowledge still haunts me.)

We finished serving patients about 1 pm and received a nice lunch, including all of the tortillas that we could eat (not usual in free lunches). Home before dark, not very tired at all.

216

Week Two
Monday, May 2, we worked at Centro de Salud doing the usual work. We took time to reinforce the traveling pharmacy a little.

Wednesday, May 4, we waited at the end of our path for the truck to go to La Fortuna. I had forgotten how bad the road is up closer to the village (see the above description of the road to Villa Nueva).

There are always a lot of patients in La Fortuna, so I started immediately to give consults. I gave 60. They cleaned up the kindergarten building for us to use. Apparently, there are no kindergarten classes this year. We were grateful for the roof as it rained once in a while.

When all of the dog immunizations were done (by Wornita), checking for malaria (done by Eliza), and immunizations (done by Litza and Carolyn), I still had 35 patients waiting. Litza gave 18 consults. 2 pm. A quick lunch (free again, not all-you-can-eat), and we were off. Big black clouds—not good for the road, so we rushed.

Stayed at Margarita and Mateo's house in Limoncito. Delmys, their 27-year-old daughter, made us welcome. We got to attend church with them that night.

Thursday, May 5
The house is right on the highway; we didn't have to walk. Chito pulled in and off we went. The traveling pharmacy was obviously more compact. I said to Hermana Confianza (somewhat mournfully), "They'll never let us pack the pharmacy again." (Too many medicines to cart around.) Later I learned that some boxes had gotten wet, so they dumped the contents of those boxes into the others. So much for the well-organized pharmacy.

West to Francia to pick up Victoria, the nurse for Francia. Then on to Brisas de Miramar (Seaview Breezes), the far west, southwest part of the county. Chito charged $79 for this trip because it was so much further.

We set up shop on the front porch of a private home. Cooper immunized dogs; Victoria immunized children. I gave 50 consults. Our goal, unknown to me, was 50. We were expected to produce 500 Lempiras (10 per patient) to help pay the transportation. But for a few consults Hermana Confianza forgave the fee, so we only produced 470 lempiras.

Another nice homemade all-you-can-eat lunch. Even a lunch break; I didn't have to wait until I finished all my work. I was very grateful. Hermana Confianza's work went with mine.

217

For all of these outreach clinics, I had all the equipment I wanted: stethoscopes for adults and kids, otoscope (ears), ophthalmoscope (eyes), watch for counting respirations and pulse, even a blood pressure cuff. It will probably never happen again! It was pretty nice to have it all because there were quite a few adults with high blood pressure.

We overloaded the truck a lot to give half a dozen folks a lift partway home—a few rugged miles (carrying babies). When they got off, Chito could return to a normal speed (10 mph.)

At Francia, we unloaded all of the medicines! What was that about? The clinic pharmacy there was pretty much depleted; the left-overs were actually planned-overs. I was so impressed with the cleverness and planning ahead to use this rare transportation opportunity.

After sharing Vespers with Victoria and Cooper, we all had time for a nice chat because another tire had gone bad. Chito finally borrowed a tire to get home. He stopped to drop off two tires at Omar's shop in Limoncito to be repaired. All of the tires looked beyond repair to me, but I'm not in charge of the car.

He dropped us at our road. We walked a mile, then got a lift for that last big, steep hill, arriving in the dark.

Scrubbing clothes using a tub and washboard, 2012

Friday, May 7
For the nuns, the immunization campaign is over. We return to our contemplative lifestyle. This day, washing laundry and cutting firewood are the physical tasks. Some rain arrived on Wednesday and Thursday so laundry washing at the house, not at the stream. We are grateful.

Vespers – *Vísperas*
From: Sister Confianza

We have our afternoon prayers at about 2:30 pm, when the shadow from the house reaches the stump fifteen feet to the east and there is a nice shady chapel space for worship. We were hesitant to call this prayer time Vespers (*Vísperas* in Spanish), since that term usually designates an evening hour, until Sister Alegría ran across Teresa of Avila's Constitutions, which have them at 2 pm.

The timing works well for us. By mid-afternoon we have finished any major physical work of the day and had our daily baths. After the fifteen-minute program, there is time for music—singing and/or playing *flautas* (recorders) together, and perhaps a rest or quiet task before making dinner. A typical 5 pm Vespers wouldn't work in a small monastery where the same Sisters who pray also must cook!

Vespers, like our other prayer times, has a fixed opening song. Besides the two readings from the Psalms cycle, we read a selection from the New Testament. We practice *lectio continuo* (a term I learned from Kathleen Norris in The Cloister Walk), which means we take one book and go through it passage by passage each day until it is finished. The Gospels—the life and teachings of Jesus—are our main sustenance, though in between we read the letters and other books of the New Testament. Often we will include something "extra," be it a third song (often pertinent to the season) or a brief reading or saying from another spiritual teacher.

Vespers is our most flexible prayer time. It's true that when we travel overnight, Compline may be replaced by a church program, but Vespers can vary in time, location, and content. On one-day trips, whether to Limón, Bonito, or elsewhere, we carry a small New Testament with Psalms. On those days we've been known to have prayers on a park bench or in the bus, but more often we do Vespers along the *desvío*, stopping in a spot of shade on the walk home, usually much later than its standard time.

Vespers is also the service most likely to include guests, as afternoon is a good time for visiting. Whether we go to a neighbor's house or they come to the Monastery, we try to accommodate by making sure the scripture is a coherent selection, singing songs that are simple or well known, and closing with an extemporaneous spoken prayer. Monastic life is known for its rigidity, but Sister Alegría and I have found that flexibility is one of the most important traits to cultivate.

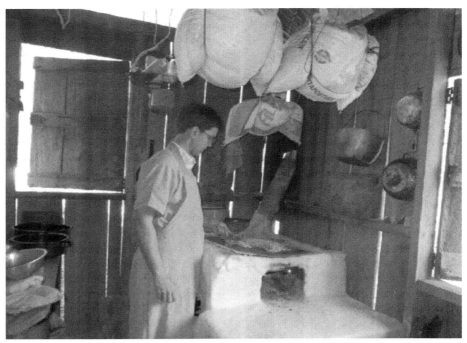

Sister Confianza toasts corn on the *comal* for *pinol*, 2016

9
A Part of the Larger Community

"*La vida es complicada.* Life is complicated."—Xiomara of Limoncito

An Interesting Visitor
From: Sisters Alegría and Confianza   Date: June 15, 2011

<u>Appetizer by Sister Confianza:</u>
Last week, following the suggestion of Sister Alegría, I started a new journaling practice. My habit had been to write about what happened during the day and do a personal *examen*, to see where God was present in my day, give thanks, and ask forgiveness for words and actions that I wasn't proud of. I noticed how self-absorbed my writing was. I have been taught that one should only speak about oneself and not try to tell others' truths, and I have tried to live that out. Unfortunately, I think it backfired. I found that my whole way of living was self-centered: I only thought about myself, how things affect me, and how to get my own way. My new practice is to notice and write about other people.

Most of the time it's just Sister Alegría and me at the Monastery, quietly doing our stuff. She's the main "other person" in my life; it is rare to have more than one visitor in a week. However, we currently have two sets of neighbors who have been coming over regularly. The young folks from Lauda have brought us milk a few times and sought medical consults for their toddlers. Now a big blended family is caring for Elías' place and they like to come over to join us in worship.

I guess that God is supporting this other-centered plan by sending people to the Monastery almost every day in the last week. Unfortunately, some of the visits have involved extra walks up from the creek, aggravating Sister Alegría's asthma. We thought you might find interesting the visitor who came by Tuesday.

Main Course by Sister Alegría:

A very upset young man gestures frantically for help, looking in through a window. The first gesture indicates a request for food. I come out right away and serve food (cold beans and toasted tortillas— poor fare, but that's what there is). He sits with his head in his hands, gathering his forces or praying.

He ignores the food and gestures more. A murder. I'm rattled enough that I speak in English as I'm trying to put words to his message. But I hear that it is English and revert to Spanish. When I reflect back to him that he had told me he had killed someone, he shakes his head and tries again. He had seen a murder. And as a witness, his life is in danger.

Suddenly he leaps up and runs off. Our friend, Don Rafa, had come up the path. Don Rafa had been working near here and the boy passed by without greeting him. Don Rafa "thought that was strange" so he came over. He recognized him; he is a good boy. When I ask directly, he says that he is also of sound mind. Off he goes to call the boy's brother. "Maybe we'll see each other a little later."

We walk around to the back of the house. No sign of the boy. I announce in a loud voice that the visitor had been Don Rafa, our friend, and someone who can be trusted.

Then he shows up again in the porch. More signs, but there is soon speaking. I notice that he is a strikingly handsome guy. A light whiff of alcohol, but not enough to explain anything. Tears flow. The murder was of his brother, 25 years old, César, by four armed men, near here on the road. There are hints that there is a family feud.

My questions combine my two principle concerns. First, a good treatment for emotional trauma is to talk about it. You know, vomit out the poison before it can do its maximum damage. Second, are there armed murderers combing the area for this kid? Should we contact the police?

I give him water; he drinks only a little (not consistent with the amount of running he supposedly has done). As he gets more nearly normal, contradictions enter the story and there is greater resistance to my questions. He still doesn't know what to do, where to go. I encourage him to stay until he can put together a plan.

Our friend, Omar, comes up the path. He calls out, "I'm Omar," not his usual greeting. The boy runs behind the house again. We talk briefly. Omar takes Rudy, his brother, home. First though, he confirms that their brother, César, is alive and well, living in Copán. Rudy uses drugs. Omar has spent all day searching for him.

The next morning Omar stopped by to give us three quarts of milk, an accent to the profuse thanks he had given us the day before.

<u>Dessert Course</u>
From: Sister Alegría

We met César in December, 2015. He looks just like Rudy except a little heavier and with striking blue eyes. In fact, at first I thought that he was Rudy—until I saw his eyes.

Omar tells us Rudy is "*completamente transformado*;" he has changed completely. No more drugs. Thanks be to God.

A New Cat
From: Sister Confianza   Date: June 15, 2011

Last month when we came to Bonito, we visited Juan Donald and Gus, the Jesuit parish priests who have become good friends. It is always so nice to spend time with these two kind men. Their presence and their hospitality are a great support to us. Like us, they have dedicated themselves to a celibate life, serving God in a foreign country. Both Juan Donald and Gus are from the south-western US and have lived in Latin America some forty years.

Juan Donald and Gus at the parish house in Bonito, 2012

When we had visited two months earlier, their cook and housekeeper, Doña María Julia, had offered us a kitten; their cat had two. We were interested but unable to decide on the spot. In May, to our delight, they still had the kittens, and again offered us one. This time we said, "Yes," without hesitation. But which one? Both were said to be good mousers. We wanted a male, but both kittens were female, so we picked according to looks—the one with white on its face and belly and splotches of grey stripes.

Gus found an apple box and we put the kitten in it and tied it with rope to carry home. We visited a few friends on the way and asked about their experience with cats. Sister Alegría had heard that female cats "go crazy" when they're in heat.

"Yes, but it doesn't last long," said one friend, "only a couple of weeks." What!? Yet cats are valued here; we would have no problem giving away kittens.

We were concerned that the kitty might run away in the first few days. We'd heard of keeping it in the house for the first week or two for it to get accommodated, but this cat is not to be an indoor cat—Sister Alegría is allergic! Our friends suggested locking it in the kitchen at night or while we're gone, and I imagined keeping it tied up at least for a while during the day.

We began to think of names. Maybe something Biblical... I once knew of a cat named Jezabel. How about *Profetisa* (Prophetess)? *Tigre* also has a nice ring to it... Well, when we got to the Monastery that evening and I took the cat out of the box, we discovered it's actually a male! That took a little readjustment—and back to the drawing board with names.

As advised, we kept it locked in the kitchen that night and also the next day when we went to the stream to wash clothes. Upon our return, Sister Alegría opened the kitchen door and the cat spooked. It jumped up on the stove and hid in the firebox. When he peeked out, he was covered in ashes. Then we knew his name: *Ceniza* (Ash). It matches his natural coloring, too.

We began to let him explore the yard and for a day or two he picked his way through the brush mewing. I imagined he was calling for his mama or his sister playmate. We were also concerned about his adjustment to our diet. Ceniza had been raised on scraps as well as dog food and rice with powdered milk. His first night he didn't eat the cheese and tortilla I left for him. Then on his third evening at the Monastery we watched him catch and eat a mouse. Perfect! This was exactly what we had hoped for. He would have a fine diet with the prey he catches and the bits of tortilla and *yuca* that we give him plus

224

the occasional milk when our neighbors give us some. And our kitchen will be clear of mice!

That night we left him loose, and he was still around in the morning. The next Monday, he was free when we went to Limón. Upon our return in the late afternoon, Ceniza greeted us with a meow. I am so impressed by how quickly he adjusted to his new home. Yes, he is now the Monastery cat.

This week, we brought home his rabies immunization from Centro de Salud and injected him. He didn't like it much, but now we're up-to-date.

Go, Ceniza, go! Catch that mouse!

A Fallen Neighbor
From: Sister Alegría   Date: June 30, 2011

On Monday, June 20, 2011, we get up and out nice and early, and walk half way to the highway when José Wilmer picks us up. He isn't headed to Limón, so he drops us off at the highway. When I go to the window of the cab to thank him for the ride, he indicates toward the west. "There's a dead body over there."

Sure enough, there is a human body lying on the side of the road. Dead or alive? That is not so obvious. I go to investigate; José Wilmer takes off to do his errands.

He is on a slight downslope. We first see his feet—bloody (various ages of blood, but no longer actively bleeding), grotesquely swollen and deformed. A few large round holes. Strong smell of blood.

The rest of his filthy body looks pretty good—a bad scrape at his left temple. But his body posture says, "I'm alive, at least so far." I feel his jugular pulse and watch his shallow breathing. He opens his eyes part way.

We begin to talk. Yes, he is thirsty and, yes, his neck works ok. I support his head and give him water from one of our bottles. He accepts it eagerly. I don't offer him food; I expect him to be in surgery this morning.

Nato (NAH-toe) is his name. He seems about 25. He had done an errand in Hicoteas yesterday and was returning. He flagged down a car for a lift. The guys in the car assaulted him and robbed him. They shot him in the feet. They took him off the highway on the La Fortuna road at least 1/8 mile and dumped him there. That was about 3 pm yesterday afternoon.

He crawled from there to the highway. A neighbor (1/4 mile from the La Fortuna road) says that he heard a scream (or shout, it's

225

the same word in Spanish) in the middle of the night. I figure that's when Nato got to the highway and hoped for and called for help.

He asks us where we live. I tell him that we are Protestant nuns and live in the Monastery on the La Fortuna road. He volunteers that he has been influenced by Mormon missionaries. I affirm that it is the same God and ask permission to pray. Sister Confianza and I put our hands on his body and I pray aloud.

It was about 6-6:30am when we got there. Soon Rambo shows up with a car full of workers. He would call for another car to take Nato to the hospital in Tocoa. No car comes.

Nato starts to shiver. The sun has not yet crested the hill. We have a small sack, which we put around his chest. None of the earlier folks who stop have a cloth, a rag or an extra shirt. The sun goes higher and warms our fallen neighbor. Yet higher and we are all toasting. Sister Confianza opens an umbrella and positions herself to shade him.

We each take a small walk up the La Fortuna road where we can have a little visual privacy. We take all of the cash out of our money belts. $37—not enough to hire a car to Tocoa, but enough to show good faith and pay for most of the gas.

Many vehicles pass by: big palm oil trucks, regular pick-ups, buses, motorcycles. Several pass by on the other side of the road, even when one of us stands in the center of the road gesturing for it to stop. Some slow down to have a good look. Some ask curious questions, the most common one being, "Is he dead?" Some say that they will call the police.

No one who stops and is going in the right direction has space. A few pass, then come back trying to help. A few trucks, loaded to the hilt, pass. We don't try to flag them down. A few elegant trucks with empty beds and dark tinted windows pass without acknowledging our presence. One of the buses going in that direction stops and the driver seriously considers. His bus is full and the wounded man would have to lie in the aisle. He decides he needs to go on.

A loaded truck breaks down "coincidentally" at this spot. Trouble with the battery. A second loaded car stops to help the first. All of the folks come over to the spectacle. Some recognize him and confirm that he was seen in Hicoteas at 2 pm yesterday. One has a cell phone and is willing to give cell phone time. Nato gives him his mother's telephone number. Her phone is turned off. Next his brother's. His phone is turned off, too. Next the local police—they don't answer. But someone does manage to call a relative of his. We call Juana Nidia to say that we think we'll have to go to Tocoa with the patient and won't be at work.

The mayor's driver, Luís, comes along. He is reluctant to lower his window. Yes, this is the same Luís who drove the ambulance in 2007 when we took the old guy with the scalping injury to Tocoa. (By the way, that man is alive and doing well. He has to use braces to walk, though.) Luís is only going to Bonito and refuses to call the mayor for permission to go to Tocoa. The government has its rules. And on he goes.

We've now been here about an hour.

The broken-down truck and the helper truck move on. They have helped a lot.

Then a troop transport truck arrives. The soldiers take charge of our patient. Some even know how to carry an injured person. Off they go. In all of this time, no one except the Sisters and the soldiers have touched Nato. Fear.

We begin walking toward Limón. Half a mile later, we are at Rosa's. They have heard about it. We sit in the shade and I drink a pint of water and start eating one of our big flour tortillas. Rosa brings us a plate of food: fresh soft cheese and fried almost-ripe *plátanos*. Sister Confianza just accepts a cup of coffee. I gratefully clean the plate.

David, our friend the taxi driver, is eager to tell us his experience. He had seen Nato on the road on his way to work. Because there was another person there as a witness he dared to approach the injured man. He was lying face down in the dirt and seemed to be suffocating. David turned him over, so that he could breathe freely; that is what he dared do.

Then a lift to town and a half mile walk to Centro de Salud. We are only half an hour late and re-enter our regular Monday schedule.

More on Nato
From: Sister Alegría

In July, 2016, we got a lift with a man who had been Nato's employer before the above incident. Nato had robbed from him, then from the next employer he had. Gossip says drugs were important in his life. He now lives an upright life. His feet and legs have recovered, and he works for the palm company.

Crime Wave

From: Sister Confianza   Date: July 20, 2011

Finding Nato, the injured man on the road, was just the beginning of a small wave of crime and other unfortunate events that have touched our lives recently.

Robbery

On Sunday afternoon, June 26, 2011, I was resting in the hammock with the cat on my lap. All of a sudden, Ceniza sat up alert. I looked up and saw two men walking quickly down the west hillside toward the Monastery. One had a rifle and I wondered if they were hunting; it's not rare for guys to go out *monteando* in the area. The cat hopped down and ran off to hide. I noticed that the young men had dark ski masks on and called Sister Alegría. When she stepped out of the house and saw the guys, just twenty yards away, she said, "Get inside!" I obeyed.

We latched the front door and began to close the shutters. As I closed the last one on the southeast I found myself face-to-face with the two men—probably teenagers, not taller than me. One in a blue mask carried a pistol and the other in a black mask carried a rifle. *"Buenas tardes,"* I said as I shut the pine-board shutter in their faces.

"Buenas," they responded automatically.

Sister Alegría and I decided to "lay low," literally, and we sat down on the floor to be out of bullet range, reciting the Lord's Prayer in Spanish together.

There is a pounding at the front door. "Give us your money." We look at each other.

"No," we respond.

Sister Alegría says, "We're poor. People who know us know that. Look in the kitchen, what do you see? Beans, corn, salt. Nothing fancy. Rich people have fancy stuff. Think about it."

I hear one of them say, "I just think about my mother." He is hoping that by robbing, he will have something to take home to his mom!

They start rattling the wooden door and I remember how previous robbers broke the latch. "We're not here to rape or kill. We just want money."

We find our money belts, hidden at the bottom of the cardboard boxes in which we store our clothes under our beds. There is 500 lempiras ($25, three or four days wages) in 100-lempira bills, just enough for us to make our planned trip to La Ceiba the next day. Sister Alegría explains in Spanish what we are doing, "I'm getting the money. We have 500 lempiras." She counts them aloud. "I will pass it under the front door to you," and she slips the five golden bills through the crack.

"Give us more," one voice says.

"We don't have any more," Sister Alegría replies.

"We want dollars," he insists.

Incredulous, Sister Alegría responds, "We don't have any dollars!"

"They told us you had dollars."

I wondered who had told them such a thing. Why would we keep dollars in the house, when they can't be used as currency? People have the most interesting ideas about how we live.

Then I remember that we have a coin purse with small bills in it. I get it out: 26 lempiras ($1.30). Sister Alegría says, "We found more: ten, fifteen, twenty, twenty-two, twenty-three, twenty-four, twenty-five, twenty-six."

"Dollars?"

"No, lempiras. I'll pass it under the door." And they take it.

"We want more. Let us in to go through the house."

"No," says Sister Alegría.

They start pushing more strongly on the door to open it. I whisper to Sister Alegría in English, "Maybe we should let them in." I'm afraid of violence.

Sister Alegría says to them, "We don't allow weapons in the house. If you want to come in, you must set your guns aside. Put them on the stump away from the door."

Two minutes later, they pound again. "Let us in."

"Where are your guns?"

"In our hands."

"Then you can't come in."

Suddenly, I remember that we have yet a few more lempiras: a stack of one-lempira bills that our friend Jyl sent us. After a trip to Honduras with Sister Alegría some years ago, she had taken them back to the US as souvenirs and recently mailed them to us to use. I tell Sister Alegría. She replies, "They'll never believe that we have no more money if we keep coming up with more to give them!"

"This is it, really!"

I get them out and Sister Alegría counts them aloud, "... fifteen, sixteen, seventeen."

"Dollars?"

"No! Lempiras." Sister Alegría slides them under the door.

"We have no more than this," she says.

We wait. Finally, the guys say, "We're leaving now. Be sure you don't call the police."

"Don't worry about that," I say. We have no phone.

As we hear their footsteps recede, Sister Alegría says, "Tell all your friends that we don't have dollars." Then she adds, "Go with God. And give thanks to God for your lives."

The whole interaction probably lasted 15 minutes. We stay sitting on the floor to recover for another fifteen to thirty minutes, going over the whole experience, what each of us said and heard and saw (not all the same things). Soon, we were laughing about the young men's insistence on dollars. We were giving God thanks for our own lives.

Gifts and Lamentations

Our plan for the week was to go to La Ceiba to visit Larry and Allison, our missionary friends. On Monday, we worked at Centro de Salud in Limón. It happened that the police had a roadblock set up at Chito's place, so we told the sergeant about the robbery. He was sympathetic. Since we had no cash (and had forgotten to borrow any from friends in Limón), he got us a free ride to Bonito—on the bus.

"Dios le pagará. God will repay you," Sister Alegría said as we got off, using a phrase we have heard sometimes when we've given a needed gift.

"Amen," replied the bus driver.

In Bonito, we got money from the bank.

We stayed at the parish house overnight, but didn't get to see the priests. María Julia told us that Juan Donald had been in a motorcycle accident a month earlier. Today, in spite of broken ribs, he was flying back to the US for his annual vacation; Gus had taken him to the airport in San Pedro Sula.

As we walked from the bus on our way back from Ceiba on Saturday, we met a young man on his way to Limón, who signaled for us to come look at something along the side of the road. "A dead man," he said. Sure enough, there was a bloated, smelly body among the brush. He had apparently been killed and dumped there two or three days earlier. The young man said he would notify the police.

We later learned that the dead man was named Nando and had been a friend of our neighbor Javier. He had worked on Dimas' land to the south of the Monastery. Some forty cattle had been stolen from that property in a big operation earlier in the month.

On top of all that, we arrived home to discover that several unripe pineapples had been broken off their stems and later in the week someone stole a ripe one—and had the audacity to plant its top in the garden!

What was this wave of violence in our neighborhood? Are more crimes happening or did we just happen to be more closely involved in these recent ones so that they affected us more? That Sunday, July 3, we had a time of lament—crying aloud to the Lord, wailing the injustices and asking, "WHY?"

Fire

On Friday, July 8, a fire started in the neighbor's field to the south (the property of Jonathan, a local man who is working in the US). As is our precautionary custom, we kept our eye on it to make sure it wasn't threatening the Monastery property. In the afternoon, Sister Alegría was on the porch and heard a crackling sound. She looked out and saw that the flames had crossed the fence line onto our land, so we started to clear a firebreak, hoping to prevent it from reaching the house.

Soon, a young couple showed up to help. Nino, the current caretaker of that property, confessed that the fire had probably started from a tree trunk that was still smoldering from a controlled burn he and Javier did a couple of weeks earlier. He got right to work cutting a three-foot wide swath with his machete around the perimeter of our yard. Sister Alegría, Nino's partner Yadira, and I followed with the rake and hoe to clear the ground of potential fuel. Their three-year-old daughter Danixa watched from the safety of the porch. We all worked hard and fast as the flames moved in from the south, then encircled the entire Monastery. Praise God, the firebreak held.

Nino, Yadira, and their children, 2016

As we could see the danger had passed, I started a cook-fire in the stove and made a meal which we all ate hungrily, somehow tolerating the smoke-filled air. Danixa whined a bit to her parents to go home, but calmed down after eating. Sister Alegría was impressed that she didn't ask for food, the way kids in the US might have. Children here are raised to be relatively passive.

After our profuse thanks, Nino and family made their way home. Sister Alegría and I are aware that it was through human strength and effort that this fire didn't burn down the Monastery—a contrast from, say, in 2008, when we just left the premises with a fire closing in, and it was purely God's Grace that kept the buildings safe. Sometimes we have to remind ourselves that we have a part to play in God's care for us.

An interesting side note: My wrists, perpetually achy from the tendonitis, had less pain for several days after that hard hoeing. It felt like a miracle healing through reverse physiology.

Trusting in God

I'm not a big believer in Satan, but I began to wonder whether these unfortunate events are the Devil's tricks to try to scare us away. Teresa of Avila framed the challenges she faced in founding monasteries as the Devil trying to stop God's plans. Well, it won't work. I feel only deepened in my trust in God. We were ready to hand over all our money to the robbers and leave the monastery buildings to the fire if necessary. Just a reminder that material possessions aren't what's really important and fear, of course, is pointless. Our protection and security come from God.

This last Thursday, July 14, we had a retreat using parts of Ruth Ward Heflin's book, GLORY. She reminded us of the power in praise and prayer. If we focus on our part—praising and praying to God—God will do the rest. May our hearts be open to God's direction, and may we have the guts to follow it.

Medical Equipment Follow-up
From: Sister Alegría   Date: August 10, 2011

Last year in July, I told you about my 15-minute sit-down strike at Centro de Salud. This is what happened next.

A certain nurse was transferred to another clinic and none of my equipment disappeared again. Everyone knows in which drawers I keep them and they are always there for me (my old faithful Eli Lily pediatric stethoscope and adult stethoscope). I also use a very nice otoscope (ears) and ophthalmoscope (eyes) donated by an international aid organization—yes, the same one that gave us bargain basement BP (blood pressure) cuffs.

One sister (in the States) sent us a high quality versatile (pediatric or adult) stethoscope with replacement parts. I checked it out and decided that for this old dog, better to stay with my old tricks. We presented the stethoscope to Juana Nidia, the R. N. The auxiliary nurses use stethoscopes only to do blood pressures, not to auscultate (listen in a diagnostic way) chests. Juana Nida can auscultate. We keep the spare parts at the Monastery; they would get lost fast at Centro de Salud.

Another sister shipped us excellent stethoscopes, but we were unable to get them. International shipping is just not straight forward. Import laws—it was all very complicated and disappointing. The stethoscopes will be sold at cut rates to other health care providers. They will not be wasted. But we are now all set with stethoscopes.

A big donation to buy BP cuffs (sphygmomanometers). Excitement. How to get them? We asked Doctora Karen to look for them in Tegucigalpa—see what is available and at what prices. She forgot.

Her sister-in-law works at a private clinic in Tocoa. She could get them for us at the same price their clinic pays (there is no data about what that amount would be).

During these conversations about BP cuffs it comes out that Dra. Karen thinks the bargain basement BP cuff is pretty darn good! *Oy, vey!* My wealthy background sneaks up behind me and bites me again! Also, it comes out that she keeps "hers" locked up in her exam room. The rest of us all share one BP cuff whether she's working or not.

By now the money has cleared the bank and we're ready to make the purchase. Two standard BP cuffs and one with pediatric, standard and "thigh" cuffs that could be interchanged. When you can shoot for the stars, why not?

Dra. Karen calls the sister-in-law asking her to check prices. Dra. Karen has never purchased a BP cuff and asks her to buy the most expensive as the way to assure good quality. You'll be pleased to know that I do NOT roll my eyes in response to that; I have already been humbled about my rich expectations. Sister-in-law will call back.

The medicine situation has been very tight all year and by now we have spent a lot. Not much money left other than the equipment money. The sister who sent the money clarifies that we should use it for medicines if we think that would be better. Her intention was and is to help provide health care.

Holy Week—clinic closed.

Easter Monday—Dra. Karen not back from holiday.

Then two weeks of immunization campaign—keeps us all occupied. Money goes out to pay for transportation for the outreach.

Dra. Karen's mother is diagnosed with breast cancer and Dra. Karen leaves to take care of her in May.

The medicine shortage gets tighter. We spend most of the BP cuff money on medicines (with some ambivalence). No news from Dra. Karen.

Two weeks ago, Sister Confianza stumbles across termites in/on a top bunk which we use for a storage shelf. She does a deep cleaning. There is a blood pressure cuff!! An excellent one! I am amazed. It is the one I bought in medical school. I don't remember bringing it down here. I don't know when. A gift from God.

A mouse had chewed a hole, but I easily patch it with a piece of heavy denim. I take it in the very next Monday.

Now we have two BP cuffs to share and it feels pretty nice.

Next on our schedule: My pre-renewal retreat. On Thursday, August 25, I will renew my profession for three years. Supposedly after that, I will be eligible for Perpetual Profession.

In Bonito
From: Sister Alegría   Date: August 10, 2011

We're in Bonito today. On Monday, we worked as usual in Centro de Salud, then stayed at Juana Nidia's house. She and her husband made us welcome. Yesterday very early we went to Villa Nueva, one of the poor, remote neighborhoods that we visited in April/May. There is a program to help the most remote, poorest (and highest mortality) neighborhoods. It requires a regular visit by a physician. Dra. Karen is not yet back, so Juana Nidia asked us to go.

There were 24 kids at school. First we dewormed them all. Then Cooper gave his Stamp Out Malaria talk. Then they did finger pokes to check them all for malaria. By then, the mothers and other kids had shown up for consults. I gave just over 20 consults. Don't you feel sorry for those kids? You just innocently show up for school one day and all of a sudden you are taking medicine, getting a lecture intended for grown-ups and having your finger stuck. *Así es la vida.* Life is like that. They were all very compliant.

When we finished there, we were served a lovely chicken and vegetable soup, with rice and tortillas on the side and *guanábana* (soursop) fruit drink. Yum.

Then to Eva's. We caught a ride with an oil palm truck to Bonito. Stayed at the priests' house last night. Unfortunately, neither priest was there, and their cook, María Julia, is in the hospital in La Ceiba. Her daughter and sister made us welcome. To bank and email today. We'll go home this afternoon.

Sister Alegría's Renewal of Profession

From: Sister Confianza   Date: August 31, 2011

Two weeks ago Sister Alegría had a five-day silent retreat in preparation for her Renewal of Profession. Because of my continued wrist limitations, Sister Alegría did a large share of the physical work (like scrubbing laundry and grinding), so it turned out not to be all that different from a normal week. I, on the other hand, was able to enjoy a bit of retreat myself.

On retreat, Sister Alegría read from various books including: The Historical Jesus by John Dominic Crossan (material poverty makes for freedom, which, in turn, allows one to rule one's own life); *Pies de cierva* (Feet of the Hind) by Hannah Hurnard (an allegory of the spiritual life); and On Beginning from Within, by Douglas Steere (what makes a saint). Her favorite quote from the week was, "The only real sorrow is not being a saint." (Leon Bloy, quoted by Steere).

I planned a closing shared retreat day, using Monastery Without Walls, by Bruce Davis, which treats aspects of the monastic life in a thoughtful way with inclusive poetic language, combined with excerpts from the Diary of Polish nun, Saint María Faustina Kowalska.

Sister Alegría made her renewal on Thursday, August 25. This time it is a three year commitment; up until now it has only been one year at a time. She found herself a little nervous! In fact, it feels so deep, she's not ready to talk about it. That's why I'm writing.

The day was nice. We were centered and prepared and able to celebrate well. The program was a reminder that we are continually in formation and that every day we have a chance for a new beginning.

Coming up in September is our Annual Monastery Retreat.

Chicken

From: Sister Confianza   Date: October 11, 2011

Sister Alegría and I have been thinking about getting chickens, so we are asking all our friends for their advice. One day in September we go visiting in Limoncito. On our way back via the shortcut, we stop by the home of Xiomara. We've admired her chickens and chicks before and ask her some details about raising them. She is happy to share. Then she gets some dry corn out to feed them. With her toddler in her lap, she uses a knife to loosen the kernels from the cob and sprinkles them around her for the chickens.

All of a sudden, she reaches down and picks up a half-grown rooster and offers it to us. *"¡Para la sopa!* For soup!" she says, smiling.

Sister Alegría and I look at each other, and Sister Alegría says, "I've never killed a chicken before." Xiomara just laughs and patiently explains the steps. I am relieved to hear that her method is similar to what I saw my father do when I was young. Sister Alegría is still wide-eyed, but we agree to take the chicken. Xiomara ties its feet together and shows Sister Alegría how to carry it under her arm—and we're off.

But what do we do with a live chicken? We're certainly not ready to make soup tonight! Happily, unlike dead chicken, a live chicken keeps without refrigeration. So, once at the Monastery, we let it run free, and it begins scratching around for food right away.

We're home late. We bathe and have Vespers as dusk settles in. Then we hear a flutter of wings. Uh-oh. We didn't get the chicken into the bathroom in time to close him in for the night. Now he's roosted in an unknown tree—or was nabbed by a wild animal, like we've been warned about so many times!

We go to bed, feeling like we've failed as chicken farmers. I wake up the next morning to a rooster crowing—from the neighbor's place half a mile away! Shouldn't our rooster respond if he's still alive? No sounds. I try to console myself, thinking we did the best we could and already gained that much more experience.

Then, in the middle of Lauds, I hear a "cluck-cluck," and a shuffle: There's the chicken, foraging around the yard—a pure gift from God.

We keep the young rooster around the house for a few days, tossing him a little corn and finding out just how messy chickens are. The second night we're able to lead him (with corn) into the bathroom and after that he goes there to roost on his own. Only once do we hear him try to crow, "Cock-a-croak!" His voice is changing; he is just an adolescent.

Our imagination is to invite our neighbors Reina and Javier over to share in the chicken soup. At age 18, Reina is an experienced housewife; she will be able to demonstrate for us how to kill and clean the chicken. But how will we get word to them?

Walking to Javier and Reina's, 2013

A few days later, right after lunch, Javier shows up. They obtained a sack of *elote* (young corn on the cob) and would like to borrow our food mill to make *tamalitos* (a kind of tamales made from young corn). We, of course, are happy to oblige.

"Too bad we don't have any meat," Javier says. "We'd really like to make *montuca—tamalitos* with meat."

"Yes, that's too bad," I say.

"We have a chicken!" says Sister Alegría.

"Would that do?" I ask.

"*¡Claro que sí!* Certainly," says Javier.

"*Vámanos, pues.* Let's go, then," I respond. Sister Alegría and I close up the house, Javier captures the chicken, and we all walk to their place—almost a mile down the road, through the woods and pasture and over the creek.

We all get right to work shucking corn, carefully saving the inner husks to use as the tamale wrappers. Sister Alegría helps Javier cut the corn off the cob.

Reina stokes the fire in the stove to boil some water, and then gives us the lesson on butchering the chicken. With its feet tied together, she hangs the rooster upside down on a fence post in the yard, then twists its wings together behind its back so they won't flap. She takes a knife and slits its throat, letting the blood drain down, (even the comb loses its color!) as it dies quietly.

Reina takes the chicken to the kitchen (one end of the single-room house), sets it in an empty pot and pours hot water over the whole thing to loosen the feathers. Then we go back outside and pluck it easily. It is a pretty small bird underneath!

Next, Reina lights some dry corn husks and moves the carcass over the flame to singe off any remaining feathers. She also singes the feet and removes the papery outer layer of skin—now they are clean enough to cook! Then we take a knife and a green scrubbing pad down to her washing rock in the stream. There, Reina scrubs the whole chicken over with soap "to remove the smoke" and rinses it. She removes the legs and wings, cuts them into small pieces, and puts them into a pot.

Now for the anatomy lesson. Reina pulls out the entrails, many of which she cleans for cooking. She names and explains all of the parts to us. The gizzard, for example, is called *"la piedra"* (the stone). "It's where the chicken cooks its food."

She finishes cutting up the carcass and puts all the edible parts into the pot; the rest are left for the dog.

Back to the house, where Reina adds some ingredients to the pot and sets it on the stove to stew. She puts me to unwrapping forty (!) bouillon cubes, while she collects other condiments. Sister Alegría and Javier work together to grind the corn; the condiments go through the mill near the end: onion, garlic, cilantro, basil, and cumin.

The batter is divided into two pots with salt, sugar, the bouillon cubes and lots of melted shortening stirred in. The smaller pot receives a higher concentration of spices plus the tomato enriched sauce from the chicken, turning it pale orange.

Now it is time to make the *montuca.* We take two overlapping corn husks and put in a large spoonful of plain batter, a small spoonful of orange batter and a tiny piece of cooked meat. Then wrap it up, fold over the ends and set it in a large pot over a layer of corn cobs to keep them from sticking. When the pot is full of the *montuca,* Reina fills it part way with water, puts a layer of plastic over the top, puts on the lid and sets it on the stove to steam—a long time.

By now it is getting dark and we're concerned about getting home. Sister Alegría wonders aloud about taking some raw tamales home to cook ourselves, but they convince us to stay.

When the *montuca* is cooked, Reina unwraps and serves us each one on a plate with a fork. They are very good. She and Javier also eat, along with their 23-month-old son who has slept most of the afternoon.

Finally, they send us home with a package of *montuca* (enough for four meals) and a flashlight to guide our way. Javier walks with us until we get to the path we're familiar with, and we return to the Monastery, tired and well-fed.

It's been quite a week!

Annual Monastery Retreat
From: Sister Alegría   Date: October 12, 2011

When my son Glenn was two or three years old, he was an exemplary big brother to his little brother. One day, he gave something to Scott and I told him, "It makes God smile to see brothers share."

He was so pleased to hear that. In one act, you can satisfy your little brother, earn compliments from your mother and make God smile! Well, it just doesn't get any better than that.

It didn't occur to me to tell him that God was grateful for his act of generosity. Grateful, why would I have said that? It was a lack in my religious education. I'm sure it had been mentioned by someone, at least in passing, that God is grateful, or at least is capable of gratitude. If I had ever heard it, I never really took it in.

Last week was our Annual Monastery Retreat. Julian of Norwich was our guest religious for the week.

In chapter 14 of Revelations of Divine Love (the long version), Julian talks about the Lord's gratitude to those who serve him/her. I like it; I like it a lot.

Besides the thoughts of Julian, we focused on Psalm 18:1-2. In these two verses, ten names or titles are given to God. A Psalm of praise.

Psalm 18:1, 2 (King James Version)
I will love thee, O Lord, my strength.
The Lord is my rock, and my fortress, and my deliverer;
My God, my strength, in whom I will trust;
My buckler, and the horn of my salvation,
And my high tower.

Our activity was to write a short Psalm of praise to the Grateful God. This is one of the Psalms that came out of that activity.

Psalm to the Grateful God
God, you who have created all food
    are grateful when we give a pineapple to a neighbor.
God, you who engendered all joy
    are grateful when I smile at a grouch.
God, you who shower us with blessings
    are grateful when I bless a narco who has given us a ride.
God, you who have the power to heal all diseases
    are grateful when we treat one of your daughters or sons
in the clinic.
God, you who have the power to demand all attention
    are grateful when I offer you a word of prayer.
God, you who created all
    are grateful when we try to care for your creation.
God, you are really Simple.

Obviously, this Psalm to a Grateful God is pretty specific to our life circumstances. You could write one more suitable to your own life.

Praying the Psalms
From: Sister Alegría

That ancient Hebrew hymnbook, the Psalms, forms the heart of communal monastic prayer. Everything is covered: love songs to God; acknowledgement of God's intimate knowing of each of us, sometimes in celebration, sometimes not (Where can I go to flee you?); complaints; public celebration and praise; private angst; calls for divine justice; calls for divine revenge.

The sensitive modern reader of goodwill flinches at the rawness of some Psalms. There are less-than-honorable sentiments expressed. How does this fit with our Lord's teaching to love our enemies? It seems not to fit at all.

This is our spiritual psychotherapy, I suppose we could say. If the psalmist can share his most vile thoughts and wishes with God, so can we. God can take it. If we insist on giving to God only our best, that means that we keep (hoard) for ourselves our worst: envy, hatred, fear, rage, greed, lust, pride. If we don't give it ALL to God we slow down God's process of refining our souls. As one woman has said, "You have to take out the garbage."

Every worship time has Psalms. It is part of monastic discipline to pray the Psalms that come up, whether they fit my mood of the day or not. This is sometimes a challenge. My spiritual path is devotion, not discipline. They can look alike and they feed each other. Practicing this discipline helps my devotion grow in wisdom and depth.

November Calendar
From: Sisters Alegría and Confianza   Date: October 12, 2011

Dates of interest for Amigas del Señor:

Sunday, November 6, 10 am
Unprogrammed Worship at Multnomah Monthly Meeting (MMM), Portland, Oregon
Amigas del Señor and MMM are connected through a Covenant of Caring. This Sunday we celebrate this connection and hold one another in the Light. "Holding in the Light" is an old-fashioned Quaker expression meaning "praying for one." It stems from the awareness that the word God and its old connotations may limit our connection to the Divine).

Wednesday-Friday, November 16-18
Pre-Renewal retreat for Sister Confianza (shh, she'll be in prayer)

Thursday, November 24
Renewal of Profession of Sister Confianza (one-year renewal)
Our usual Thursday fast will be replaced with a feast day.
Please include us in your prayers that day.

<u>Sunday, November 27, 9:30 am</u>
> Worship at Sellwood United Methodist Church, Portland, Oregon

This is Sister Alegría's church of membership and the church that accepts and forwards donations to us. This First Sunday in Advent, both they and we will have a special day of celebrating our connection.

We cordially invite you to participate in both of these public worship opportunities if you happen to be in the Portland area on those dates.

We'd love to have you for the Renewal of Profession ceremony, too. If you happen to be in the neighborhood, just drop in. We'll cook up a few extra tortillas.

Ceibita

From: Sister Alegría   Date: October 13, 2011

I'll tell you about this week's trip to Tocoa. On the 31st of August, we knew that we didn't have enough money to live on for five weeks, when more would be available in the bank. This is not like the guessing of the early years. We know what things cost now. We look at each other, laugh and say, "I wonder how God will provide THIS time."

I won't bore you with all of the details: the gifts of milk, lovely meals, chicken, *platanos, chatas*, corn on the cob, *yuca*, cool sweetened drinks, *mandarins*—I'm sure I'm forgetting lots. As it turned out, we lived at a higher standard of living than usual (diet-wise) and the money lasted six weeks. We started this week with $15. The bus fare to Tocoa is $5.

<u>Monday, October 10</u>
The government medicines had arrived. *Ay! Ay!* (local for Woe is me!) Not nearly enough: not one tablet of acetaminophen or antihistamine, not one drop of liquid asthma or allergy medicine. Trouble. We made our list.

We talked with Sor Leonarda when we went there for lunch. We told her about the medicine woes. She has a strong relationship with the medical teams that come to Limón fairly regularly from February to October. They do not collaborate with Centro de Salud, but do with her. She said she would write a letter (a real tear-jerker) explaining that when they aren't around, her only resource is Centro de Salud and please, please, donate a bunch of medicines. She had

242

me write a list of medicines that would be especially useful and will add, "and anything else you can spare." She practically guaranteed results.

OK, time to leave town. Before we even got to our usual hitch-hiking spot, a truck passed. It is a concrete carrier—sometimes cement blocks, sometimes sacks of cement. Big letters on the doors: PASSENGERS PROHIBITED. I didn't flag them down. They stopped. The helper guy signaled us to come. We climbed into the cab and he went to ride in the back.

It is a crude, rough truck on a crude, rough road. My teeth were clacking together. We were grateful for the ride and noticed that we weren't being passed by faster moving vehicles. My asthma is active this week and I felt pretty tired. (My asthma had not bothered me for a few months. I had lots of time feeling better and walking so fast Hermana Confianza had trouble keeping up.)

We get to the bridge just before Bonito and the truck breaks down at the police/military stop. Two of the soldiers come over to the cab, look at the sign and read aloud, "Touching the Passengers is Prohibited." All laugh. It soon becomes clear that the plan is to wait for some mysterious help. I pass around mandarins—we have just enough for one each for the driver, helper guy and each cop or soldier.

We ask the soldiers to help us hitch a ride to Tocoa. The very next car to come is the Limón mayor's son in his elegant, air conditioned car. We know one another. He brings us right to downtown Tocoa.

By 5 pm, we are in Ceibita, walking to the parsonage of a new pastor, one we have never met. We are assured by a passing young man of the church: "They'll make you welcome." They do.

We go to Irma's house for dinner. This is our tradition when we come to Ceibita. Once we skipped it and she was offended. Irma served us fried *plátano* slices and refried beans. We're not used to this. We are rural poor; we don't cook with much oil.

Tuesday, October 11

Pastor Jesús, our host, has a computer and can buy *saldo* for $2 for 24 hours of internet access. He offers this to us. That's what we pay for two hours at a business. We snap it up. We spend most of the day at the computer. We are given lunch as we are working.

Late afternoon, we visit Sister Cándida (I forgot to give the proper title to the others. In Honduras, everyone in the church is Sister or Brother.) She feeds us dinner—refried beans, fried hot dogs and corn tortillas.

The evening church meeting is for the leaders only. We are not invited. We are disappointed. The internet connection doesn't work. We spend a few hours typing in documents to send the next morning.

Wednesday, October 12

Columbus Day, now called *Día de las Razas* (Race Day). But it will be celebrated next Monday. The bank will be open after all.

After morning prayers, we get to work on the internet and work until the time runs out. We catch the bus to Tocoa. The bus stop is very near the bank.

The bank is air-conditioned. I notice that I am breathing significantly harder than I was earlier. I am the designated bank person, because we persons of the *tercera edad* (third age) have a special line. I transfer $500 from our account to Eloyda's to buy medicines. I withdraw $74 for us to live on.

Next stop: telephone for hire. I call Eloyda, giving her our order, telling her how much is for her and how much for us. Her medicines are all by donations—sometimes medicine donations, sometimes money to buy them. This time of year, the budget is always used up. $300 for Limón, $200 for *Clínica Metodista*. She is grateful. We have an expression, *"Algo es mejor que nada."* Something is better than nothing.

We buy a treat: lychees are in season, five cents each. We buy a bag of ten. Yum. (I am forbidden to eat mandarins because of the acid reflux.)

Next stop: pharmacy. The asthma medicine costs too much; I refuse to buy it. The woman immediately gives me a discount. $30 for asthma medicine. *Así es.* (That's the way it is.)

Back in Ceibita we get off the bus at Centro de Salud, hoping to see Gilma, the nurse. I've worked with her before and haven't seen her in a few years. The evening before, as we were talking with Pastor Jesús, I commented that I felt ashamed to visit her because I had nothing to give her. Well, I had to listen to that. I am a nun. If I feel shame to not have something to give, that means that I feel pride when I do. Now I know that I must visit.

Gilma is not in. But her supervisor, Elizabeth, R. N., is there and makes us welcome. She has been there about two years now. I had hoped that they get their medicines from a different warehouse than we do. But no, they also have to go all the way to Trujillo to get their medicines and they are missing all that we are missing and even more. We commiserate together. I leave greetings for Gilma. The paint on the lovely new clinic (from only three years ago) is peeling and she is trying to get the mayor to pop for paint.

We walk, very slowly, the half mile to the parsonage. I am really tired. The house and fence are locked up. We relax in the shade and do afternoon prayers. I take a dose of my new expensive medicine.

Jesús and his wife show up on his motorcycle and we all go in. We get another long talking session with him. So interesting, but I just need to rest. I go to bed for an hour and Hermana Confianza and he talk. They feed us a light dinner: chopped up wieners in scrambled eggs with two slices of white bread.

The women's group is scheduled to meet. I was looking forward to this. Irma, the president shows up and opens the church. Then the sky opens up and there is a tremendous downpour. As we are on the way across the yard to the church, we meet Irma running to us. No one showed up. Called on account of rain. Sigh. We do prayers and I go to bed.

Ceibita Feeding Program

We had hoped today to visit the feeding program, run by the church. Well, it won't be open today because the cooks are cooking for a special church dinner and worship this evening.   This feeding program was started several years ago. The founding pastor was embezzling (in the construction and the management). It was a mess. They accept the kids who come, 1 year old up to age 12. They serve 150-180 kids a day. Everyone knows the menu. Chicken day has a big turn out and rice and bean day has a small turn out. They cook 15 pounds of rice. When it is chicken they cook only 12 pounds. No vegetables—too costly. It is not a big meal-sized plate of food. *Algo es mejor que nada.* Some children (with their mothers, who don't get to eat) walk as far as a mile to get this small meal. Meals are served five days a week. Jesús buys the groceries and stores them at his house, dispensing the groceries for the day only. There had been a problem with groceries walking away.

Now I will talk in lempiras, not dollars. One dollar is worth 19 lempiras.

Our friend Irma is now one of the cooks. She earns 1,500 lempiras a month for six hours of work five days a week. The two week budget for groceries is about 4,000 lempiras—small. Jesús sends all the receipts to the central office of the church every 2 weeks. Tight now. This is very important.

In August a work team came from the states and painted the parsonage, inside and out. Bright green—it's fabulous, and best of all, the pastor's wife got to choose the color. Even the refrigerator (which sort of works) sports a new coat of green paint.

245

For several years, the financially corrupt pastor was here. Then he fathered a child in the neighborhood. He's not the same race as most of the neighborhood, so this was pretty noticeable. He was removed because of the financial irregularities. The reputation of the church was in the toilet.

An experienced woman pastor came two years ago and began rebuilding practically from scratch. She paved the way for Jesús (they have had only good things to say about each other). Now the church is growing. He says that his main effort is to "erase the footprints of the past." Not an easy job. The ex-pastor still comes to visit his extra woman and illegitimate son from time to time, so he continues to damage the reputation of the church. Jesús says he won't even go walking without his wife along. He is very aware.

Violence in the Aguán River Valley

Jesús also brought us up to date a bit on the violence in "the Aguán" right here in Colón. A week ago, Paul Jeffrey was here. He is an international reporter and photographer for the UMC. He was a missionary in Honduras for some years before that. He and Jesús went together to where the *campesinos* are trying to reclaim land taken by Facussé. Facussé is famous. He is the head of a consortium of very rich people who own anything worth owning in Colón. In the name of the consortium, he bought up all the private banana plantations. "It's like this. You can sell your land to me at what I consider a fair price. If you don't, who will take care of your widow? It's a free country. You decide." Well, in this free country, they, each and every one, decided to sell.

Oil palms produce more money than bananas, so banana plantations have been replanted in palm. Jesús was very impressed with the squalor—living in tarp tents, mud, masses of mosquitoes. There had been a murder (which group of armed men? the company goons or the government soldiers, does it matter? The guy is dead.). Paul photographed everything.

Thursday, October 13

In the night, I woke up coughing and took extra asthma medicine again. After morning prayers, I told Hermana Confianza, "I'm ready to admit that I am sick with asthma."

She smiled kindly and said, "I'm glad that you're ready to admit that." (Saying "I told you so," is not good nun behavior; she would never do that.)

We took the dirty clothes out to wash. I am the designated scrubber and wringer since her wrists still trouble her. She is designated to "do everything that Hermana Alegría doesn't HAVE to do." That went well.

I am under voluntary house arrest as part of my asthma treatment. We bought another batch of internet time, so I can write this to you. I am also the designated typist (again, those pesky wrists). So far, my fingers are fine.

I am going to walk to the worship service tonight in a private house, just on the other side of the public health clinic, no matter how long it takes. I am determined. I am reminded of our old friend, Teresa of Avila. She recommends that the Sisters have "very determined determination."

Renewal of Profession
From: Sister Alegría   Date: December 13, 2011

We had a beautiful feast day on Thursday, November 24, for Sister Confianza's Renewal of Profession. We worked (the essentials only) for a few hours in the morning and then did Unprogrammed Worship (Quaker-style), had a lovely dedication worship service and had a general holiday atmosphere with relaxation. We made chicken and dumplings and wild berry cobbler for our special meal. The dumplings were heavy, but that didn't dampen our mood.

It was kind of neat for us to think about our US friends and relatives celebrating Thanksgiving and praying the same day we were celebrating.

This was a very special celebration. It was the first "milestone" day in which we felt like we weren't re-inventing the wheel. We had experience. We had a tradition. We could just do it.

I preached. II Chronicles 20:1-30. The short version: Three armies were converging on Jerusalem. The king was scared. Called for fasting and prayer. A temple prophet said, "This isn't your fight; it is God's." He told them where to have their picnic and watch. By the time the king arrived (with the choir, the army and the people), the three armies had attacked and killed one another. It took three days to carry away the plunder.

All those challenges that look like a battle to you, well, they're God's battle. Just pray, fast, take your position, trust in God and watch as God does the hard stuff. We've watched God do a lot of hard stuff in the last year. A lot to celebrate. Celebrating, among other things, that some of those hard things are now in the past, not the present.

Sister Confianza wants to add her comments:

In this first year as a Professed Sister, I have really come into my own as a nun. Some weeks ago, I was meditating on what Peace Pilgrim wrote about finding one's place in the Grand Scheme of Things. I thought to myself, "How lucky I am to have found my role. I'm a nun, and I get to pray all day. What an easy job!" and I smiled.

Baby Jesus 2011
From: Sister Alegría   Date: December 20, 2011

On December 5, I gave 45 consults, all age people, some with complicated problems. I'll tell you about just one.

An 18-day-old is brought in for her routine newborn exam. She is not nursing well. I guess not! She is gravely ill with pneumonia. I tell mom that she has to get the baby to the hospital.

"Can I wait two days?"

"No, certainly not."

Mom has no money. Neither do we; we've been living on credit for three weeks. We talk about the mayor's office (they've helped others). A clear "No." I suppose she's not in his political party.

I tell her that even if she has to hitchhike to Tocoa, she must go. I know that it is possible because I've done it—also taking a sick baby to the hospital. If I could do it, she can do it.

We talk about Sor Leonarda as a possibility for help. She'll go see Sor. I have the nurse give the baby intramuscular penicillin and gentamycin. I write out the pink hospital referral form. I tell her to show it to Sor. "She knows me."

The next day, I think about what I said. This is a racist place. I with my white face can hitchhike to the city. Mom has a black face. I award myself a Cultural Insensitivity Prize; I repent.

The next week they are back for follow-up. She had gone to Sor, who gave her $16.

Then she hitchhiked to Tocoa. A ride in the cement truck to Bonito and then another ride to Tocoa! Amazing! I'm impressed. She says, "I could do it because you gave me so much encouragement."

The baby worsened on the ride, even turned blue. At the hospital she was immediately given oxygen and IV therapy. She stayed five days.

"So you didn't even need the money from Sor?"

"Yes, I did. I had to buy a medicine the hospital didn't have and I had to pay my bus fare home."

The baby is fabulous. She is perfect; she is healthy; she is beautiful.

I take the baby out to the waiting room, holding her high, "Look at this child; she is a miracle—the child who lived because her mother was so brave as to hitchhike to Tocoa to the hospital." I weep.

Unto us a Child is born.

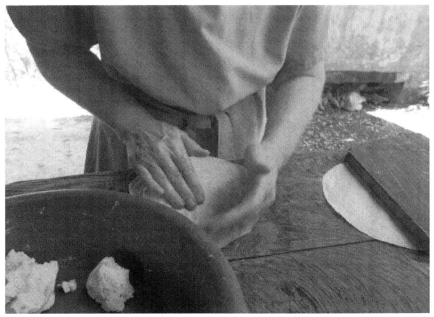

Sister Alegría forms corn tortillas, 2016

Sister Confianza walks the *desvío* near the Monastery, 2013

10

Seeking Health Care

"Come unto me, all ye who labor and are heavy laden, and I will give you rest."—Jesus the Christ

A Month of Ups and Downs
From: Sister Confianza   Date: December 27, 2011

This month took place between about October 10 to November 10. We now manage to tell you.

UP: The check with $605 of donations finally cleared the bank.
UP: We spent $500 of that on medicines for Centro de Salud and the Methodist clinic in El Pino.
DOWN: There was no news of new donations.
DOWN: That left "not enough" money to live on.
UP: When there's no money, we find we're really able to trust in God.
DOWN: Even with our donations, the pharmacy at Centro de Salud looked like it would run out of medicines in two to three weeks.
UP: Sor Leonarda asked the last North American medical team of the year to donate left over medicines and they agreed.
DOWN: They didn't leave any medicines.
UP: Sor Leonarda gave us a five-pound bag of rice and lentils enriched with vitamins.
DOWN: It tasted awful.
UP: We found that it was more palatable by adding half plain rice.
DOWN: A cold front came, bringing rain that lasted seven days.
UP: We were able to do the yearly tank cleaning and it refilled within 24 hours.
DOWN: There was too much rain to go into Limón as planned.
DOWN: We were down to one day's worth of food.
UP: Our neighbor Javier came over and brought us fat pork.

UP: The three of us went to dig *yuca* and got enough to last a week or two.

DOWN: Most of it was bad.

UP: It still fed us for several days.

DOWN: While we were out, someone came by the Monastery and stole our hammock from the porch.

UP: We came up with a pattern to make a hammock from left over denim fabric.

DOWN: We ran out of thread and couldn't sew it.

UP: We finally made it to town.

DOWN: Both of us had lost weight in recent weeks (probably due to the icky food).

UP: Lupe, the cook at Sor's Home, showed us how to rinse all the bad-tasting stuff (yes, the vitamins) off the rice and lentils, so they would taste good.

UP: They gave us two more bags of it.

UP: Our friend Fela gave us *cassave* (a sort of "cracker" made of *yuca*)

UP: She also sold us thread.

UP: Noemí let us buy groceries on credit at her store.

UP: We got our hammock made.

UP: It is fabulous.

UP: We had the idea to make a trip to the US to raise awareness about the monastic life and Third World poverty.

UP: Our first inquires got a positive response.

UP: We spent several weeks imagining the possibilities.

DOWN: Our next requirement (a tour coordinator) was not met. We will not be going anytime soon.

DOWN: Dra. Karen left the Limón Centro de Salud for good and took her position and salary with her.

DOWN: Head nurse Juana Nidia is very discouraged that such government corruption extends to the Public Health System.

DOWN: No one knows when or where the money will be found and the effort made to get a new doctor.

UP: We got a free ride to Bonito to use the internet and go to the bank.

UP: We received news of more donations, including a big anonymous one.

DOWN: It would not be available for another month.

UP: Eloyda confirmed that we can order medicines on credit.

UP: We did.

UP: We received an inquiry from a woman interested in checking out the Monastery.

UP: We ran into old friends who took us to their property to visit.

UP: They gave us a bunch of oranges.

DOWN: Because of the time spent with them, we did not get back to the internet and did not get this update sent out.

UP: A stranger paid our bus fare to get home so we did not have to ride in the back of his truck.

UP: We get by with a little help from our friends.

Health
From: Sister Alegría   Date: January 31, 2012

In October, we started seeing patients with what looked like influenza—lots of them. I've seen well over 200 in these months. Our flu shots arrived in late November. As health care workers we both received them (even though Sister Confianza is young!). Well, 13 days later she got sick, really sick, with obviously the same crud. It takes 14 days for the immunization to take effect. On day 17 I got sick, not so sick, but sick enough. Then I got a little sicker.

Soon Sister Confianza was back to full strength and my stuff got worse and worse. Bad lower gut, general feeling of sickness, cough. It seemed to last a long time. We decided to treat me for amoebas. Then for H. pylori—the bacteria that is often responsible for high stomach acid. I have been taking high-dose meds without results. The cough is from the acid reflux irritating the throat and its secondary effect of worsening the asthma. I lost weight.

Sister Confianza's parents sent us a fabulous Christmas package which included dried fruits and nuts. With that and local foods, purchased and grown, we did a full-court press of nutritional rehabilitation. We ate well. It seemed to Sister Confianza that she was gaining weight (not our goal). Gradually, I became able to eat volumes in the normal range again. Felt better and better. Gained a tiny bit of weight.

Right after Epiphany (January 6) we started our Yearly Review. In it we each tell what we remember that is relevant about the specific topic of that meeting. Our meeting on health was an eye-opener.

First, Hermana Confianza with her wrist tendonitis (pain). She has been taking anti-inflammatories faithfully for over a year. She wears splints 90% of the time, waking and sleeping. She has learned how to protect her wrists and hardly ever makes an "oops" in that direction. Her Mom sent some wrist range-of-motion exercises which she does regularly. My sister and sister-in-law sent another set of splints—also excellent, but allow just a little more movement.

She now wears them in the day and the more restrictive ones at night. Things get better a little, then worse again. She hasn't had a normal day in 15 months.

Second, my acid reflux and asthma. I, too, have been taking all of the medicines, high doses. We do all of the life style changes recommended (e.g., raised head of the bed, restricted diet, asthma medicine before exercise). My body has taught my taste to dislike things like a tiny bit of black pepper in a dish, any spices, fruits that aren't really, really sweet. In short, I, too, have been doing all the right things and the problem lightens and worsens. Discouraging.

We decided that perhaps we have been a little too good at accepting what comes our way and it is time to look for more expert help.

Money was available in early December. We spent some on medicines for the clinics and held on to the rest because we thought that we would need some expensive (by Honduran standards) health care.

After the Yearly Review meeting, I looked up both problems in my 2001 Internal Medicine book. The things I had worried about for Sister Confianza were probably not worries (i.e., we wouldn't have to go to Tegucigalpa for the top-of-the-line sophisticated laboratory). What I learned about my acid reflux is that I should have had MUCH better results with the aggressive regimen we had been following.

First priority, gastroenterology consult for me, as it looks like a more serious health problem, even though it doesn't cramp our style any more than her wrist problem.

We decided to come to La Ceiba (I say come, because that's where we are right now), for the GI (gastro-intestinal) consult, expecting an endoscopy to be part of the work-up. We had no idea what that would cost. We decided to do this in spite of the fact that we had already planned our 6th Founding Day anniversary on February 1.

Yesterday morning, on our way to Centro de Salud, we got down from the truck in which we were riding to talk to our friend, Alex. He gave us the name of his GI doctor in La Ceiba and recommended him highly. He also told us the cost of the consult and his colonoscopy—much lower than we had feared. He just glowed being able to help us in this way.

We walked (with our heavy traveling backpacks) the last half mile to the clinic chatting cheerfully. We were now convinced that we could get consults for both of us this week. Hoorah!

We had a ridiculously busy day. We had planned to travel to Bonito to stay at the priests' house and leave from there this morning. I finished my 57ᵗʰ consult after 3 pm. Then I rested a bit, finished the lunch I had barely started at noon, drank a lot of water, and we did afternoon prayers. I had been entirely immersed in patient care. Hermana Confianza was our practical manager. She told me that if we tried to get to Bonito, we would arrive in the dark (after the priests' normal dinner hour). We have never arrived that late there and it is a long walk from the bus. She had asked María Elena (Sor's helper) if we could stay at the orphanage.

We took our empty food containers from lunch over and were welcomed warmly. Doña Lupe gave us dinner and soon we were given a small room (storage room with a bunk bed) in their large hovel. We were very grateful. Doña Lupe even made us some jelly sandwiches to carry for our breakfast this morning. A mouse got one in the night.

We caught the 6 am bus and here we are. We are registered at the GI doctor's office (first come, first serve). We will return shortly for the consult. I am very excited and hopeful.

Hold us in your prayers. Big stuff for us this week.

We'll keep you posted as well as we can.

Health Update
From: Sister Alegría   Date: February 1, 2012

I got my GI consult late yesterday afternoon. I am impressed with the doctor and am scheduled for endoscopy tomorrow morning. He doesn't think that there is much possibility of the more serious problems.

We just got out of the orthopedist's office. Also an amiable physician. He injected Hermana Confianza's carpal tunnels—both sides. It is not tendonitis. There had been no numbing, so I got fooled. The conservative treatment is still the same and we did that well. The expectation is that she should feel improvement tomorrow and in five days can gradually reduce medications and increase activity. The injections often last as long as three months, often without recurrence.

He did not charge us. He also offered to take care of any of the kids I refer for free. If he can't handle them in his office (he can't offer free hospital service), he'll refer them to CURE (like a Shriner's hospital) in San Pedro Sula. Tears came to my eyes with gratitude.

I don't like to cry in front of people. I went to the bathroom for a few minutes.

Gratitude, gratitude, gratitude.

The Latest in Health
From: Sister Confianza   Date: February 3, 2012

Yesterday, Sister Alegría and I got up early and had prayers outside our room in El Pino as the sun rose. We hopped a bus to La Ceiba, both of us fasting. Sister Alegría was not even allowed to drink water before her endoscopy. Since Thursday is our regular day for fasting, I also did not eat, though I did drink water.

An accident on the highway made the rush hour even slower and we got to Medi-Centro close to 8 am. When we registered at the doctor's office, we were number 7 on the list, with an expectation to be seen about 11 am, so, we found a quiet corner and spent time in silent worship. Then we went to the internet a couple blocks away.

When we returned, they were ready for Sister Alegría. She went in as I waited and read the previous day's newspaper.

About an hour later, she came out, looking a little dazed, and sat down next to me. She told me how they put an IV in her hand with sedatives. They instructed her to lie on her left side, put a mouthpiece in (to keep the tongue out of the way), then gave her the "real anesthesia." She remembers nothing after that, until she woke up on the other side of the room.

The doctor informed her that she would have another office visit with him in the afternoon to get the results and his recommendations. We decided to stay at the building this time. We went down to the cafeteria and had a very nice lunch of grilled sandwiches and *tres leches* dessert.

Then we waited, and waited, and looked at the newspaper. Sister Alegría would have liked to lie down, but there was no place for that.

Finally, at about 3:30, we were invited back into the doctor's office. He reported that the endoscopy was completely normal. He gave her the report, including colored pictures of the mucosa of her normal esophagus, normal stomach, and normal duodenum. No hiatal hernia is present (that would probably have called for surgical intervention). He affirmed that the aggressive anti-acid reflux treatment that we had been using had been excellent and very effective. Certainly, stomach contents continue to rise, but with the acid under control, they don't cause damage.

He advised her about managing medicines (to actually try to decrease one medicine) and emphasized the importance of continuing the rigidly restricted diet. Sister Alegría is always in hope that the diet could be liberalized, but no such luck. No tomatoes! no citrus! no chocolate! no fried food! How will we keep her weight up? (Actually, we've been doing very well with that on this restricted diet. I make sure she eats a little something five times a day. The hard part is to keep from gaining weight myself.)

The doctor gave the opinion that allergies are probably the more important cause of asthma, not acid reflux as we had thought. We're very relieved.

This morning we ordered Zyrtec (a stronger allergy medicine than she had been taking) through Eloyda. It will arrive for us in about a week. We also ordered a meager amount of medicines that we are completely lacking at Centro de Salud. As usual, we gave money for Eloyda to buy medicines for her pharmacy, which is in the same bad shape as ours.

Our original hope had been to return to the Monastery today, but after spending three days in the city, we decided it would be better to take a little more time here in El Pino to visit our friends in the church. Hopefully, we'll go back tomorrow.

Other exciting news:

We expect a Friend whom we have not yet met to visit in the next week or so. She is a photographer and has offered to update our photos, so, we've got to get back home and get ready!

Thanks for all of the good thoughts that you have sent to us by email and by mind-messages and prayer. We appreciate that very much.

More Continuing Health
From: Sister Alegría

We lived with the "knowledge" imparted to us by the GI doctor for three years. We have since learned that I did have a hiatal hernia. We used increasing amounts of allergy and asthma medicines and followed the diet more and more punctiliously. I had surgery in 2015, but that's another story.

Sasha
From: Sister Alegría   Date: February 20, 2012

Sasha (Alexandra Bosbeer) is the Quaker photographer who visited us last week. She went by Hermana Alejandra while here. Her classic Dutch beauty wowed everyone who met her.

It was a whirlwind visit. She came to give us the favor of updating our photos. It was a five-day photo shoot! She also showed us how to double twist twine to make a clothesline that requires no clothespins. Very cool, very useful. She also dropped tidbits of forestry lore.

Twisted clothesline, 2012

Then she was gone. Her visit was a great blessing and a very big change of pace for a contemplative monastery. She continues traveling.

We are grateful for the blessing of her visit and for her life.

Worsening Wrists
From: Sister Confianza   Date: February 20, 2012

After Dr. Salazar, the orthopedist, injected my wrists on February 1, they hurt a lot. I held out for the five days of rest (no using force in my wrists) as prescribed.

When we got back to the Monastery and I returned to doing household chores, the pain increased. The expectation was that it would have lessened and gradually improved over the next couple of months. However, by Day 10, it seemed to me about as bad as when it all started in October, 2010. We cut back my activities even more— no hauling buckets of water, but continuing to run the cook-stove. We began Reiki (healing touch) and considered the next steps to take.

Since January, it has been sinking in how long I have gone with restricted activity and continued achiness in the wrists. I'm tired of it. If there is something that can be done to alleviate the pain and have me return to normal activity, I'd like to do that. If nothing can be done, I'd like to know so I can mourn the losses and move on with my life. I turned 30 on February 15. I feel too young for this.

On Monday, February 13, I called Dr. Salazar. He reiterated that the next step is to go to San Pedro Sula for a nerve conduction study, then come back to see him in La Ceiba. When he sees the results of the study, he may want to operate. It is outpatient surgery, one hand at a time "so you can still do personal care." The sooner we can move on it the better. Trouble is, we only have $86 available in the bank account. Though Dr. Salazar won't charge us, the study costs $200 and the hospital bill would be about $550.

Last week, Sasha helped with tasks that I couldn't do, but Sister Alegría and I both overdid it physically. When she left on Friday, my wrists ached so much, I decided I had to stay out of the kitchen entirely to protect myself. Now even cooking falls to Sister Alegría. It is too much, too soon. At least I can still bathe myself!!

We had hoped not to do overnight travelling during Lent, which starts on Wednesday, but it looks like we have to. Today we are arranging to have money transferred from the USBank account to our account here so we can travel within a week.

Please keep us in your thoughts and prayers.

Wrists
From: Sister Alegría   Date: February 24, 2012

On Wednesday, February 22, we travelled to La Ceiba. First stop, the bank. The money had arrived and we withdrew some. Made an appointment for the nerve conduction study the next day in SanPedro Sula. Arrived at El Pino, happy to see our friends there.

On Thursday, February 23, we spent all day traveling to San Pedro Sula (three hours one way), waiting for test, having test and returning to El Pino. The nerve conduction test was NORMAL. There is no carpal tunnel syndrome. Thoughts of imminent surgery are put aside.

This morning, Friday, February 24, we presented the study to the orthopedist and he examined Sister Confianza's wrists again. He decided that she has "de Quervain's disease," which is a "stenosing tendovaginitis of the first dorsal compartment of the wrist." Basically, tendonitis of the thumb and wrist.

He injected both tendon sheaths and sent us to buy new splints. These are SPLINTS. They completely immobilize the thumb, plus the same immobility of the wrists as before. If she was helpless before, she is doubly so now.

We are very hopeful that with this new diagnosis and treatment she will do well.

Thanks for all of the good thought and prayers that you have sent our way.

Money Management as Spiritual Practice
From: Sister Alegría

You notice how casually I wrote about transferring money from the States to meet our immediate medical needs. Oh, so casual, as if it were nothing. This is a hold-over from Middle Classness.

Money management is a spiritual practice, whether you like to see it that way or not. Spiritual growth is often about giving up something good for something better. In my life, that has included going from being OK financially by US standards to depending wholly on God.

When we founded the Monastery in 2006, we sought material poverty. We were called to material poverty. Not very many people told me to my face that I was crazy, but enough did to inhibit me from free-flowing conversations with people who might.

In the first few years of the Monastery we used what had been "my" money for most of our expenses. We stopped doing that early in 2011. The money that we sent for in 2012 had been "mine." This was an emergency decision and within two months we were convinced that we had made a mistake in our spiritual practice of money management. By early 2012, I had divested myself of about 1/3 of my net worth. My goal was to reduce my holdings to nothing before Perpetual Profession (lifetime commitment). I would otherwise be eligible for it in August, 2014. When one has lived "prudently," that divestment is technically difficult to accomplish. It took all of that time.

Soy Libre—I'm Free
From: Sister Confianza   Date: March 5, 2012

Within three days of our last update, my life completely turned around. I went from almost total disuse of my hands to complete freedom of movement, from moments of agonizing pain to only occasionally achiness, from an emotional down to a high. I feel like I have been resurrected—and we're only at the beginning of Lent! Many of my thoughts are too new and profound to put into words, but I'd like to share some of the moments, feelings, and reflections from those few days.

Friday, February 24, evening

During an open-air worship service in El Pino, my right hand and wrist were really hurting me, so I adjusted the thumb-immobilizing wrist splints. A young man at the keyboard led a song:

"Somos libres. Libres para cantar, libres para saltar. We are free. Free to sing, free to jump."

He encouraged us to sing out and "jump up and down for God." I didn't feel very free, but I jumped anyway.

After the program, we ran into our old friend, Carlos, the former pastor in El Pino. Sister Alegría asked if he would pray for me, and then and there, he and his wife, Wendy, did so.

He has seen miracles, and asked me how I would know if I am healed.

"If the pain goes away."

"Muy bien. Very good."

I wanted to tell him that I thought the ego might be involved, but before I could, he said, "There could be some pride going on."

"Yes," I responded.

He then asked me pointedly, "Do you have faith in Jesus?"

Almost hesitating, I said, "Yes," and added to myself, "Lord, help my unbelief."

The pain in my hand was slightly alleviated after the prayer, which Carlos took as a good sign. "Healing can take time," he said.

Saturday, February 25, morning

I woke up feeling pretty low. I had great pain in my right hand and wrist. The splints seemed to be holding my thumb out in an unrelaxed position and I wondered if they fit properly. I cried, and Sister Alegría suggested we might stay near La Ceiba so that we could return to the orthopedist for follow-up. At first, I wanted to go in the same day, but as the pain subsided, I decided to let it wait. I was losing confidence in the doctor: On February 1, he gave me one diagnosis that turned out to be wrong, and now had given me another which I didn't show strong signs for (I didn't have sharp pain in the telltale spots and had never suspected that my thumbs were involved).

The challenges of daily life for the coming weeks were becoming apparent. Have you ever tried to brush your teeth without using your thumb? How about feeding yourself? Not only was it hard for me, it hurt. We tried to think of things that could make it easier. (For example, we have some lightweight plastic utensils.)

We decided to go spend a few days in Las Mangas with our missionary friends, Larry and Allison Smoak, where I could learn to adjust and Sister Alegría wouldn't be burdened with all of the physical tasks awaiting her at the Monastery.

Evening

We attended worship at the Pentecostal church next door to the Smoaks. Again, there was a song about our freedom in Christ. I raised my splinted wrists and sang, *"Me ha hecho libre.* He has made me free." At the end, there was a general intercessory prayer that included asking for healing for the sick. I felt personally included. The sense of being covered in prayer continued through Monday, including specific prayers from individuals where we were staying and folks in the US who emailed me. I knew that I was in the good hands of God.

Sunday, February 26, morning

I was still feeling pretty vulnerable, and more and more dependent. At breakfast Sister Alegría had to put the toppings onto my pancakes for me, and even cutting them myself strained the hand. Accepting all this help and sometimes having to ask for it wasn't easy. I was like a child again, just like Larry and Allison's fourteen-month-old daughter, Eva, but without the same sense of entitlement.

Mid-morning

Sister Alegría and I had Unprogrammed Worship looking out over the Cangrejal River valley: tree-covered hillsides, blue sky, myriad shades of green, flying egrets, singing birds. I wept. Here I was, hardly able to do a thing for myself, and yet I still had eyes to see and ears to hear: I could enjoy the beauty of creation, if I chose to. I looked down at my practically useless hands on my lap, held in a single position: open to receive. This was my only option: accept God's grace. The tears continued to flow.

One of the struggles I have had during these sixteen months of restricted use of my hands is the desire to do the work that is prohibited. On one level, it is a desire to do my share. When Sister Alegría is stuck with the majority of the hard physical work, she often gets tired out. It can be horrible for her, being so tired, sometimes with asthma. I feel bad, because I can't help relieve her by taking on the tasks. (Though we did learn that I can sing or read aloud to help provide companionship and encouragement.)

Then I ask myself: *Are my desires to pitch in pure? Do I want to relieve her for her sake or so I don't have to be bothered by seeing her suffer? Do I truly want to contribute, or do I just want an ego boost, seeing how much physical work I can accomplish? Do I think I am only worthy when I can do something obviously productive and that I am a useless lump and a burden when I can't? It is said that one can't live on bread alone, but by the Word of God. Am I way too focused on apparent physical needs and wants—like getting dinner on the table and having clean clothes?* Sometimes I can remember that my main job as a nun is to pray and to seek God, and that I can contribute to the world through non-tangible ways like positive words, a listening ear, and prayer.

Lord, help me to accept your boundless grace, knowing that I can do nothing to gain your love, freely given.

<u>Monday, February 27, morning</u>

Larry and Allison completely surprised me when they said I could get a consult with a physical therapist (PT). There is a charity hospital run by North Americans in a town further up the river, and they have a PT on staff. There was also a PT as part of the medical mission team in town this week. On Monday morning, the Smoaks drove us up there to check things out.

The guy on staff was actually an occupational therapist (OT), specializing in hands! God certainly arranged everything for my benefit this week! Moreover, the PT on the team specializes in lower extremities. Everyone told me to take advantage of our time there, so I asked him about my knees, which sometimes get sore and even swollen when I do a lot of squatting or climb up and down hills. He gave me several exercises to strengthen my leg muscles and get the knee cap tracking properly. He said it is a common problem among women.

Kevin, the OT, asked me my history and did a few tests for pain and strength in my hands and arms. He said that I don't show any signs of de Quervain's disease (though that could be because of the injections three days earlier). In fact, he said, most of my problem right now is that I've been wearing wrist splints and been immobilized for so long that my hands and wrists are weak and the muscles atrophied. (I had been suspicious about that.) If there is something else going on it can't be detected at this time.

Kevin gave me some exercises (which include a wad of green silly putty!) for strengthening the muscles and the tendon glide. He said, "Stop wearing the splints."

"At all?"

"What for?"

Moreover, there is no need to take anti-inflammatories unless I have an obvious reason like a headache or sore muscles. (Both the OT's and PT's eyes had widened when I said I'd been taking them around the clock for sixteen months.)

Then Kevin told me, "Pain is subjective. It is what the patient feels and reports. Increase in pain may be from an actual physical cause, or it may be just one's perception. It cannot be objectively measured. Stress in whatever form can magnify it.

"You are likely to have pain and other wacky sensations without the splints. Your wrists may get tired and achy, like your body does after doing a lot of work. Don't let the pain control you."

Then he added, "You know, it could be the Devil trying to keep you from doing the work God wants you to do." I can see something to that. Whether you call it the Devil or the ego, something was keeping me from living fully, from being all God made me to be.

Later

The rest of our day at the hospital was very nice. Several people prayed over me. We had interesting conversations with lots of folks and got all kinds of affirmations about our call and work in the Monastery. Sister Alegría gave a few consults to children and I translated briefly for a doctor. They even invited us to join them for lunch.

Tuesday, February 29—Saturday, March 3

"Pick up your mat and walk." That was the miracle I received on Monday. I immediately returned to doing kitchen tasks, like washing dishes. The only warning I had been given was to take it slow in adding force and weight (I won't be scrubbing laundry, cutting firewood, or carrying five-gallon buckets full of water for a while) and to not do any one thing for too long at a time (that repetitive-use issue). I notice that sometimes I feel a little naked without the splints on.

We returned home on Wednesday, and gratefully settled back into our monastic prayer and work schedule. We no longer have to be on "survival mode," just getting by on the strength of one Sister.

Sister Alegría helped me look more deeply at some of the issues about why I might have held on to the pain so long and the self-absorption of that. We both want me to come out of this a better person, learning all I can from the experience, and maturing personally and spiritually. I hope that I am able to be more compassionate and caring (having now experienced suffering), more alert to ego traps, and more able to share love in all circumstances. That is, less self-centered and more attuned to God and others. God is great! How could I ever doubt?

2011 End-of-Year Financial Report
From: Sister Alegría   Date: April 16, 2012

EXPENSES	
Provisions	$425
Household	230
Communication	203
Health	494
Clothing	28
Transportation	68
Library	29
Taxes	3
Robbery	30
Total cost of living	$1,510
Alms	$6,859
TOTAL EXPENSES	$8,369

INCOME	
Donations	
-General	$5,075
- Alms	3,180
Book Income	752
Earnings	2
TOTAL INCOME	$9,009

We have a lot of good news: donations received—up; cost of living—a little down; and lots more money spent on needed medicines for Centro de Salud in *Limón* and Clínica Metodista in El Pino.

We had a few milestones in the spiritual practice of money management this year. For the first time ever (in September), we bought medicines knowing that the remainder was not enough to live on. God came through, of course, in the form of friends and neighbors giving us food—lots of food and a wide variety.

The second milestone was asking for and receiving credit at a local store and in medicine purchasing (in November). I really noticed how much I hated to ask for credit at the local store. Still lots of worldly pride.

Thirdly, the amount of money that went out as alms was far higher than any past year, and more than four times what was spent on Monastery expenses. We celebrate.

A few notes:

- Transportation: This is only for overnight trips. Bus fare (or car fare) to Limón and Bonito come under Household expenses. Two stories:

  In September, we needed to go to Bonito and decided that we should do that without paying at all (the usual bus fare for us both ways would be $8 total). We walked to the highway and watched a bus pass (that was hard!), then hitched a ride. When it was time to come home, we walked the half mile from downtown Bonito to the gas station where hitching rides is usually pretty easy.

  We approached the first car. Yes, they were going in our direction, but there was the bus right in front of us! Wouldn't it be more comfortable to ride the bus? "But we're in a tight spot financially," I say.

  "OK, climb up." A few minutes later, one of the guys tells us to get into the bus; they paid the fare.

  In December, we had to pay the medicine bill (purchased in November). We were both pretty sick that day—a nasty virus that we had brought home from the clinic—but we had to pay the bill. We walked to the end of the path and waited. Don Julio pulled up soon and dropped us off at the bank in Bonito. We made a date for him to pick us up for the same door-to-door service going home. Our travelling cost $15 that day. There was money to pay it and we kept our word.

- Robbery: The robbery was in June. Life is a university; you have to pay your tuition.

- Income: We received more money in donations this year than before. Of that, $752 was "sort of" earnings—Rosalie Grafe, our publisher, refused to accept earnings from the Amigas book (published in December, 2010), sending it on to us. It went into the Alms Fund. We think the book spurred more donations, too. But we can't exactly publish a book every year, now can we?

Thank you for your support!

Immunization Campaign

From: Sister Alegría   Date: May 7, 2012

We just finished. This was the every four years BIG campaign. Every child under 5 gets an extra dose of oral polio vaccine and all children 1 to 4 get a measles and rubella booster. This is also the usual time of year to clean up all the backlog of missed immunizations. Frankly, I have been dreading this campaign since its 2008 predecessor.

After our last outreach clinic last year, I reminded Juana Nidia that I am of the third age. I also asked her to notice that I work longer and harder than anyone else on these outreach clinics. There are usually multiple nurses immunizing with one doctor giving consults. A nurse sometimes steps in to help me after all of the immunizations are done. Often I am still working after they have already eaten their lunch. Riding in very uncomfortable positions is hard on me, too, as it is on all of us. She listened to all of this. I get exhausted from outreach clinics. I've told you before, but I hadn't told her.

Monday, April 23

Most of the nurses went out to neighborhoods to immunize. Juana Nidia, Sister Confianza and I ran the clinic. I gave 51 consults. Juana Nidia gave injections as prescribed and immunized. Hermana Confianza checked people in and dispensed medicines. Then Hermana Confianza and I packed the traveling pharmacy. By then the nurses were returning and checking in with Juana Nidia. We prepared medicines for La Fortuna, then reinforcement meds for the second week—separately. Made a list of the needed medicines that would arrive later that evening.

We finished our work and left the clinic at 5:30 pm. One of the grocery shops was still open so we could buy provisions. Our dear friend, Alex, gave us a lift to our road. We walked the last half hour in full dark, a little tired but well satisfied with our work and our endurance.

Thursday, April 26

To La Fortuna. We took the cat with us to the road since he was due for his rabies shot. As we were waiting, along came Don

Chepe on his motorcycle. He stopped to chat. When he heard about the day's plans, he said, "I'll call Wendy (his adult daughter) to make you a nice soup." Soup, by the way, is a special meal here because it is based on meat. Meat containing meals are just not very common. If you've never eaten soup made from homegrown, free-run chickens, you have missed out on a treat. Then off he went.

We got the poor cat immunized and off we went (with a seat for me in the cab in honor of my advanced age).

Very organized project. This is unusual. A post for rabies shots (dogs and cats) near the gate of the school yard. A post for the three nurses for immunization of children. A post for Hermana Confianza to check in patients and do pharmacy. A post for me to give consults.

The school students, various volunteers, the nurses that felt energetic, and Sister Confianza carried the heavy wooden tables and benches from the school rooms to the yard—even a long string of benches for the folks waiting for consults.

We dived in. After a few hours, Juana Nidia started giving consults, too. I gave 65 and she gave 34. We had huge shade trees and occasionally a light breeze. The nice soup showed up as promised, delicious and plentiful.

Wornita came to help Hermana Confianza in the pharmacy when she was trying to keep up with two prescribers. We were done by 2:10. Home just after 3. It was a lovely day.

<u>Wednesday, May 2</u>

Our next assignment was Nueva Esperanza, twin town to Plan de Flores. We showed up at Chito's house at 6:15 am (quickly got lifts with fast drivers)—an hour early. Chito wouldn't be our driver after all. The mayor came through and would provide a car and driver.

We hung out for a while at Chito and Rosa's, drinking hot milk with sugar (with coffee for Hermana Confianza). I gave Rosa an injection she needed. We admired her baby chicks.

We rode to Nueva Esperanza in the back of the pickup. The school yard had little shade, but we set up as well as we could. When I had done about 70 consults, I looked up and saw the nurses relaxing in the shade. I asked for help. I gave 76 consults that day. Juan Nidia gave seven.

Back to Centro de Salud (riding in the cab this time, I taught the nurses about high blood pressure). The nurses did their paperwork; Hermana Confianza and I re-organized the pharmacy for the next day. Juana Nidia let me use the internet to study my long distance consultants.   Teachings on adult cardiology.   Sister Confianza shared the cold flour tortillas and soft cheese that we had made the day before. That was our dinner that night. Juana Nidia hosted us at her house. (We gave her five brown eggs from our hen as a hostess gift.) She stayed up until 12:30 doing paperwork. I am grateful not to have her job.

Thursday, May 3

Gave a few unofficial consults at Centro de Salud before we left for Plan de Flores. I rode in the cab this time. I gave 73 consults that day and Juana Nidia 17.

I measured blood pressure on all of the adult patients. During the campaign, I picked up six people with high blood pressure who didn't know it. Half, when pushed on the subject, admitted to having received treatment for it in the past. The others—completely new. Very sobering. Taking blood pressure on every adult is not routine.

Each day a meal showed up for me at my work space (at about noon, I suppose) and for Hermana Confianza, of course; I don't know about the auxiliary nurses. I just shoveled it in as fast as I could. Yes, I ate in front of my waiting patients, many of whom were probably also hungry. Then I went back to giving consults. I could do this huge volume because on outreach clinics we don't do proper medical records. I also didn't wash hands between patients. I just focused on the patient in front of me—a murder could have taken place ten feet away and I wouldn't have noticed.

Chito drove us back, dropping Hermana Confianza and me at Doña Eva's house (his mother-in-law). We had Benadryl to give Don Clemente, her live-in partner of 50-plus years. We joked for a while, then climbed the hill to Rosa's place. I had promised to give her another injection that day. I did. She had promised to give us some homemade cheese. She did.

She also gave us several *chatas* to take home. We chatted longer than we had realized, but it didn't matter. We got rides and were home well before dark.

We sailed through this campaign. We are healthy and strong. I am grateful for the concessions to my age and limitations. We even got our pineapple patches weeded! I won't dread the 2016 campaign.

This week, the nurses are still on mop-up duty, but our duties are back to normal.

Sister Alegría splits firewood, 2016

Bad News
From: Sister Alegría   Date: June 4, 2012

Our faithful support from Sellwood United Methodist Church will be no more after the end of June, when it closes. In spite of falling membership, it hung in there with us, providing the service of receiving and sending on tax-deductible donations to the Monastery. They pray for us every Sunday in their worship service. Sellwood has been with me from the start of my Honduran mission trips in 1999. I have many fond memories of the folks there. Sellwood has been a blessing to me for 26 years, a blessing to the Monastery for these years and a blessing for several thousand poor Hondurans who have never heard of Sellwood.

On the practical end of things, we do not have another church or 501(c)3 group standing in the wings ready to take over. We're open to suggestion. We'll keep you up to date.

Right now we have money. We'll be able to buy medicines at the end of the month. We have bought corn and beans in bulk from Don Julio. We have a laying hen.

Our Master forbids us to worry about tomorrow, so we don't. As our old friend, Teresa of Avila, says, "If God wants us to eat, God will send us food." And if God wants us to have money, God will send us money. By definition, therefore, we always have enough—the amount God prescribes. Life is so interesting. We just wonder what God is up to next.

Sister Confianza picks wild berries and *nance* fruits, 2013

Chickens eating from a termite nest, 2016

11

Raising Chickens

"¡Jesús nació! Jesus is born!"—every Honduran rooster

Chickens!
From: Sister Confianza   Date: June 4, 2012

That's right, we have chickens! Here's a timeline to tell the story. Below that, a list of advices we have received from friends and neighbors here in Honduras. Which ones do you think are worth following?

Timeline:
- October, 2011—Sister Alegría and I gather advice and recommendations from our friends about raising chickens, and we feel ready to start. We think three hens would be a good number, and start making it known that we are ready to purchase young birds.
- January 9, 2012—Nurse Wornita gives us a pair of golden three-month-old chickens and a few pounds of corn to feed them. We have them roost in a tree by the house. I'm impressed by all the interesting sounds they make; actual clucking is rather rare.
- Jan. 16—During the night, the young rooster is nabbed by a possum. We saw it, but didn't realize it was a predator!
- Jan. 17—We set up a perch in the outhouse, with a sheet of plastic under it to catch the droppings, and close the hen in there at night.
- February 17—We buy a *quintal* (100 pounds) of corn at a low price from Don Julio of La Fortuna. It is also low quality. We give more than half to friends for their chickens, and toast and grind some to make *pinol* porridge for ourselves, besides feeding the chickens.

Sister Confianza carries 40 lbs of corn to the Monastery, 2013

- Feb. 27—We go to La Ceiba and neighbor Javier takes the hen to his house. After two weeks he brings her back, assuring us she is ready to lay: *"El gallo la ha machucado."* "The rooster has mashed her."
- March 17—The hen acts agitated. We set up a nest (a small cardboard box lined with a sack) with an egg in it under a bench next to the front door.
- Mar. 18—The hen lays her first egg, and lays one a day (minus two) for 24 days.
- Mar 19—We give the first egg to María Elena, one of Sor Leonarda's helpers at the orphanage. We enjoy eating the others ourselves.
- Mar. 19—Doña Eva gives us a three-month-old black hen.

- Mar. 21—Javier's partner Reina gives us a two-month-old black-and-white speckled hen. It is interesting to watch them all interact, scratch for bugs, and preen.
- Mar. 24—I make a more "natural" nest using a circle of rocks filled with dry grass. The hen rejects it, breaks the egg that I put in it, and finds a spot under a bush to lay. I put the sack back and hollow out an egg to use as a decoy next time.
- April 10—The big hen gets *culeca* (broody), sits in the nest most of the day, and won't lay.
- Apr. 18—The hen lays an egg again, and continues through number 34.
- May 1—Hen gets broody again, this time for two weeks. On Javier's advice, we finally take away the nest so she can't sit in it. She soon returns to normal behavior.
- May 11—We buy another *quintal* of corn from Don Julio, this time of good quality from the new harvest, at a higher price.
- May 15—We sell an *arroba* (25 pounds) of corn to Javier and Reina for their chickens.
- May 21—Friend Wendy from La Fortuna gives us a sandy-gray (ostrich-colored) hooded hen and a red-and-black rooster, both about three months old.
- May 23—The golden hen lays again.
- May 25—The hollowed-out egg gets broken, and the hen doesn't lay.
- May 26—Friends Margarita, Mateo, and daughter Delmys come over and place a sheet-metal barrier around the trunk of a tree to keep possums from climbing it. However, the long pole they set up is too slippery for the chickens to climb into the tree branches. They continue sleeping in the outhouse, making their stinky mess that we have to clean up every morning.
- May 28—At dawn, the little rooster crows for the first time.
- May 28—The big hen is such a bully to the smaller ones (and to the cat!) that we are ready to make her into soup. Wornita convinces us to give her more time as the others grow, and gives us a young rooster to make our soup with instead. We butcher the bird all on our own—a first for either of us! The other chickens and the cat eat up the bones and other leftover bits.
- May 29—We find that the hen has laid three eggs in the brush. With a new decoy, she begins laying in the nest again.
- May 30—We cut a new pole and put notches in it, and the chickens are able to climb into the tree in the evening. The

big hen makes sure she gets to roost higher up in the tree than the others. In the morning, they all fly down.

- June 4—We decide to try selling a few eggs. Our friend misunderstands and accepts them as a gift, giving us some *pan de coco* (coconut bread) in return.

And so the saga continues...

Tips and Advices we've received on raising chickens

1. If you can raise chickens you should. You'll come out ahead economically.
2. It's good to have chickens—to keep you ladies from getting bored.
3. You should have a rooster so he can sing *"¡Jesús nació!"* ("Jesus is born!") every morning.
4. Feed the chickens in the morning and at night.
5. You can't go wrong with corn.
6. They will eat chopped-up *yuca* if there isn't corn.
7. Feed ground corn to the chicks.
8. Give rice to the chicks. Ground corn can make them swell up and die.
9. Chop up a termite nest to feed the chickens.
10. Termites are the best food for chicks.
11. Pluck out a young hen's tail feathers so she will develop well and grow big. (Don't do it after she starts laying eggs.)
12. Place a notched piece of wood as a ladder to the tree where the chickens roost.
13. Have a dog who will bark in the night and scare away predators.
14. Secure a piece of sheet metal around the tree trunk so the predators can't climb up.
15. If the roosting branch is too high, and a laying hen jumps off and lands hard on the ground, the egg inside her might break. She won't be able to lay, the eggs will build up, and then she will die.
16. Don't have the chickens sleep in a very enclosed space; they'll get the plague.
17. A hen will start laying at six months of age.
18. Make a nest by putting a sack in a corner or in a box.
19. Put an egg in the empty nest so the hen will know where to lay.
20. You need a rooster so the hens will lay.
21. The hens begin to lay at a younger age if there's a rooster.
22. If the hen is broody and you don't want her to set, tie her up for a few days. Try bathing her in water.

23. If the hen is broody and you want her to set, get fertilized eggs from other people.
24. Place a nail or old file under the nest to protect the unhatched chicks from thunder.
25. For success in raising chickens—to have a healthy flock—dedicate the *primicias* (first fruits) to God: Give the first-hatched chicken to a servant of God. (This came from a pastor.)
26. *Pollo es el plato favorito del tacuacín.* Chicken is the possum's favorite dish.
27. Weasels may come and kill partly-grown chicks, eating only the head.
28. If the chickens get intestinal worms, give them saltwater to drink. They will get diarrhea and excrete the worms.

Are you ready to raise chickens yet?

Three Days of Retreat and Fasting
From: Sister Confianza   Date: July 9, 2012

Ever since we learned that the little Evangelical church in Limoncito has a retreat with fasting the last three days of each month, I've been wanting to participate; I relish every chance we get to worship and pray with local congregations. When we discovered that the June retreat would start on a Thursday, our regular day for fasting and extra spiritual practice, it seemed like the perfect opportunity. With numerous stresses in our life, we could use extra prayer and fasting.

Limoncito is over an hour's hilly hike from the Monastery. One option would be to spend the night there; Mateo and Margarita have hosted us before. However, our place is in the Monastery; we ought to be on location as much as possible. Besides, we have chickens to feed and put to bed at night, and a cat too. We have been feeling physically very strong, and we know God always takes care of us. We decide to just go for it, walking to Limoncito and back each day.

Thursday, June 28
We get up just before sunrise and sing *"Me levanto hoy con el sol en mi alma"* ("I woke up this morning with the sun in my heart") instead of having our usual program for Lauds. We should get to Limoncito by the 6 am start time. We walk in silence to center ourselves, sometimes singing, but not chatting.

Walking the path from the Monastery to the road at dawn, 2012

When we arrive at Margarita and Mateo's house, we find Margarita outside doing chores. Are we early? No. It's already 6:30. At the worship service the night before, the pastor had announced that the retreat would be postponed one day.

Sister Alegría and I look at each other. What should we do? This is our fast day; we've dedicated these three days to retreat. We return to the Monastery and do familiar spiritual practices there.

We have a lovely day with shared readings, music, Unprogrammed Worship, and individual prayer time. At 3 pm we break our fast with watermelon, and then fix beef stew for supper! (Margarita felt so bad that we had walked all the way to town that she sent us home with fixings for dinner.)

Friday, June 29

We get up earlier than on Thursday to achieve a 6 am arrival. When we get there, no one is even up yet, so we rest—Sister Alegría in a hammock and me on a bench. When Margarita is ready the three of us walk to the church next door. She has the key and opens up. I'm not quite sure what to expect. We sit on a bench for some time, occasionally singing a chorus. Over the next hour or so a few other people show up: Mateo, a woman named Lidia, and the pastor, Baudilio. They each kneel at the step at the front of the sanctuary to pray—sometimes audibly, sometimes in silence—and we join them.

Finally, *Hermano* (Brother) Baudilio pulls up a small lectern and begins his teaching. His theme is the New Birth—what it means to be born again, and what the "new man" looks like. He says that if we have "put on Christ" then we should be filled with love and joy, and it will show in our actions.

Brother Baudilio is a good storyteller, and does a lot of dramatization. At one point he expounds on Jesus' teaching that "You have heard it said, 'an eye for an eye and a tooth for a tooth,' but I tell you, love your enemies and pray for those who persecute you." What does that look like?

"Hermana Alegría," Brother Baudilio says. "Hermano Mateo here is your brother. I come over and beat him up—" and he mimics punching Mateo.

"Oh! Oh!" exclaims Sister Alegría.

"I am your enemy, but now I come to you in need." He walks up to Sister Alegría, crouches over, and looks up pitifully with his hands cupped. *"¿Comida?* Food?" Sister Alegría mimes handing him something.

"We must forgive our enemies and give to them when they ask, "Brother Baudilio concludes.

At noon we have a stretch and bathroom break, and then Brother Baudilio continues till about 1:30. "I prefer to go from six to six," he says, looking at Sister Alegría and me, "but since you have such a long walk, we'll stop early today." We are grateful; we'd been told they usually end around 2 or 3 pm.

"Does that mean you'll start at 6 am tomorrow? "Sister Alegría asks. Brother Baudilio just smiles.

To close, the six of us stand in a circle and all pray aloud simultaneously. Then Brother Baudilio invites Sister Alegría and me to share something, and we sing *"Benditos son,"* our translation of "Blest are They." The others hum along.

Margarita's son and daughter-in-law have prepared a soup for us to break our fast: chicken noodle with potatoes. Then Mateo graciously drives us back to the Monastery. We have a relatively relaxed afternoon. We bathe, then wash the day's clothes. We don't have to cook dinner—there are ripe bananas and leftover toasted corn tortillas and cheese from the day before. We do our regular Weekly Review, have Compline, and go to bed promptly; it was hard work to listen well in Spanish all day.

<u>Saturday, June 30</u>

We don't get up quite as early today, but still arrive before the church is opened. We happily rest in the hammocks under the bougainvillea until Margarita is ready; Sister Alegría has a tummy ache.

I'm feeling more comfortable about what to expect today, so when we enter the church, I go to the front step and kneel to pray aloud with the others. I am more accustomed to praying in silence, so this is a good practice in letting myself go without being self-conscious.

The same five participants are there again, plus Domitila, Margarita's mother. Brother Baudilio won't be leading the retreat today; he's been called to attend a conference in La Ceiba. When we are all gathered, Sister Alegría says, "Sisters and Brother, I have something to share with you today." Ah, now I understand the tummy ache; she is carrying a burden.

She continues, "I'm sorry Hermano Baudilio isn't here today. I don't want to be teaching against him, but I regret that I participated in yesterday's drama where I gave food to the man who beat up my brother." Sister Alegría goes on to recount the robbery of 2007, when the two of us returned to the Monastery after an exhausting trip to find the house open and robbers nearby. They were in the process of taking things from the house, but when we arrived had a new idea: one of the young men pulled me aside and said he wanted to "make love" to me. Another started closing the doors and windows, and Sister Alegría followed behind opening them back up until the oldest put his arm around her neck and a .38 to her head.

We were saved when Chito, who had dropped us off, returned to the house and shouted. The three young men ran off. The police were called, came out in a borrowed pickup, and looked over the scene. They fired a shot in the air before leaving.

We spent the night at our friend Gloria's house in Limón, and the next day made an official report to the police. To press charges, we would have to do our own investigation and bring the names of the perpetrators to the Justice of the Peace.

Gradually, we were able to gather that information: two of the young men were brothers from La Fortuna, and the third was their cousin from Limón. However, almost everyone who told us anything said, "but you didn't hear it from me." Only one friend, a woman pastor from La Fortuna, confirmed information without a caveat. Potential witnesses were clear that they wouldn't testify, or would only share limited information.

At the same time, we were doing a Spiritual Formation course on forgiveness. Sister Alegría and I decided that we would not press charges; we just prayed a lot for the boys (who were falling fast) and their families. About a year later, the young man who had brandished the revolver killed someone, and some months after that his father and brother were killed in revenge.

The retreat participants have been listening quietly, sometimes nodding, as they are familiar with the characters in this local tale. At this point, though, Sister Alegría socks it to 'em: "Because we decided not to prosecute the robbers, people were killed. In yesterday's drama, I wish that, while my 'enemy' was eating, I had called the police. I think we Christians have become supporters of violence when we do not report or testify about crimes. We piously say, 'Oh no, I don't want to seek vengeance,' and leave the perpetrator free to harm others."

One retreatant defends the drama: "Brother Baudilio was saying that we should love our enemies."

"Yes," I respond, "but what does it mean to love them? It isn't to let them continue their bad behavior. It is to help them see what they have done so they can change."

"It is time, "Sister Alegría says, "for us Christians to take the side of the victims, and support them in their search for justice. That means reporting crimes and being willing to be witnesses. Honduras has a system where the witness can be behind a screen and use voice-altering technology for anonymity."

She tells about the Honduran *Asociación para una Sociedad más Justa* (Association for a More Just Society) which works in crime-ridden neighborhoods in Tegucigalpa and San Pedro Sula, walking alongside and advocating for victims as well as encouraging the police and other officials to do their job of enforcing justice. Crime has gone down significantly in those neighborhoods.

Sister Alegría has finished her story, her exhortation on what she figured was an unpopular issue. Her tummy ache disappears.

Raising Chickens

The group spends the rest of the retreat day singing choruses and hymns for and with one another, as well as chatting casually and praying some more. We again finish around 1:30. Margarita's family serves Sister Alegría and me a small meal before we walk back to the Monastery. We stop at a little store and buy cupcakes, and the storekeeper gives us small bottles of juice for the road. When we get home, we cook ourselves a nice big dinner.

I have to admit, we're pretty pleased to have been able to do it—three days in a row of fasting with long walks. We fully appreciated our day of rest on Sunday!

A Mysterious Death
From: Sister Alegría   Date: July 18, 2012

It seemed like an ordinary week. We wanted an ordinary week, the constant returning to God. It's very good stuff, this contemplative life.

Monday—ordinary.

Tuesday—ordinary.

So far, so good.

Wednesday morning at Lauds, Sister Confianza noticed only four chickens wandering around. Later, she found the black hen dead under the roosting tree. She had been dead for a while—stiff. The only sign of trauma was blood on her feet: one foot with a small cut. She had acted normal just the afternoon before. We were mystified. We buried her in the back yard.

Thursday night, the littlest chicken got spooked (she is a timid little thing) and refused to go roost in the tree. She even hid in the little protective plastic box (for the cat on rainy days). Sister Confianza picked her up and put her in the *sanitario* (outhouse). I put the plastic tarp in place to catch the droppings.

Friday morning at Lauds, Sister Confianza noticed three chickens wandering around. We found the big hen hunkered down beside the house, her comb very pale, blood on one foot and acting sickly.

By the way, we've heard two new bits of chicken lore:
1. When the chicken is ready to start laying eggs her comb turns bright red.
2. Black chickens are good for witchcraft.

We saw no sign of witchcraft (as if we could recognize it) near the dead black hen. Her comb had been bright red, but no eggs yet.

The data about combs is what had us really notice the paleness of the big hen.

Back to the narrative: By afternoon, the hen was acting more normal. We decided to put them all in the *sanitario* at night until further notice. The big one and the little one entered willingly. The rooster and the *"empedrada"*(pebbled) chicken took a little herding.

The hen seems to be recovering well, but she's not laying eggs.

Javier, our neighbor, says it was probably a vampire bat. Doña Eva, our friend who gave us the black chicken, says it was probably a snake.

What do you think?

New Sponsoring Church
From: Sister Alegría   Date: July 23, 2012

You're wondering about our precarious situation—that is, without a sponsoring church. We wondered, too.

A lot has happened since I wrote about that. I'll skip the low dark valleys and the high sunny peaks.

When Randy (the erstwhile treasurer at Sellwood UMC) mentioned the idea to the church where he will become a member, the pastor and treasurer responded with enthusiasm. Our new sponsoring church is Oak Grove United Methodist Church in Greater Portland.

We're actually a bit nervous. It is sort of like entering into an arranged marriage.

Many people came through with donations during that time when it looked like the opportunity would end. We are very grateful to you and for you. We're running behind on thank you notes.

By the way, when Sellwood closed, it had an endowment fund to deal with. The members decided to send us $50,000. It will be available in August. Do you remember our financial report for 2011? We spent just over $8,000 in the entire year. We have some homework to do to decide how to best use this money. Please pray for us to receive Divine guidance.

This is a challenging time for us. Some of our most important counsels come from the "Q source"—the teachings of Jesus of Nazareth. One of the very comforting teachings for me in these last six years has been (my version): "When everyone is criticizing you, you're probably doing the right thing." Remember how Jeremiah was treated? He's one of my heroes.

Now the criticism (overt and covert) has fallen off. Hmm. Does that mean that we're no longer doing the right thing? This being faithful can be pretty tricky. Pray for us, that we stay faithful.

Prosperity generally destroys faithfulness. Whether approval or material prosperity, it always seems like a little more would be a little better.

Babies, Babies, and an Ambulance
From: Sister Confianza   Date: August 16, 2012

July was a month with babies on the mind. It actually started back in June, when we stopped by Margarita and Mateo's house in Limoncito and discovered that their younger daughter (age seventeen) had just given birth to her first child, a daughter. They'd had trouble at the hospital when Ledy's blood pressure went sky-high and then plummeted in response to treatment. She ended up having a C-section. Sister Alegría was concerned about mom and baby's health at first, but they have recovered well.

In mid-July, Javier came by and invited us to their place. He and Reina had just returned to Jonathan's property (bordering the Monastery's) which they care for after she gave birth at their home in Lauda on July 1. I got to hold their second son, as yet unnamed. Reina was looking pale, and it seemed to us awfully soon to return to fulltime housewife work. About a week later they left without notice, so we had them in our prayers. We've just learned from Javier's mom, Suyapa, that they are fine. (Suyapa, her partner, and their two sons recently moved to the house we can see from our porch on Dimas' property to the south.)

Through the internet we heard good news of a healthy second daughter born to Allison and Larry, our missionary friends near La Ceiba.

We celebrated new birth with our Christmas-in-July one-day retreat. My baby connections continued when I got to hold newborns at Centro de Salud on several different Mondays. That doesn't happen too often.

The first week in August we had an urgent situation at Centro de Salud with a baby in for its 40-day checkup. He was not being well-fed or well-bathed by his mother, and Sister Alegría was concerned that he would die if left in his mother's unaided hands. She informed me we would travel to Tocoa to make sure the mom and baby were admitted to the hospital, so mom could learn to care for him (it worked so well for Deiber and his mom two years ago).

Trouble was, Mom didn't have money to go, nor someone to care for her other children. Nurse Wornita talked with Mom till they could come up with a childcare solution. Thankfully, Dad could get off work for the emergency.

Reina, Javier, and their two sons, 2013

Just then a woman with a snakebite arrived at Centro de Salud. Since it was not known whether the snake was poisonous or not, we all decided to go with prudence and send her to the hospital, along with the dead snake for identification.

As it turned out, she could afford to pay the local ambulance to go to the hospital. Yes, Limón now has an ambulance donated by Spain. It is an SUV retrofitted with a gurney and all the equipment. It had been announced in town that the service was free, but, of course, there is no budget for it, so families have to pay 600 lempiras (about $32, or several day's wages for a laborer) for fuel and the driver. There are no medical professionals to accompany the patients, and who knows what they'll do when the equipment wears out or the oxygen tank gets drained, but for now, it is a resource that is being used regularly.

Sister Alegría and I were assured that the mom and baby could go along in the ambulance without having to pay, and gave them a little cash for the bus fare coming home. We were glad to not have to make the trip ourselves.

Passports
From: Sister Alegría   Date: August 16, 2012

We spent yesterday in San Pedro Sula. The purpose was to renew our passports. The short version is "mission accomplished." The long version is too long.

We really enjoyed our day in the city. We bought stamps and mailed letters at the post office. We bought and ate tiny soft-serve ice cream cones. We bought a Spanish book of "all the gospels." There is in Spain, apparently, sort of a "Jesus seminar," and we bought their book—$50. Gag. We had imagined getting such a book, and were delighted to learn that it exists (and we had the money to buy it). We also found a book about nuns in Argentina, *Mujeres de Dios*. I can hardly wait to start reading it.

We splurged with a big lunch at a Chinese restaurant— chicken and broccoli over rice.

The consul was only open in the afternoon. We were amazed at how many people were waiting. We had imagined a one-person office, since the same man always answered the phone. There were four people: the armed guard/doorman, two people processing paperwork and one who arranges for the delivery of the new passports.

We are now without passports until the new ones come. We paid $75 each to have them delivered to Bonito. We weren't expecting that. We took the last bus out of town and arrived back at El Pino about 8:30 pm.

Time to run.

Saga of the Sombreros
From: Sister Alegría   Date: August 27, 2012

Usually a monastery or a religious order is founded by a person or persons with years of experience (for example, the Teresas). Well, we didn't have anyone like that.

The founding and maturing of a monastery has lots of big and little challenges. Hats make a pretty good example.

We arrived in Honduras in 2006, each with a sun hat. There was never a consideration of NOT having sun hats. Mine was a classic Tilley hat. Sister Confianza's was a green foldable hat. We talked once in a while about what we should do about this lack of uniformity. Just talk. There were lots of more important decisions to be made.

One day in 2007, Sister Confianza was facing toward the rear as we were going to Bonito in the back of a pickup. The wind grabbed her hat. (The chinstrap was useless facing away from the breeze.) End of green hat.

We found a nice generic straw hat near the bus station in Tocoa ($5). We liked it and sewed strings on it.

We still didn't match, and we talked. My Tilley hat was obviously years from wearing out—and it's obviously a style not available here. One day we were visiting Fela. She held my hat, looked at it wistfully and said, "I would really like to have a hat like this."

Instant clarity. The Tilley hat had to go. The next trip to the city we bought me a generic straw hat—same shop, same price. I gave my hat to a beggar in La Ceiba (it was not Fela's size).

The hats weren't identical. Mine was fairly rainproof. Sister Confianza's drooped in the rain. It drooped and frayed—more and more. She stopped wearing it on rainy days. Finally we decided we should replace it (August, 2011). We learned that it was not a "generic straw hat"—it was a fashion statement that had now passed! We couldn't find a new one.

We talked about a handmade hat. There used to be a guy in Limón who made them, but he died. Then there were the *buscanovia* (look-for-a-girlfriend) hats; also part of the past, not the present.

Sister Confianza cut out a cardboard visor, with an extension fold-up inside the crown. This allowed her to see and get some sun protection. NO ONE ever made a remark about this look.

We kept looking. In February, we found a perky (brim turns up and is not as wide) straw hat in a hole-in-the-wall place at the La Ceiba bus station. $5.

That same trip, we had received a lift from our friend Wendy. We rode in the cab and I forgot my hat in the truck!

She returned it two weeks later. It had been pretty dirty and she had had her hired woman wash it. It drooped and was frayed. Now I was the one who couldn't see. We were told that new hats would be available during Holy Week. Yeah, right—if you want hot pink! So I adjusted to my droopy hat.

Sisters Confianza and Alegría purchase groceries at Noemí's store in Limón, 2012

On our way home from San Pedro Sula this month, we found a perky straw hat similar to Hermana Confianza's in the very same shop in Tocoa where we'd bought the original ones! $6.25. This time mine is the one with the coarser weave. We sort of match. So that's where we are now. The habit definitely includes a straw hat when we're out in the sun, and we remember to not worry about tomorrow.

Counting the Days
From: Sister Alegría   Date: September 6, 2012

Our second hen began laying eggs. We are so pleased. Very soon, the golden hen got broody again. We started saving eggs. When we had ten, we consulted our neighbor. She assured us that we didn't have to wait for the traditional fifteen before letting the hen incubate the eggs. She also gave us goat's milk to drink—freshly boiled and with sugar, very good. Neither of us had ever tasted goat's milk before.

That was yesterday morning. In the afternoon, we completed all of her detailed instructions and put the hen on the eleven eggs (yes, the other one had laid an egg that morning while we were gone).

It takes 21 days for eggs to hatch. We're counting. This is the acid test of whether our young rooster is fertile or not. A few of the eggs (that we opened before to eat) did demonstrate the spot that my mother taught me said the egg was fertilized.

Day Two and counting.

Donations
From: Sister Alegría   Date: September 24, 2012

We have been able to start using the Endowment Fund money we received from Sellwood UMC. I like to think that the folks who donated it (most of whom are now dead) would be pleased with how it is being used.

Becas con Bendiciones (Scholarships with Blessings <www.becasconbendiciones.com>) provides uniforms, shoes, school supplies, vitamins, worm medicine and adult mentorship to poor kids so that they can attend public school. There is also a great end-of-school-year party. Usually if a child needs glasses or something similar, that can be managed, too. This year 715 kids in at least eight communities in Honduras receive this help.

We learned about these scholarships because one of the communities that receive scholarships is Ceibita, a suburb of Tocoa, where we visit at least once a year. Delmys, one of the sisters at the *Iglesia Metodista Unida el Buen Samaritano* (Good Samaritan United Methodist Church) administers the Ceibita part of the program.

Fortunately for us, *Becas* uses the same Honduran bank that we do. We were able to transfer $3,000 from our account to theirs. Slick. (I'm sure you notice how rare "slick" is here in Honduras.)

Henry and Sara Clines founded and direct this program as a living memorial for their son. We met up with them last week at

289

Ceibita. They had hand carried a care package for us from the States and took a packet of letters to mail in the States.

We were so happy to meet up with Pastor Jesús, who kept us up until 8:30 at night! Remember, we had gotten up before 5:00 and had worked much of the day at Centro de Salud before hitching a ride to Tocoa. We were tired. We got to see Irma and Cándida, too. They all fed us, of course. Lots of news from there. If you want it, write specifically asking for it.

After our morning meetings, Henry and Sara gave us a ride to Tocoa, where we did a little shopping and caught our bus home. It was a very busy two days.

More Donations
From: Sister Confianza   Date: October 1, 2012

The same day we transferred money to the Clines' bank account for *Becas con Bendiciones*, we transferred $10,000 to Sor Leonarda. Those are undesignated funds to use as she sees fit in her work.

We have told you many stories about our friend and collaborator Sor Leonarda. She is a former nun (*Sor* is the formal title in Spanish for a religious Sister) who began laying the groundwork for an orphanage in Limón in the early 2000s, at the same time that Sister Alegría was coming here frequently to work at Centro de Salud and prepare for the founding of the Monastery.

Sor's organization, *Comunión H*, is a Honduran non-profit whose board of directors, she says, "keeps electing me president." Her focus is on helping the poor, particularly in the Garifuna community and those affected by HIV/AIDS. She helps individuals with money for medical care or food, and distributes clothes and school supplies to poor persons and communities. Sister Alegría emphasizes that Sor has saved numerous lives.

Her main work is running the *Casa Hogar*, a home for children, many of whom are AIDS orphans. Others come from *la calle* (the street), abusive homes, or families that cannot assure their wellbeing. She keeps children through age twelve or so at the orphanage in Limón. Older kids are sent to other specialized programs, while a few are in junior and senior high school in Tegucigalpa, living with families and still under Sor's supervision. All of the children are in her legal custody through the Honduran Department for Childhood and Family.

Sor Leonarda does not have a dependable source of money or support. Many of the mission teams from the US who come to Limón through the Carolina Honduras Health Foundation (the "gringo clinic" where Sister Alegría worked on her first trips to Limón collaborate with Sor. Almost all of these donations are designated to a specific purpose.)

Sister Alegría, Sor Leonarda, and Sister Confianza in the yard of the orphanage, 2013

Sor also receives many in-kind donations, from American, Honduran, and other sources. "If I'm not here, it means I'm out seeking," she once told us. She's come back with clothes, mattresses, cleaning supplies, and food.

The current location of the orphanage is in a concrete block building next to Centro de Salud. The fifty or so kids sleep dormitory-style in two big rooms: boys and girls. They've been threatened with eviction numerous times in the last couple of years. The owners/neighbors want Sor and the kids gone. A few months ago the owners decided to renovate the second story where Sor and others slept in tiny former hotel rooms. Her "office" space downstairs (a former grocery store) is now storage, piled high with all the goodies she's collected. More than once in a rainstorm everything got soaked.

Happily, one US couple decided to organize for a new building. Ken and Peggy Hook have been working with Sor for a couple of years to secure the land and funding. A US architect friend designed a first-class orphanage, and now an engineer from Tocoa and his crew are constructing the two-story building on what used to be our friend Gloria Lacayo's property next to the Junior High School.

Last Monday, September 24, I talked to Sor while Sister Alegría rested at Centro de Salud after a long morning. Sor had sent over the lunch she gives us every week: spaghetti with chicken. (She's been feeding us now for three years, always the same menu, though the recipe varies. We only buy meat on special occasions and never spaghetti.) I went to return the dishes and Sor came out to meet me with a radiant smile.

"Thank you both so much for that donation!" she gushed. "I looked at my bank book yesterday for the first time. I hadn't realized the quantity until then. When I saw it, I prayed, *¡Gracias, Jesús!* Thank you, Jesus!'"

"Yes, thank God," I replied. "And thanks to the church who entrusted us with the money."

"It really lifts a burden," she said. "Now I know we'll be OK. I don't have to worry about things for a while. I'm so happy!"

"Oh good," I smiled.

"We will invest it well," she assured me.

"Oh yes, we know. That's why we gave it to you."

Then Sor tells me about her weekend caring for the kids and doing all the cooking. She'd given Lupe, her regular helper and cook, time off to go visit her daughter and other girls in Tegus. "You know, I used to be white," Sor jokes, grinning and patting her cheeks. "But now, after this hard kitchen work, I'm brown!"

I laugh. "You're burnt!"

"With some of this money, I'll hire a helper for Lupe in the kitchen."

"What a good idea!" I respond. Honestly, we've thought she needs to hire several more helpers, but pretty much everything is on hold until the new building is finished.

"Can you give me the name of the church so I can write a thank-you letter?" Sor asks me.

"Well, the thing is," I say, "that the church closed. The money came from them divesting their endowment fund. But we stay in contact with the folks there. It's really a privilege for us to be able to be the channel to get this money to you."

"*Son enviadas.* You are envoys," she tells me.

Maybe we are. Sor Leonarda certainly is one.

Planting Pineapples
From: Sister Confianza

On September 25, 2012, Sister Alegría and I had a big work day and planted 55 pineapple starts, completing the *ronda*. In that calendar year, we planted over two hundred piñas in a large oval around the Monastery that defines the yard.

Sister Confianza clears the firebreak below the line of pineapples, 2016

Raising Chickens

The idea first came after the fire in July, 2011. Flames went down the east hillside toward the garden, but stopped at a row of pineapples—these plants with their spiky leaves are relatively fire resistant!

Another reason we decided to focus our efforts closer to the house was the continued discouragement with our garden. In 2010 we did a lot of work to clean up and thin out our pineapple patch in the garden. We even applied sulfur to combat the supposed heart rot fungus, but by the end of August we were convinced that, in fact, it was rhinoceros beetles damaging the plants: we arrived to find them eating fruits and even young blossoms. When fruits got close to being ripe, other animals—jay birds and rodents—pecked and chewed holes in green and ripening fruits.

Beginning in 2011, there was evidence of human theft as well: almost-ripe pineapples completely gone—and a few times, the crown had been planted nearby! We figured that by planting near the house, our regular presence would discourage others from helping themselves.

One day in May we went over to Elías' property. There was no caretaker living there, and the large pineapple patch that Martín had planted more than two years earlier was overgrown. Wearing our pants and rubber work boots, Sister Alegría and I climbed between the barbed wires of the fence to take a closer look.

Pineapples reproduce vegetatively. Each "eye" on the fruit starts out as a purple flower, but normally doesn't produce a seed. Instead, the plant makes sprouts or shoots. Some grow on the stalk right at the base of the fruit. Some grow from the base of the plant. These sprouts can be removed and planted in small holes. The larger the shoot, the sooner it will produce fruit. The crowns can also be planted. A base sprout may be left on the original plant and it will bear fruit the next year.

Sister Alegría and I discovered that Elías' pineapple plants had lots of shoots, so we helped ourselves to a number of them when there were several on a plant. We did the same thing in June and continued extending our *ronda* row to encircle the yard.

In August we finally ran into Elías in Limón and told him what we'd been doing. He gave us his blessing, and on Friday the 31st, we made a special trip to bring back 62 sprouts of all sizes—from seven inches to two feet long. We lay them out like a prize catch along the south side of the house where they could dry a bit before planting, as recommended by our ag books.

Satisfaction. In a couple of years we figured we should be harvesting lots of pineapples!

Annual Retreat
From: Sister Alegría   Date: October 22, 2012

The first week in October we had our Annual Retreat. We did something a little different this year.

Usually our guest leader (in the form of the written word) has been a European-born female Christian religious. This year, we used the writings of Eknath Easwaran, an East Indian (very ecumenical) Hindu, married man and university professor. We were able to buy his book <u>Climbing the Blue Mountain</u> in Spanish translation in August. It was returning to an old friend.

I recommend Easwaran for those struggling to overcome past injuries related to organized religion, for those committed to respect for other religions, and for those who may benefit from a reminder and encouragement with regard to the human-side responsibility in perfecting the God-human relationship.

It was a good retreat. We're now back to normal schedule.

A Self-Renewing Life
From: Sister Alegría

Contemplative monastic life should be self-renewing. We have friends who are rich (i.e. middle-class people who live in the US) who take vacations. They wonder about us and vacations. We don't take vacations. Gandhi, in his later years, said that he was always on vacation. He spent fifteen hours a day receiving supplicants and helping to manage the ashram where he lived.

There is a rhythm to monastic life. A daily rhythm, structured around prayer. A weekly rhythm, structured around Sunday, the day of rest; and our one day a week out in the community. A monthly rhythm: first Thursday, Meeting for Worship with Attention to Business; second Thursday, monthly day-long retreat; third Thursday, whatever clearness committee comes up; fourth Thursday, Music Committee. A yearly rhythm: Advent, Christmas, Epiphany, Ordinary Time, Lent, Holy Week, Easter, Pentecost, Ordinary Time. Our Annual Retreat is eight days in September each year. It is one of our renewing activities.

Storm? What Storm?

From: Sister Alegría   Date: October 26, 2012

Our water tank is now completely filled, thanks to lots of rain this week. Today, we are told it was a big-deal tropical storm. The big risk from tropical storms is flooding. We are above all that—quite literally.

We have lots of email catching up to do; that's why we're in town today.

Sister Confianza has a crummy tummy today, so I'm doing as much as I can.

The News

From: Sister Confianza   Date: November 16, 2012

There is a lot of news, but we haven't been able to use the internet in recent weeks to share it all with you. I guess I've already gotten accustomed to having more frequent access, now that there's a place to use internet in Limón. Today we've come in especially for this task. The last time we came in, I got sick and we couldn't do all we'd planned. This morning, the electricity was out briefly, so we'll just see what we'll be able to get done!

First, I just completed an eight-day retreat of continual prayer, beautifully prepared by Sister Alegría. It is in preparation for my Renewal of Profession next Thursday, November 22. I am excited to be making a three-year commitment to continue in this monastic life, deepening my relationship with the infinite loving God. I really feel I am where God wants me to be. Do keep us in your prayers.

Second: Chicks! We told you about putting the golden hen to set, but haven't had a chance to tell about the chicks. (One nice email I wrote about them got lost in Cyberspace.) The short version is, ten of the eleven eggs hatched on September 24 and now we're down to six chicks. They are fascinating for us first-time chicken-raisers to watch as they develop. They are already adolescents, with scraggly feathers coming in, and each one is a different color combination: yellow, brown, black, and speckled.

Besides the loss of chicks—one to a skunk that clawed its way through a termite-eaten board into the outhouse where the birds sleep—we were also saddened when an unseen predator nabbed the rooster in the middle of the day a few weeks ago. It is all being quite a learning experience for us!

The last big news is really quite awful: There was a murder near the road at the entrance to the Monastery. I actually heard the shots the night of Saturday, October 27, after Sister Alegría had gone to sleep. Gunshots aren't so unusual, but I could tell these were close, so I said a prayer for whoever might be involved. I didn't think more about it—except to tell Sister Alegría the next day—until we were coming home from Limón on Monday evening and noticed a bad smell and vultures hanging around the entrance to the Monastery path.

Two hens with chicks at the water dish, 2014

I was anxious until we could finally investigate in daylight Tuesday morning. We went close enough to recognize clothing, confirming that it was a human body and not an animal. We were able to notify the police through a neighbor who was going to town. The three National Police officers assigned to Limón, along with the brother of the deceased, eventually came to investigate around noon. They explained that Efraím Guevara, who is from *La Mosquitia* (The Mosquito Coast) but was working in Limón, had been kidnapped by a group of unidentified persons because he supposedly knew something about a robbery.

The police asked what I knew. I told them how I was up late reading Saturday night and heard a car coming up the road from the creek. It was a late hour for traffic and I didn't hear it continue much past our place. Then there were loud shots—about seven—and shortly, the sound of a car going back down.

"Was it a green truck?" one officer asked.

"I don't know; I didn't see it," I replied.

Satisfied, they took my name, Confianza del Señor (they didn't need my legal name), and left.

An hour later, a couple of women and a man walked up to the house. They were relatives and friends of Efraím, and wondered if we had any rubber gloves they could use to help lift the body and take it home. We didn't. We could only offer them some water to drink and our prayers.

Later in the week, Sister Alegría and I had a memorial service for Efraím. We prayed for his family, for the community affected by this violence, and for the healing of the Monastery land, that this might be a sanctuary of God's love.

What's really so awful is that this sort of thing is not terribly uncommon in Honduras. I recently read in the newspaper that the murder rate in our Department of Colón is about 140 per 100,000—higher than the national rate of 100 or so and much higher than the worldwide rate of eight. My sense is that because of the corrupt and ineffective police and justice system people take things into their own hands, knowing that they also are unlikely to be punished.

Let us all continue to pray and to work for peace in this world, our home.

Gun Control
From: Sister Alegría

In 2013, the government decided that things couldn't go on as they were. Colón had a high murder rate, the highest in the nation (for a basically rural area).

It became illegal in the Department of Colón to carry a gun in public places, in buses, even in your own car. It matters not if it is licensed. It will be confiscated. A pilot project.

Murders dropped from 307 per year to 207 per year in 2016. There is now consideration of extending the law to larger parts of the nation.

Honduras is no longer the murder capital of the world and Colón is no longer the murder capital of Honduras.

Renewal of Profession
From: Sister Confianza   Date: December 3, 2012

When I had the Clearness Committee about renewing my Profession, the question before me was" "Is there any reason I shouldn't make a three-year commitment at this time?" For the nearly seven years I've lived at Amigas del Señor, I've committed one year at a time to continue in this monastic life. According to custom, this was my first opportunity to make a longer commitment.

I couldn't find anything to keep me from doing so. Actually, I've been looking forward to it: the chance to be a little more settled, not continually questioning and discerning if I should keep sticking with it. I have the sense that I am where God wants me to be, doing what God wants me to do. There is a beautiful peace in that.

After these three years (which will make ten at the Monastery, longer than I've lived in any one place), I will have the opportunity to make a lifetime commitment or continue with temporary professions, as seems fit.

The day after my eight-day pre-Renewal retreat (which was the last time we were in Limón to use the internet), we visited our friends Margarita and Mateo in Limoncito and invited them to attend my Renewal of Profession. They said they would plan on it. It's the first time we've invited anyone to a special event since my Reception into the Novitiate in 2009. They are some of the people with whome we connect spiritually who respect our life. They are also more likely to keep their word than a lot of folks.

On Thursday, November 22, we anticipated their arrival in the afternoon; we had told them 2:00. I had a busy morning baking sweet bread while cooking breakfast and Sister Alegría washed the laundry. After the flurry of work we danced and played recorder together and then had Unprogrammed Worship.

It had been rainy all week, and off and on during the day. We knew the road was muddy—bad for driving—so it was quite possible that Margarita and Mateo wouldn't be able to make it. It crossed my mind that if for some reason they didn't come, it was because God had a reason for us to not be sharing these special occasions with others at this time, so I wasn't perturbed when they weren't there by mid-afternoon. We went ahead with our program: a joy-filled service with songs, scripture, and even anointing me with oil.

Then, just as we were singing our closing song, Mateo, Margarita, their daughter Delmys, and their granddaughter (the five-month-old baby of their daughter Ledy) showed up! Even though the formal program was over, we sang together and shared encouraging words in a brief worshipful time. Then we celebrated with sweet bread served with pineapple jam (made earlier in the week from Monastery-grown fruit) and punch. It was a lovely afternoon.

Thanks for all your thoughts and prayers.

Sister Alegría fills a gallon with drinking water from the tank, 2013

12

Preparing the Way

"Prepare the way of the Lord." –Isaiah

All in the Name of Progress

From: Sister Alegría   Date: December 3, 2012

The window, two-and-a-half by three feet, no glass, no screen, is the only source of light for my exam room. My desk is right below it, so I get the full effect of the chilling breeze this cold, rainy day. I don't feel cold; I'm working. But the patients suffer.

To my right is a twin size bed. I have the patients sit on it. To my left—a long high exam table. Between them, a two and a half foot wide aisle. At the end of the exam table is the door. At the end of the bed is a four-drawer cabinet. A temporary wall provides visual privacy.

There is one other exam room. Then there is the everything room: a small area for patients to wait, the microscope on a desk where Eliza does malaria tests, the nebulizers, the pharmacy shelves, a spot for immunizations, the shelves of medical charts, the treatment area. (How would you like to get your shot in front of everyone?) There is no running water in the building.

All of this is in the name of progress. The "real" clinic is closed to be repaired (the roof that has leaked since it was put up, the plumbing that never worked right, and more). We are hopeful. We are told it will take several months.

Related news: Doctora Diriam, the new government physician has arrived. She is charming and helpful. She has heard enough about me to approve of me sight unseen. This is a great relief! Her predecessor made it clear that I was on trial for several months. Dra. Diriam is our chief. I am grateful.

———

Preparing the Way

I wrote that a week ago. Today I see that the old clinic building has been razed to the ground. This is really beyond my expectations.

Summer Program Coming
From: Sister Alegría   Date: December 17, 2012

It will be intense. We'll open up the Monastery to as many as four women for seven weeks, June 25 to August 15, 2013.

You've read a lot about our life of prayer, poverty, and physical work. You may know someone who is ready for this kind of a challenge. Pass on the invitation.

Unlike the year-long stay, the summer women will pay their own way, a $500 fee and air fare to San Pedro Sula, Honduras.

Feliz Navidad
From: Sister Confianza   Date: December 21, 2012

"¡Gloria a Dios en las alturas y paz para todos en la tierra!"
"Glory to God in the highest and peace to all on earth!"

We joined the angel choir this year!

Enjoy this and other photos taken by Sasha Bosbeer in February on Flickr <www.flickr.com/photos/amigasdelsenor/>.

There are even songs we've written and translated, including several Christmas carols in English and/or Spanish.

We don't have any interesting Baby Jesus stories this year, although last week five women brought in their newborns to Centro de Salud for their seven-to-ten-day check-up. The *puérperas* (new moms) were easy to spot in their customary get-up: heads wrapped in scarves (often a diaper cloth), cotton in their ears, a bundle in their arms–tiny baby hidden among blankets and pillows. After being checked in, they sat proudly in the front row of the waiting room. As *puérperas*, they receive priority and would be seen before the other patients. Yes, there's room at this inn!

Celebrating Christmas
From: Sister Confianza   Date: January 25, 2013

New clothes, tamales and sweet bread, evening worship services, and fireworks. We got to participate in some of these Honduran Christmas Eve and New Year's Eve traditions this year, as well as the Monastery's own traditions like midnight worship, the 12 days of Christmas (no fasting!) and Epiphany on January 6.

Here's how it all unfolded:

Friday, December 21—Winter Solstice
The Mayan calendar ended so some people thought the world was going to end. We decided to ignore that and made plans to go to Limón to use the internet. From the Monastery porch at sunrise we watched for a car to come down the road from La Fortuna—visible because the trees have been cut down for pasture. When I heard one, I walked ahead quickly carrying both backpacks to meet it. Sister Alegría wasn't far behind.

Just as we hoped, it was Don Julio. He makes a trip in his pickup to the small city of Tocoa every Friday, carrying passengers and cargo for a fee. To our great appreciation, he has never charged us for a ride to Limón. (That's probably because of our volunteer work at Centro de Salud, where he often brings patients.)

"Where are you travelling to today?" Julio asks.

"To Limón," we answer. "Also, we'd like to buy an *arroba* (25 lbs) of beans."

"OK. I can bring them next Friday." The bed of his pickup, outfitted with a rack that allows passengers to stand, is already jam-packed with people and luggage, but they cram together even more to make a little space for Sister Alegría and me to squeeze in. There's a lively discussion about what day Jesus was actually born. One young man says, "I always thought it was December 25, until I started reading the Bible. It doesn't say when he was born!"

Someone else says, "Wasn't he born the night of the 24th? That's why we celebrate the *Nochebuena* then!"

Another adds, "In some places they celebrate his birth on a different date."

Sister Alegría says, "The Orthodox celebrate Christmas on January 6, what we call Epiphany."

The first man is a bit consternated to think that Christians have "invented" Jesus' birthdate. "The important thing, though," he concludes, "is that the great King of Kings was born."

"Yes," adds Sister Alegría, "and that is worth celebrating. If someone else hadn't picked a date, we'd have to, so we could celebrate!"

Don Julio drives us to the *desvío de* Limón. Ever the gentleman, he helps Sister Alegría down from the back (they are about the same age), and asks, "What are you doing for the 24th?"

"We'll be at the Monastery," she replies.

"You don't want to be there by yourselves," he says. "Why don't you come for the worship service in La Fortuna? I could come pick you up."

Now, this is appealing. "OK," says Sister Alegría. "What time?"

Julio consults with someone else and says, "It would have to be 4:30."

"And can you bring us back afterwards?"

"No," he laughs. "You'd stay till the next day."

"Oh, then we can't. We have to be at the Monastery for our midnight service."

So Julio takes off with his carload of folks to Tocoa. We climb the hill to visit our old friends Chito and Rosa. They now have a pretty nice setup, living rent-free on their *patrona's* (boss's) land. They are really liking it, because they can plant crops as well as raise milk cows, pigs, and chickens, and Chito can still do taxi work with his pickup. In fact, the income from selling milk pays for their groceries. "We like it so much here, we don't want to move to the house we built in Limoncito!" he tells us.

Rosa gives us cups of sweetened hot milk while we chat. "Why don't you come over on Sunday to help me wrap tamales?" she asks us. "I'm going to do all my Christmas cooking that day so on the 24th we can just be relaxing and eating."

"Hmm..." I say. "Sunday is usually our day of rest."

Sister Alegría is tempted. "Maybe we could rest on Monday instead, like them..."

Rosa says firmly, "No, no. Take your day of rest and come on Monday to eat."

"OK," we agree.

December 24—_La Nochebuena_—Christmas Eve

In the morning, I cook what will be our breakfast and lunch: bean soup with vegetables we had purchased on Friday. This will finish our cooked beans so we won't need to make a fire to boil them in the evening. I also bake a cake—gingerbread—which we will share with Rosa and Chito. I take coals from the firebox and put them in the oven below to heat it up. Once the batter is in, I keep a fire going above to keep the oven hot. Sometimes it's been a challenge to keep it hot enough, but today it's actually hotter than ideal.

After breakfast, we go to the creek to wash laundry. (This time of year we usually wash at the house, but we had done our annual tank washing late in November, which turned out to be after the significant rainfall, so there isn't much water at the house right now)

When we get back up to the house, we hang the clothes indoors, eat our lunch, and have afternoon prayers early. Then we are off.

We walk along the road as far as the creek, where we run into a family from Bonito Oriental. They have come out to gather pine branches to decorate with. The back of their pick-up is stacked high with trunks of _ocote_ (pine that has aged into greasewood) and sacks of pine greens. They brought along their dogs and the men hunted, catching two big armadillos (good eating, we know).

They kindly make room for us in the double cab and give us a ride all the way to the highway. The driver offers us tamales, but we demure since we plan to eat at Rosa and Chito's. Then we walk the almost-level half mile to our friends' house.

As we come up their drive, Chito sees us and gives us a friendly welcome. We are offered plastic chairs with arm rests under a structure with a palm-branch roof for shade. Chito sits in a hammock as we chat, and Rosa brings us each two delicious pork tamales. We have a lovely afternoon just relaxing and watching them prepare for their evening festivities: bringing pop from town as well as white bread to make sandwiches with the fried pork meat from the Christmas pig they'd butchered the day before. In their spacious dirt-floor kitchen, their daughter Angela has set up a Christmas tree on the table—a small pine sapling decorated with strings of colored beads and small stuffed animals. "If only we had electricity," laments Rosa, "so we could put lights on it."

As evening begins to set in, Rosa and Chito express concern about us getting home before dark, so we prepare to leave. We were hoping to go to worship in Limoncito with them, until Rosa told me they wouldn't be going after all; the car's headlights don't work. Instead, Sister Alegría and I sing a few Christmas carols for them. Rosa fills the container I had brought the gingerbread in with pork meat and sweet rolls, and packs up tamales for us to take home.

Along the main road, a pickup stops to give us a ride without us waving it down. We climb in the back with a young man and his rack of hot pink cotton candy which he had been selling in a nearby town. When they drop us off at our road, we buy some, and happily eat it as we walk. A nearly-full moon lights the way as darkness settles in, and we sing Christmas carols as we walk along.

Back at the Monastery, we eat some of the food Rosa sent before Compline and then go to sleep. At midnight we rise for our special program of scriptures and lots of Christmas songs. After worship, we go outside and light some fireworks. Last year we discovered that sparklers are available here, which are favorites for Sister Alegría and me, so this year we bought some. We also got another kind that shoots colored balls into the air. (We prefer lights, not noise.)

December 25—*La Navidad*—Christmas Day

Unfortunately, I got chilled going outside and couldn't get back to sleep very well, so I wake up tired. After Unprogrammed Worship and another service of scripture and song, we take naps. In late morning we go to visit our neighbors, taking them a small pineapple from our garden. We can see their house and hear them often from our porch, but it's a 20-minute walk to get there.

Suyapa, the young matron, is home along with her 15-year-old daughter and two sons aged 8 and 4. (Neighbor Javier is her oldest child.) We are again served tamales and sent home with more. We watch as they adjust the straps on a zebra-striped dress for the daughter. She will debut it on New Year's Eve, just as she had debuted an outfit in town on Christmas Eve.

All of these outings were enjoyable, but we got overtired. As the season continued, we cut back on our physical work and included lots of singing and treat foods to keep the celebratory spirit.

January 6—*La Epifanía*—Epiphany

We decided not to have a big Epiphany bash this year. We did, however, buy grated coconut and made *tableta*, a candy. It was our first time and took a lot of work melting the sugar and stirring it over the fire, but it came out chewy and delicious.

On January 5, we take some of the candy to Suyapa's house to share with her family. I read aloud to her and her kids the Christmas story from a little picture book we have. Suyapa gives us some *badú* to take home. It's a starchy root vegetable that they harvested from a swampy area nearby. Later in the day, she sends over a tiny pot of a special dish she had made: chunks of meat from a *guatuza* (similar to rabbit) that the guys had hunted, cooked in milk from their own coconuts. We serve it with the *badú*, which turns blueish when boiled. It was a delectable, gourmet, extremely local meal—a lovely way to end the 12 days of Christmas.

Finally, on Sunday the 6th, Sister Alegría and I celebrate Epiphany with a relaxing day of rest at the Monastery.

Peace to you in the New Year!

Thank You
From: Sister Alegría   Date: January 25, 2013

Thank you, anonymous donor(s).

Our process of accepting gifts is a bit rough. If you've been with us from the beginning, you know that it has always been this way.

If you have given us money and not received a thank you note, please know that we are grateful. Some thank you notes went into the mail this week, but we know that we have received money without names.

Thanks again.

Bennett College
From: Sister Alegría

Sister Confianza and I were both born into the (United) Methodist Church, which in the US, is mostly composed of white people. The Society of Friends is the same. We understand that this is not our fault, but it is our problem. We are committed to a multi-racial monastery. Obviously, just letting things flow will not achieve that.

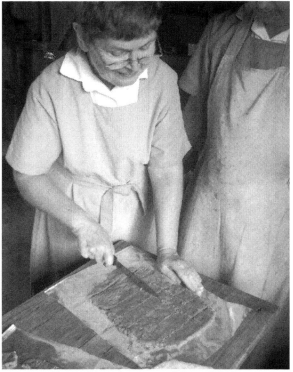

Sister Alegría cuts *tableta*, 2013

In January, 2013, we opened a relationship with Bennett College, founded by the Methodist Church in the 19th century to provide education for African American women. Most Bennett students are the first generation in their family to go to university. We offer scholarships for Bennett women to attend our summer Spiritual Formation program, the first session of which we were planning for 2013. This has remained a strong, mutually beneficial relationship.

A New Henhouse
From: Sister Alegría   Date: February 18, 2013

Mateo built us a new chicken house last week. We have been talking about it for months and now those ideas all came together to produce reality.

A week and a half ago we stopped at his house on the way to Bonito to talk details. I asked him how much money to withdraw from the bank for it. His quick response: "$2,500." We all laughed. I took out $200.

On Monday, Sister Confianza and I realized that we needed to take one of my old patients to the hospital in Tocoa on Tuesday. We stopped at Mateo's on Tuesday am to tell him what we were doing and that we hoped not to stay overnight at Tocoa, but couldn't be sure. That's fine. His first job was to cut down a big pine tree. He didn't need our presence or access to the house to begin.

We were able to return Tuesday. We spent $75.

Wednesday, Mateo came. He was now ready to give us a price: $200. I told him that I had spent some of it already on the patient and that we'll finish the project with us in debt to him. He's OK with that.

The chicken coop turned out to be more work than Mateo had expected. He and his son will return tomorrow to start on the bunks, then the book shelf and benches. You don't think we'd pay $200 and only get a chicken coop, did you?

The new chicken coop, 2013

Summer Session Announcement
From: Sister Confianza   Date: February 18, 2013

Planning for the 2013 Summer Session is proving to be an invaluable practice. Sister Alegría and I are facing our hopes and fears and clarifying the values we live by. With seven years of monastic experience (February 1 was Founding Day) we feel ready. We are encouraged by what we see and by the positive responses from others to this idea.

We have placed classified ads in Quaker publications and sent out email announcements to colleges and universities in the US through chaplains and campus ministries networks—and we've already gotten a response!

Please share the announcement below with persons, groups, or networks where it might reach interested women. We're hoping for diversity in age, race, and life experience!

Summer Session at Amigas del Señor
Seeking something more in your spiritual life?
Stretch yourself this summer at Amigas del Señor Methodist Monastery for women in Limón, Colón, Honduras.

Experience our communal life, which includes:
- daily prayer/worship times in Spanish
- the rustic living conditions of rural poor *campesinos* (no electricity)
- physical work (scrubbing laundry, cutting firewood, etc.)
- diverse spiritual practices like Unprogrammed (Quaker silent) Worship, singing, and spiritual formation
- non-hierarchical governance

Spanish language, particular beliefs/doctrine, or specific skills are not required, just a willingness to participate fully.

7-week Summer Session: June 26—August 15, 2013 (option to stay on for a full year)
Cost: $500 plus airfare
Interested?
- If you don't have a valid passport, start the process now.
- Learn more at
- www.oakgroveunitedmethodist.com/amigasdelsenor
- Contact Sister Alegría by email at
- amigashonduras@gmail.com

Sleep Tight
From: Sister Alegría   Date: February 25, 2013

We sleep on thin mattresses over planks. The guys showed us how to make more comfortable bunks. They make a frame and weave twine very tightly. Nice.

Our house has changed a lot. We now have sleeping for six easily. We have a study nook. (OK, so I'm classing it up a bit.) We also have a nice bench behind the house. We have a corn-grinding table in the porch.

All of this with chain saw rough cut pine. We got our $200 worth. Since it was much more work than Mateo had anticipated, we gave him another 200 lempiras ($10).

2012 Financial Report
From: Sister Alegría   Date: March 4, 2013

EXPENSES	
Food	$555
Household costs	181
Communication	581
Health	1,082
Clothing	66
Transportation(overnight)	88
Library	117
Immigration	346
Taxes	3
Education debt	266
Total cost of living	$3,285
Alms (given)	$22,854
TOTAL EXPENSES	$26,139
INCOME	
Donations	$63,852
Earnings	4
TOTAL INCOME	$63,856

We spent a lot of money this year. We spent a little more on food because we could. We had no significant periods of really inadequate nutrition.

We bought some of the Amigas books to give away because we could. (under "Communication")

We spent a lot on health care because we needed it. It has paid off well. We are in good shape.

Preparing the Way

We bought ourselves some books because we could and because we had to go to San Pedro Sula to renew our passports. (under "Library") That's the big immigration expense—passport renewal.

We paid part of Sister Confianza's educational debt because it was due.

We gave Sor Leonarda $10,000 because she needed it to care for her kids and because we could. (under "Alms")

We gave *Becas con Bendiciones* $3,000 to help poor kids attend public schools and because we could. (under "Alms")

We spent about $9,000 on medicine for Centro de Salud and Clínica Metodista because we could. (under "Alms")

Alms were 87% of outflow.

Our data flow is slow. I suspect some money spent in December in the US will show up in the 2013 financial report.

New Arrivals
From: Sister Confianza   Date: March 18, 2013

With chickens in the yard, a cat, and now a dog and a crowing rooster, the Monastery is starting to look like a more typical *campesino* home these days.

The dog arrived a month ago. His name is Watchiman, and that's the reason to have him—to scare off predators who would eat our chickens. Unfortunately, he is very timid, blind in one eye, and sleeps most of the day! He had been abandoned and is skin and bones, with sores showing through his black fur. Happily, we have hit upon a recipe that tempts him (corn mush with oil and beans), so hopefully he will fatten up a bit and gain some spunk.

Along with the dog, Mateo and Margarita gave us a young rooster. He has long golden feathers and a naked red neck—a breed known for being good layers. A bent beak doesn't keep this *"gallo más gallo"* from doing his job: he has been servicing hens since day one.

We had thought that the gray hen was celibate since she'd resisted the previous rooster, but not so! Sadly, the dog didn't save her from a daytime predator a few weeks ago. That left us with just one laying hen.

Then a few days ago the first two of the four pullets (the chicks we raised) have begun to lay, at not quite six months old. Now with fertilized eggs, we are ready to set another hen, and it looks like the speckled one is getting broody!

Hope your world is full of new life as well, as spring arrives and Easter comes!

312

Lauds
By: Sister Confianza

I awake in bed to the crowing of the rooster. All else seems quiet until I attune my ears to the humming of the insects. Feeling rested, I decide to get up. I untuck the mosquito net from around the three-inch foam mattress, poke my legs out, and sit up. I walk in the dark to the west end of the house and feel around on the shelf to find my glasses in their case. I put them on and go out the front door. Looking south from the porch, the black sky is strewn with stars. The crescent moon, visible when I went to bed, has set, and the stars sparkle brightly. I recognize the constellation Scorpio, with its curled tail, and the Milky Way floating like a narrow cloud across the eastern sky. The stars give enough light for me to be able to walk around the house without running into things; bushes and trees have a dark shadowy presence. I look north, and the Big Dipper hangs like an upside-down ladle above the trees and the horizontal string of lights that is Limón. The position of the stars tells me that it is not quite morning.

I return indoors and decide to read for a while, using a flashlight. I begin to hear more sounds: the barking roar in the distance from howler monkeys, the croak of a toucan, the cawing of jaybirds. When I go back out, only the brighter stars are visible. Scorpio has tilted to the west, and the sky is gray in the east: Morning approaches. I put on my habit and comb my hair. Standing outside in the growing light, the leaves now look green, and I can make out the lines in the palms of my hands. It is time to ring the wake-up bell: a rapid single-tone *ding-a-ling-a-ling*. There will be just enough time for Sister Alegría to get up, get dressed, comb her hair and take her pills before morning prayers.

I check today's page in the *Aposento Alto* (Upper Room) where we have written what psalms and songs we will be using. I get out the necessary Bibles and hymnal from the new bookshelf just inside the back door and place them on the bench outside to the east. The text in the books is now readable in the dawn light and I can see the color and fainter creases in my palms: time for Lauds.

I go out the front door, slip on my flip-flops, and take the few steps through the breezeway to the bell, which hangs from a roof beam to the north. This bell was a gift from a couple in a church I visited when I went to the US in 2007. It had once been a wind chime, with a clapper inside that sounded the three panels, each of a different tone. I use a whittled stick, which we have hung on the wall

313

next to the bell, to strike one side: four rings in a row, indicating it is time to come to prayers. I begin to sing *"En Santa Hermandad"* ("United by God's Love") and Sister Alegría joins me from inside. We chose this gathering song, which celebrates the Trinity and Christian fellowship, because it gives us a minute and a half to stop what we are doing and to get to the back bench. The bell is the voice of God; we come when it calls.

Sister Confianza rings the Monastery bell, 2015

Before sitting down, I walk to the chicken coop to open the door and let the birds out. On the last verse of the song, I walk back to the bell to announce the beginning of worship: three slow, deep tones. The gravelly stones along the side of the house crunch as I return to our outdoor chapel. I sit down and we sing the opening song, *"Vengan, todos adoremos,"* ("Come, Come, Everybody Worship"). A psalm is read in unison, not too fast, so we can savor each word and take in the meaning. After a minute of silence, another reading that is part of the psalm cycle, though today not from the Book of Psalms. Then we stand to sing. After reading the <u>Upper Room</u> scripture passage and meditation, we sing a second song, then read the prayer

314

and suggested Prayer Focus printed in the booklet. Finally, we have ten or so minutes of silent prayer and meditation.

I love to watch the sky brighten and the clouds change colors as the sun rises, and to take in the beauty of the scene around me. The first rays of sunlight make the needles of the pine trees glimmer. A slight breeze rustles the green leaves of the *nance* trees. The chickens cluck softly and scratch for bugs among the wild plants. More than one Christian teacher from the past has written about meditating on God's Word revealed in both the Book of Scripture and the Book of Nature. It is in the Creation that I have most often felt the Divine Presence.

We end our morning meditation singing an "Amen" chorus. We bless each other as is done in churches here, shaking hands and saying *"Bendiciones.* Blessings." Having started the day praising God who is Creator, has experienced human life, and is with us in Spirit, we can begin our other work centered in our purpose, knowing who and whose we are.

Asthma
From: Sister Alegría   Date: April 1, 2013

The baby got sick on Sunday afternoon, an asthma attack. As the evening wore on she worsened. In the night, even worse.

At 2 am, Dad saddled the horse, took the available cash and carried her down the mountain to La Fortuna to catch the pickup truck that would leave at 6 am. He knows she needs to go to the hospital in the city. It is her only chance.

At 7:15, they arrive at the place where he'll wait for the bus. This is when Sister Confianza and I connect with them in our walk to town. Don Marcos is the owner and driver of the truck. He signals to us, which we interpret as meaning there is room for us in the back and we climb in, knowing nothing of the little girl struggling to breathe.

Don Marcos comes to tell me about her. He has been arguing with Dad. Dad is determined to take her to the hospital. Don Marcos has asthma and I have treated him; he sees me as a good asthma doctor.

I take the backpack and go to see her. Dad is right. She is gravely ill: nostrils flaring with every breath, sweating profusely, grunting, intense concentration just to breathe. I take out my salbutamol inhaler and a piece of paper. I roll the paper to make a "spacer" to contain the aerosol medicine near her nose and mouth. I give her two puffs. I tell Dad, "Now she has had her first treatment. I can give her another one in 20 minutes."

She doesn't improve instantly and Dad still thinks he should take her to the hospital. They continue their argument. Don Marcos does not want to leave them. He wins the argument and we all climb into the truck.

The nurse (with the key) has not yet arrived at Centro de Salud. We all wait on benches. Dad and little girl are across from me and I watch her gradually improve. At the appropriate time, I give her a second treatment. Dad is still worried; he can't see the difference. She is still intent on breathing, but she has stopped sweating and grunting; her nostrils don't flare; the retractions have stopped.

Don Marcos in Limón with a car full of folks from La Fortuna
and the Sisters, 2012

Now I tell him, "I've given her the second treatment. She's exhausted from working so hard to breathe all night. Pretty soon she'll fall asleep."

The nurse arrives and we take care of all the patients; by now the little girl is not the sickest one.

We give her a nebulization treatment and send medicines home. Back to La Fortuna, back up the mountain, no hospital after all.

Do you have any idea how much time and energy I have spent complaining to God about having asthma? (Asthma so bad that I carry the medicine with me when I go out.) On that day I stopped; well, mostly, anyway.

Reflection
From: Sister Alegría

When I wrote that update, I wanted to help you imagine yourself as the mother or the father in this poor rural family far from any health care. But as I read it, I see that it soon becomes all about me. Another opportunity to grow in humility.

Day 18
From: Sister Alegría   Date: April 8, 2013

Today is Day 18. The chicks should hatch on Day 22. Stay tuned.

Sharing *El Aposento Alto*
From: Sister Confianza   Date: April 15, 2013

Sister Alegría and I are big fans of *El Aposento Alto*, The Upper Room daily devotional. We read it every morning as part of Lauds (dawn prayer). One of the things that makes it so great is that the meditations are written by regular people from all over the world.

A year ago, we discovered that the bimonthly booklet is now being distributed in Honduras. This seemed like something to be a part of. In the First Letter to the Corinthians, Paul talks about the different functions people may have in the work of the church: some plant, some water, and some harvest. We recognize that we're not evangelists trying to convert people, but rather we water—trying to help Christians grow in their faith. So in August, we ordered our first batch of *El Aposento Alto* and began selling it in Limón.

I was designated head of this project. Since I'm not a businesswoman nor very outgoing, it's been a real stretch to talk to people about it. I put the little books on display at Centro de Salud, and sometimes there are interested patients (most notably, literate women who live at a distance with little access to reading material).

Some of the staff are regular customers. A couple of stores in town have even taken copies to sell. Strangely enough, they won't accept a profit, but just pay me after the booklets have sold. I'm averaging 10 sold per month so far.

It's a little complicated to get the booklets here. The distributor in Tegucigalpa, who is the Superintendent of the United Methodist Church in Honduras, sends them through the pastor at La Ceibita. Then Alex, a vendor we've made friends with who lives in Tocoa and comes to Limón on Mondays, brings them to Limón. They often arrive well past the beginning of the month, but the date doesn't seem to matter too much to the purchasers. *"La Palabra de Dios nunca se vence.* The Word of God never expires,"our friend Fela said to me.

I have been encouraged by the many positive comments from those who buy it. Over the months I've gotten past some of my self-consciousness and let go of my ideas of how a business ought to be run, so I can be content with what is. I certainly have the sense that if something good comes from this, it's not because of me, but all from God.

Baby Chicks
From: Sister Alegría   Date: April 15, 2013

Thirteen adorable baby chicks. I make sure to have several sessions a day of *pollito* meditation (poe-YEE-toe, baby chick). They have two mothers caring for them.

See, we had eggs and no broody hen. Reina, our neighbor, had a broody hen and no chicks. She jumped at the chance to loan us her hen. When we got her home she wasn't that interested in setting. Our over-sexed rooster only sort of cares whether sex is consensual or not, and jumped her. Then one of our pullets (pullet—female chicken in the first year of life) got broody. We let them tag team the eggs. Four days before hatching day, they both got REALLY serious. Finally, we divided the eggs between them. They are doing co-parenting. They do well.

Some have naked necks like their father. They really look funny, sort of like they have helmets on.

The Letter from James
From: Sister Alegría

Every April at Amigas del Señor, we read the Epistle of James. It is short—only five chapters. Tradition says it was written by James the Just, Jesus' brother, who led the Jewish Christian community in Jerusalem. He was highly respected for his ascetic life, righteousness, and sanctity. He died a martyr.

The short "letter" could have been written by any serious Jewish theologian or humanist philosopher for the most part. It was written in fluent well-educated Greek, not the Aramaic that James of Nazareth (James the Just) would have grown up speaking.

This book of the Bible was a great favorite among the early Quakers. It was also a very important book for John Wesley, the founder of the Methodist movement. We come to our fondness for this book quite naturally, since our roots are both Quaker and Methodist.

I invite you to read James this month. Let me know what you think. Where do you see yourself in the text?

Fire
From: Sister Confianza   Date: April 22, 2013

The bi-annual fire came through last Wednesday. Neighbor Javier planned to burn only a certain field to rid it of ticks, but the wind came up and the fire escaped. He showed up at our place mid-morning to tell us of the danger. Then he and his hired hand helped us clear the *ronda*—a three-to-four foot wide ring of bare ground around the house and yard—to protect the Monastery. I was so grateful for his conscientiousness, and that we'd defined the perimeter by planting pineapples along it after the last fire in 2011.

Javier even had us light back-fires just outside the barrier so that these "cool fires" would burn up the fuel (leaves on the ground) and the bigger "hot fire" wouldn't come so close. It worked. The big fire did eventually go up the hill to the west and burned much of our seven acres. One part even jumped the road and burned Mateo's land. It also burned Javier's pasture to the east, but stopped at the edge of our garden. God is good to us.

In the evening, Javier returned to check on us, and brought his partner, Reina, and their two kids. We were able to give them their hen and her five chicks, as well as a dozen eggs—none of their hens are laying right now. That leaves us with the black hen and her five chicks (three of the original thirteen died), the three layers and the rooster.

The dog, Watchiman, by the way, ran away a month ago. I guess it wasn't meant to be.

A Working Motorcycle
From: Sister Alegría   Date: April 22, 2013

My eyes filled with tears of gratitude. I blinked them back; in this meeting I'm the "donor," not the recipient. Dra. Diriam, our chief; Cooper, the supervisor of health promotion; and I are standing in that funky little exam room I told you about, all of us very grateful.

The topic is Cooper's motorcycle. It had been out of commission for several months. He uses it to supervise the 14 small water treatment plants, the mosquito control efforts, the local health collaborators (who can collect blood for malaria tests, give a few doses of malaria medicine, treat worms and amoebas, give oral rehydration salts and dispense birth control pills and condoms), among other things.

We had given $1,000 to get it repaired (practically rebuilt). It cost almost another $100, but they could get that. They showed me the list of parts purchased.

The motorcycle is available in time for the annual immunization campaign. Sometimes Cooper and a slender nurse go up into the hills to immunize children and dogs. Sometimes they go part way on the motorcycle, then a few hours on horseback or on foot.

We're in the immunization campaign right now.

The Annual Immunization Campaign
From: Sister Confianza   Date: May 13, 2013

"What do you want from us during the immunization campaign this year?" Sister Alegría asked Doctora Diriam.

"Well," she replied, "Juana Nidia told me you have always helped out on the outreach clinics, so we are hoping for that again. The parents are more likely to bring their kids for their shots if consults are also being offered."

Sister Alegría admitted to me later that she was hoping not to go out as much this year since there are two other doctors, but we assented to join the team on three extra days over two weeks (April 15-27), besides our regular Mondays at the clinic.

Thankfully, the government shipment and the Monastery's order of medicines arrived just in time so I could pack a reasonable pharmacy for the outreach clinics. In each village, we set up shop in the schoolyard. The students brought out tables and chairs from their classrooms to set up a vaccine station for the nurses and another area for the doctors to give consults. I checked in the patients, writing their name, date of birth, and (for adults) blood pressure on a slip of paper. (I learned to take blood pressures during last year's campaign.) The patients brought those *papelitos* with the prescriptions from the doctors back to me after their consult.

The first day, out at La Fortuna, there were three doctors giving consults and I was overwhelmed with prescriptions. I ran out of some medicines and was missing others, so for the next days out I prepared better. I was extremely grateful the other days to have a student helper and only two doctors. Since there was always at least one other doctor along, Sister Alegría didn't have such a big burden as last year when she saw almost all the patients herself. That was good, since more people sought consults than in the past: 115 in La Fortuna, and over 80 each in Plan de Flores and Nueva Esperanza.

Sister Alegría and I discovered that we are in good physical shape because we could do these two weeks even with the wildfire and then catching cold. We still got tired and Sister Alegría's asthma flared, but we have recovered well. I'm especially grateful for the gift of a rice-and-lentil mix from Sor Leonarda that kept our food costs low when we decided not to boil and grind corn, as well as for numerous rides we were given (including by the doctors!) which meant we didn't have to walk as much.

Last year, Limón was #1 in immunization coverage at over 95% out of ten municipalities in the Department of Colón. At this rate, we will keep our top spot. It's lots of work, but everyone on staff enjoys going out into the villages to do this important task.

An Interesting Invitation
From: Sister Alegría

Mostly we are ignored by the "official" church. In May, 2013, that changed. Juan Guerrero, the Superintendent of the Honduras Mission of the United Methodist Church decided to visit us. He is also an Upper Room fan and promoter (and the regional distributor).

One Saturday, he, his wife, and their son visited Sister Confianza and me at the Monastery, personally delivering the next issue of *El Aposento Alto*. We showed them around. Juan enjoyed eating cashew apples. He plied me with lots of questions. I found myself sharing a lot of intimate details of my journey to found Amigas del Señor Monastery.

They couldn't stay long.

Preparing the Way

Within a month, we received an email from Juan, inviting us to Tegucigalpa to visit a site that might be good for a monastery. "I'm just asking you to pray about it—and to come and look," he said. We sat with that invitation for the next several months.

Kudos
From: Sister Alegría   Date: May 25, 2013

Here at the Monastery, we often give thanks to God for food, for rain, for rides, for friends, for health. Today I'd like you to join us in thanking God for a few faithful and fruitful women who have helped us immeasurably.

Our method of transferring donated money from Oak Grove UMC to us is as follows: The treasurer deposits money in a personal checking account in my name. Then I write out a check to deposit it in our savings account at Banco Atlántida here in Honduras. (That personal checking account is also used to pay bills that we generate in the US.)

For our first two years, Jyl Myers, a past travel companion on Honduras trips, managed that account. In 2008, she decided that the job should go to a younger person.

Marguerite Blodgett, my sister-in-law, stepped into the breach. She has done this work during five very complicated years. In these years, I have done the majority of the "sell all you have, give it to the poor, then come follow me." Not so easy to do across international boundaries. Sometimes we achieved our goal; sometimes we spent a lot of time cleaning up after missed communications.

This spring, a freak house fire destroyed much of the guts of her house. She decided it is time to give up this work.

My friend, Judy Billings, has agreed to pick up the pieces of this messy puzzle.

We thank God for these women, their willingness, their ability, their faithfulness, their guts. Please say a little prayer for each—as a personal favor to me.

Fifty Cents
From: Sister Confianza   Date: June 30, 2013

Some things we've purchased recently for 10 Lempiras (50 cents) each:

1 pound flour (corn or wheat)

1/2 hour of internet time on a computer
2 small ice cream cones
4 ounces cumin
1 tiny watermelon
1 pound rice
1 pound carrots
1 homemade baked good
1 can fruit juice
1 plastic bar eraser
2 ballpoint pens
14 green bananas
1 kitchen scrub pad

Other things available for 10 lempiras in Limón:
A consult plus medications at the Centro de Salud (Public Health Clinic)
2 big coconut bread rolls
20 pieces of candy
10 *topogigios* (frozen Kool-Aid treats)

Sounds like a bargain! Then again, a laborer here earns in a month what a minimum-wage worker earns in a week in the US (about $250). In Honduras, one day's wages buy a gallon of gasoline. Cell phones are ubiquitous, but they cost the same as in the US. So do computers, cars, and brand-name prescription medications. Loans and mortgages are becoming more common, with outrageous interest rates. It costs a lot to live "well."

Tornado
From: Sister Alegría   Date: June 17, 2013

A tornado hit Limón last night at about 9 pm. Sister Confianza and I were happy with our lovely rain on the mountain, we had no suspicion that the storm was the least bit unusual. When we arrived at the temporary Centro de Salud we noticed electric lines down, signs down, roofs missing—including the roof over our two exam rooms. We just started work. I gave consults in the "porch" (actually a bar at night).

We worked until about 11:00. I was pretty worried about Sor and her kids. Next we went over there. They had lost almost the entire roof.

There were workmen putting zinc on the roof. Then the ceiling started falling in. We were in the great room. There was a light mist going on outside. The foreman of the workers said that he couldn't continue working with the children present, just too dangerous. It was obviously not an easy thing to say. The new home is still not ready to be occupied.

It is sort of ironic. We've been concerned that the ocean might "eat" the temporary building for the last two years. And now a freak tornado.

We're in Bonito. We came to take out some money to help Sor.

She just keeps trucking; when we left she had secured approval to take all of the kids to the school for shelter.

Sister Alegría gives a consult in the covered porch of the temporary
Centro de Salud, 2013

Leishmaniasis

From: Sister Alegría   Date: June 25, 2013

In 2000, I had malaria for the first time. In 2010, Sister Confianza had dengue. We figured we had had our quota of exotic tropical diseases.

It was the dry season (April) and we went to the cool environment of the stream to do the laundry several times a week. Sister Confianza got an insect bite on her right calf that she hardly noticed. I paid attention to it as we would climb the steep hill back up to the Monastery. It got bigger instead of smaller. I asked—no itching, no pain. Hmm. Then it developed a central ulcer with red, hard swelling around it. Oh, oh.

We got out the Tropical Medicine textbook. Sure enough, it was typical of leishmaniasis. We were grateful that the "New World" leishmaniasis is pretty benign (not a systemic disease) and we don't have to deal with the "Old World" strains.

A month ago, she got a consult with Dra. Diriam, who did a diagnostic scraping (teaching me how to do it as a fringe benefit). Sister Confianza says that hurt a bit. Two weeks ago the results and the medicine arrived (pentavalent antinomy, in case you're interested).

There's been sort of an outbreak of leishmaniasis lately. That's why the remarkable efficiency of the public health program. It is a protozoan carried by a harmless insect that lives in damp wooded areas (like by our stream).

Our routine for the last two weeks has been injections of 5 ml each in *las nalgas* (the buttocks), both sides, every morning after Lauds. It will go on until all 40 injections have been administered.

I'm pretty grateful that I'm the injector, not the injectee.

Ready or Not, Here They Come
From: Sister Confianza   Date: June 10, 2013

We're ready. Sister Alegría and I celebrated that fact Sunday, June 9, with a pancake breakfast, giving a grape Kool-Aid toast to God for bringing us this far.

We spent most of April and May preparing for the seven-week program we are offering for the first time this year. We had many conversations about aspects of the program, from details about the daily schedule and how many pots to buy, to what spiritual practices to teach in this short time. We took an hour after breakfast each day to plan the curriculum—the hour we will use for the Spiritual Formation courses for the *alumnas* (students). Sister Alegría brushed up her Spanish by doing daily exercises until completing a grammar workbook. We finished rearranging the house using our new bunks and furniture, and sewed blankets and mosquito nets. We also made two significant shopping trips to Tocoa to buy foam mattresses and other items and arrange flight details. We have spent a lot of time on the internet communicating with women who contacted us. We have experienced lots of anxiousness and excitement as we wondered how many women would come and imagined possible scenarios.

On June 26, we'll meet our two summer apprentices at the San Pedro Sula airport. One is a Roman Catholic who lives in London, England. One is a Baptist who lives in Washington, DC. She is a recent graduate of Bennett College and the first recipient of our Bennett scholarship.

Now we declare ourselves ready. We are spending these last few weeks immersed in our regular monastic life, living in the now (the only time that really exists).

Geographic Orientation

North and Central America

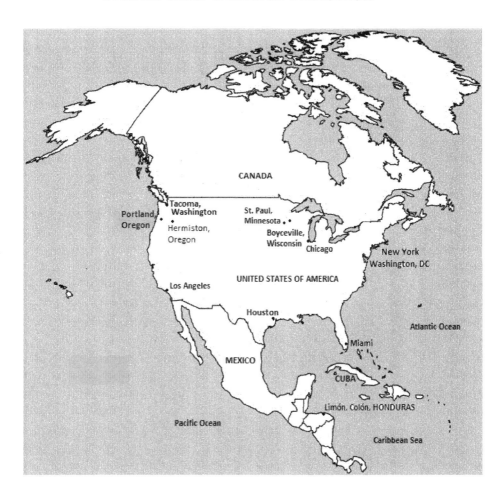

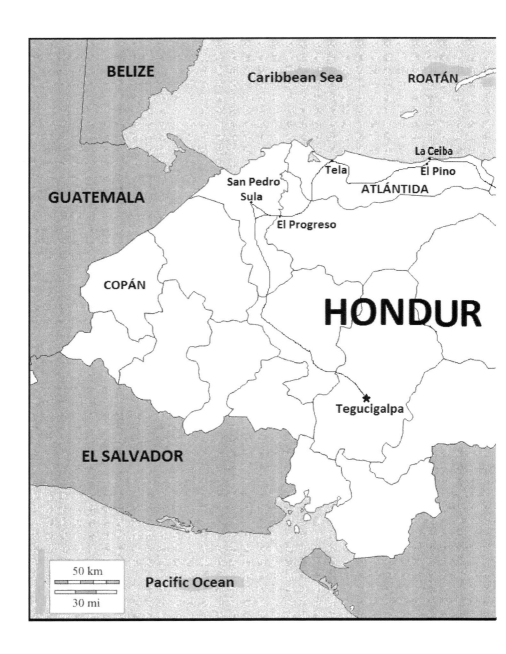

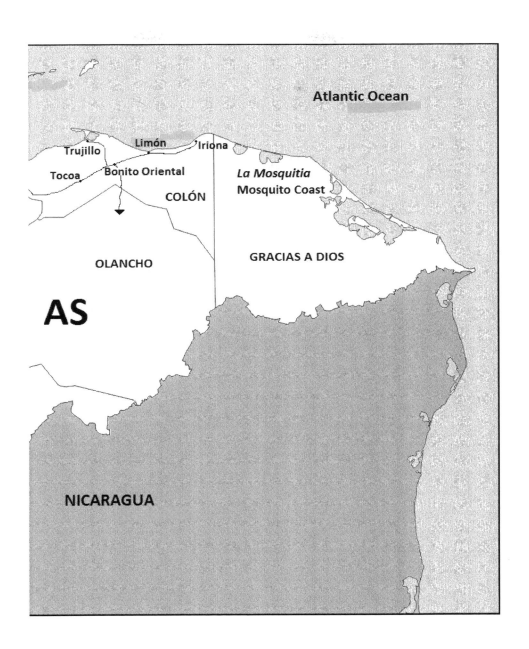

Our Corner of the World
From: Sister Alegría

Amigas del Señor is located in Limón, Colón, a rural area in the foothills on the north coast of Honduras.

One paved two-lane highway connects the population centers of the north coast. San Pedro Sula, the second largest city in the country (600,000 souls), is the point furthest west that is relevant to our life. It has a US consulate and the nearest medical specialist who can do a Nerve Conduction Study. This highway touches El Progreso and Tela before arriving at El Pino, just 20 minutes before La Ceiba, the fifth largest city in Honduras (120,000 souls). La Ceiba is a three-hour bus ride from San Pedro Sula. All distances are measured by the travel time in a bus (or occasionally on foot). You are invited to think like a poor Honduran.

Emanuel Methodist Church is in El Pino, whose members always welcome us when we visit, giving us a place to stay and even feeding us sometimes. Sister Blanca lives there and sometimes preaches, Brother José, her son, lives with her. Blanca's son, Marcos, lived and died there. Emanuel is part of the Methodist Church of the Caribbean and the Americas. Eloyda is the R. N. who runs *Clínica Metodista* and collaborates closely with us and with her local public health clinic. We are very grateful for all El Pino means for us.

La Ceiba has a Migrations Office, where we were irregular visitors for the first several years of the Monastery. Medi-Centro, a medical office building, houses Dr. Pintor (ENT), Dr. Salazar (orthopedics) an X-ray department and our Gastroenterologist, among others.

Two hours east of La Ceiba is Tocoa, population: 50,000. It is the nearest city for shopping. It has a very busy, understaffed, undersupplied public hospital that has saved the lives of some of our patients. Tocoa boasts several branches of Banco Atlantida (our bank) and a few public internet businesses. Our friends Alex, and Ingrid and Angel live there.

One of the suburbs of Tocoa is La Ceibita, where Good Samaritan United Methodist Church is. We visit there sometimes, staying in the parsonage when we have to stay overnight. Names in the book include Irma, Cándida, and Pastor Jesús.

Another hour east is Bonito Oriental, often called Bonito, where our friends, Jack and Gus, Jesuit priests, were living. They were very kind to us. When we had to on-the-spot have our passports sent by carrier, we had them sent to the priests, without even calling for permission. All went well. We are very grateful. Bonito has the closest bank to us. Bonito is where the pavement ends.

Francia, big enough to have a public nurse, is 40 minutes from Bonito. Victoria is that nurse; she is nurse Wornita's older sister. Just before Francia, right after the Limón county line, is a road headed south to Brisas de Mira Mar. After Francia you pass Lauda and Limoncito. If you went from Bonito to Limón it would take an hour, two minutes more than to the La Fortuna road, where we live.

The county seat of each county (*municipio*) has the same name as the county. We usually mean the town when we use the word, Limón.

Limoncito shows up a few minutes before the La Fortuna road. Omar lives there, with his automotive repair shop. The Limoncito church is there (Evangelical). Margarita and Mateo, our friends, live there.

OK, so you have passed through Bonito, Francia and Limoncito. You get off the bus at the La Fortuna road. As you walk, you will notice the county dump on the right side of the road. One hour of walking brings you to the Monastery (after you ford the stream and climb the really big hill). If you were to continue on another two hours you would arrive at the town of La Fortuna. It is big enough to have a two-room school, a kindergarten, and three small churches.

Limón has the mayor's office (mayor of the county). That is where we pay our yearly real estate taxes. The old hands at the public health clinic are Juana Nidia, R. N., and Wornita, auxiliary nurse. They are both about 40 as the book begins. Cooper supervises the outreach health workers. Dra Karen comes and goes; Dra. Diriam arrives later.

Fela is a friend in Limón. She sells snacks in front of the public health clinic. Hernán is the postmaster. Noemí runs a little store. She gives us credit when we need it and lets us use her phone free. Sor Leonarda runs an orphanage for 50 children. María Elena and Doña Lupe are her helpers.

The road from the highway to Limón is called a *desvío* (detour or crooked road). At the intersection of that *desvío* with the highway, live Doña Eva, who runs a small store, and her live-in partner of 50 years, Don Clemente. Their daughter, Rosa, and her live-in partner of 20 years, Chito, lived right next door for a while. Then they moved up the hill, off the road.

The highway continues on to Nueva Esperanza, then Plan de Flores, where a road to the south leads to Villa Nueva, From Plan de Flores, the main road goes on to Hicoteas, and finally to Iriona, a different county, three hours later. We call it the highway, even though it is a dirt road, because it is the main road and it connects us to the cities.

Neighbors

From: Sister Confianza

More than one young man has commented to Sister Alegría and me, "Wow. You two came to live in Honduras, and we all want to go to the United States." We have chosen downward mobility in a world where most want to move up. It is clear to us that a more equal distribution of wealth and resources across the globe would lessen the massive migration of populations, and we hope our life is a witness to that possibility.

Honduras is a small sovereign nation about the size of Tennessee with a population of nine million. Two million more Hondurans live in the US—over half of them legally. Every year, some $4 billion is sent as *remesas* to Hondurans from family members working abroad. That's more than comes in from all exported products combined, including coffee, bananas, shrimp, raw materials, textiles, and more. Every family here seems to have a relative in the US who sends back money. Some settle down there, while others, like the owners of the properties neighboring the Monastery, earn money to set up a business and return to their homeland.

The sixty-*manzana* property to the south of us is owned by Jonathan, who worked at a turkey-processing plant in Minnesota for fourteen years before moving back to live on his land in the spring of 2016. Much of his family (children and siblings) live in Lauda and Limoncito, and he would wire money regularly to support his kids and pay Javier or Nino, the caretakers of his property. Dimas, who with his family owns the large terrain south of Jonathan's, and Omar, whose land is to the southeast, each spent several years working illegally in the US. They were able to get long hours at well-paying jobs so that within a few years they had amassed enough to purchase vehicles and large acreages (over 150 *manzanas*), then return to run their businesses. Elías, owner of a property across the road to the southwest, worked on ships (like many Garifuna men) as a merchant marine to gain his investment and retirement money. Of neighboring property owners, only Mateo earned the cash to buy his land across the road to the west by working locally.

The Monastery Yard

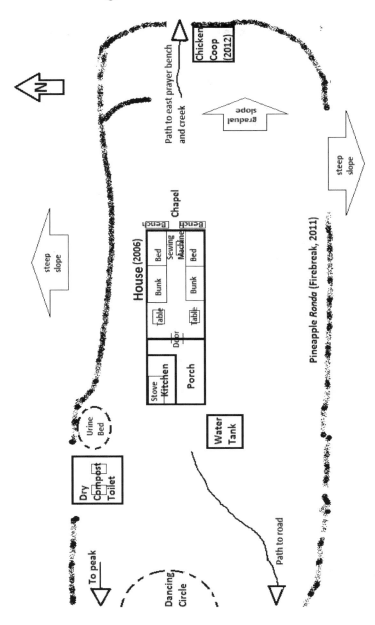

Sister Confianza consults the dictionaries, 2016

Glossary

A Love of Language
From: Sister Confianza

Sister Alegría and I both love words and seek to use the ones that most accurately describe what we are trying to say. At the Monastery, we regularly go to our fat English and Spanish dictionaries to check our understanding of a word or learn its etymology (roots). Now that we are bilingual, we sometimes find that the best word is not in the language we are using at the moment!

We include in this glossary many words from the text that have particular meaning in our life. The monastic terms are defined as they pertain specifically to Amigas del Señor. Spanish words are in *italics* and defined as people use them in our rural region of Honduras. Succinct descriptions of people and places may be found in the Index.

Abbreviations Used in Glossary:
Abbr. = Abbreviation
Ch. = Chapter
Eng. = English
Span. = Spanish

Spanish Pronunciation Tips:
Each vowel has only one sound:
    A = ah E = eh I = eeO = oh U = oo
Some consonants have different sounds than in English:
    J = h LL = y Ñ = nyZ = s

The Word List

Afternoon prayers > see **Vespers**

Alegría Happiness; joy.

Almoner One whose task is to give alms. (See "Beggars" in Ch. 1,)

Amigas del Señor Women Friends of the Lord.

Aposento Alto, El The Spanish edition of The Upper Room.

Glossary

Arroba 25 pounds.

Aspirant A woman in the first stage of monastic formation who is trying out monastic life for at least a year.

Bedtime prayers > see **Compline**

Broody Describes a hen that wants to stay in the nest and incubate eggs.

Campesino A peasant farmer or "country person."

Cassave A cracker-like food made usually by Garifuna women from grated *yuca*. It is a way of processing and preserving the otherwise poisonous "bitter" *yuca*.

Centro de Salud (Literally "Health Center")A front-line public health clinic staffed by one or more nurses and sometimes a doctor. We refer most often to the one in Limón.

Chata A short, fat variety of banana with a marshmallow-like consistency when ripe.

Clearness Committee A small group that meets to help someone come to clarity about a leading or a major life decision by listening and asking thoughtful questions.

Coconut bread > see *pan de coco*

Comal The flat iron stovetop of the traditional wood-fired clay stove.

Compline (*Completas*) Evening or bedtime prayers, done around 7:30 pm by candle-, lamp- or flashlight. (See "A word about prayer" in Ch. 6)

Confianza Confidence; trust.

Cuajada Fresh soft cheese made by placing a fragment of a rennet tablet in raw (un-pasteurized) milk, letting it separate, then removing the settled curds from the whey and kneading them with salt.

Culeca Broody (hen).

Department (*Departamento*) The largest political division in Honduras, something like a state but with no autonomy. (Each of the 18 Departments has a governor appointed by the president.)

Desvío (Literally "detour") A crooked road with a single final destination (as in *el desvío de La Fortuna:* the road to La Fortuna).

Doctora Title for a woman doctor.

Don Courtesy title for a mature or rich man.

Doña Courtesy title for a mature or rich woman.

Dra. Abbr. of *Doctora.*

ENT Ear, nose and throat doctor.

Evening prayers > see **Compline**

Examen (Latin) A spiritual practice that involves reviewing or examining a period of time (several hours, a day, a week, etc.) to notice how conscious one was of the Divine presence and how faithful or unfaithful one was to God, giving thanks and asking forgiveness as appropriate.

Friend A member of the Society of Friends; a Quaker.

Gallina Hen.

Gallo Rooster.

Garifuna [gah-REE-foo-nah] A cultural and ethnic group and its language, descended from escaped African slaves and Caribe/Arahuco indigenous peoples. They were exiled from the island of Saint Vincent in 1797 and settled on the island of Roatán and the coast of mainland Honduras, Guatemala, and Belize. The town of Limón is a majority-Garifuna community.

Gracias (Literally "graces") Thanks; thank you.

Gracias a Dios Thank God.

Grand Silence Monastic silence kept to facilitate prayer, which means no talking (except in emergencies) between Compline and Lauds.

Gringo, gringa A white man or woman.

Guatuza (Eng. "agouti") A large brown rodent, much like a rabbit with small ears and no tail. Eaten as game.

A *guatuza* in the Monastery yard, 2016

Guineo [ghee-NAY-oh]   Green banana.   Often peeled and boiled whole (eaten like potato) or sliced thin and fried as *tajadas*.

Hermano, Hermana   Brother, Sister.   Titles used among Christians and especially for monastics. (See "A new name" in Ch. 3)

Katuk   A spindly perennial plant with nutritious, edible, dark green leaves.

Lauds (*Laudes*)   Daily sunrise service, held outdoors when there is enough light with which to read the Bible (anywhere between 5 and 6 am, depending on the time of year), or indoors if there is bad weather or we are up early to travel. (See "Lauds" in Ch. 12)

Lectio divina   (Latin. Literally "divine/holy reading")   The prayer practice of meditating on a passage of Scripture or other spiritual literature.

Lempira   Honduran currency, named after the indigenous Chief Lempira, who resisted the Spanish *conquistadores* (conquerors). During the timespan of this book, the exchange rate was pegged at 18.9 lempiras per 1 US dollar.

Lutheran Volunteer Corps   An organization for young adults to spend one or two years doing full-time service work for a small stipend, and explore and live out their spirituality and the values of intentional community, peace with justice, and sustainability.

LVC   The Lutheran Volunteer Corps.
(www.lutheranvolunteercorps.org)

Machete A two- to three-foot-long, single-bladed tool used for cutting grass, plants, and trees. It is ubiquitous in rural Honduras, where every man carries one for work and sometimes hunting or self-protection.

Mano a mano Hand-to-hand.

Manzana (Literally "apple") 1.7 acres.

Masa (Literally "mass") Dough, ranging from the simple mixture of ground corn or corn flour with water to leavened bread or tortilla dough.

Meeting A Quaker "church" and its congregation.

Meeting for Worship with Attention to Business A gathering in which a group seeks divine guidance for conducting its affairs and making decisions. Amigas del Señor uses this Quaker process for our governance.

Methodist (From the early Wesleyans' methodical devotional lifestyle.) A name for Christians who follow in the tradition of John Wesley, a reformer of the Anglican church in the mid-1700s, emphasizing Grace, God's love for all, and works of charity and social justice.

Monastery The building where monks or nuns live, especially those who are dedicated to prayer. ("Convent" denotes the home of Sisters of Brothers who are involved in an outward ministry like running a school or hospital.)

Monja Nun.

Monteando Ambling through the brush (*monte*) with one's dogs in hopes of killing game.

Montuca *Tamalitos* with a meat filling.

Morning prayers > see **Lauds**

Municipality (*Municipio*) The political division within a Department, roughly equivalent to a county.

Nance A hardwood tree with yellow and orange flowers that grows on Monastery property and is top-quality firewood when dry. Also, its sour yellow fruits with a pit (somewhat like small cherries) that make a great drink when mashed and mixed with water and sugar.

Navidad Christmas.

Nochebuena, La (Literally "The Good Night") Christmas Eve, December 24.

Novice A woman in the third stage of monastic formation, when she takes a new name and trains to become a professed nun. (See "Monastic Formation" in Ch. 3)

Novitiate The period of time (one year or longer) when one is a Novice.

Nun A woman who dedicates herself to God by living in a monastery and committing to be celibate, poor and obedient.

Ocote A type of pine tree that grows on Monastery grounds, and the resinous greasewood that it produces after dying, useful for starting fires.

Pan de coco Coconut bread. A sturdy roll made with white flour and coconut milk.

Pastelito A savory snack food, made by placing a spoonful of cooked filling such as shredded chicken or rice with ground beef (we use beans at the Monastery) on a raw flour or corn tortilla, folding it over, and deep frying.

Piña Pineapple.

Pinol Ground toasted corn that is cooked with water or milk to make a warm drink or porridge (mush).

Plátano Plantain. A usually large, calorie-dense variety of banana with yellow flesh. May be boiled, fried, or grilled at any stage of ripeness.

Pollito A chick or baby chicken up to about two months of age.

Pollo Chicken meat. Also, a young chicken two to six monthsof age.

Postulancy The period of time (one year or longer) when one is a Postulant.

Postulant A woman in the second stage of monastic formation after time as an Aspirant or Sojourner, when she is seriously considering becoming a professed nun. (See "Monastic Formation" in Ch. 3)

Profession The moment of full commitment to monastic life, when a Sister takes the vows of material poverty, celibate chastity, and obedience to the will of God as discerned by the Monastery. Temporary Profession is made for one or more years at a time. After five years, a Sister may make Perpetual Profession, a lifetime commitment. (See "First Profession" in Ch. 3 and "Sister Confianza to make First Profession" in Ch. 6)

Programmed Worship Protestant worship with a designated order including hymns, scripture readings, and often spoken prayers.

Pullet A hen under one year of age.

Quaker (So-called because many of them "quaked" when moved by the Holy Spirit.) Of the Religious Society of Friends, the denomination begun in England by George Fox, Margaret Fell, and others in the mid 1600's, which recognizes that there is "that of God" in everyone.

Quintal 100 pounds.

R. N. (Registered Nurse) A professional nurse who has a university degree.

Rapadura The boiled-down juice pressed from sugar cane, sold in solid blocks. Syrup can be made by shaving off some of the brown sugar from the block and boiling it with a small amount of water.

Remesa ("remittance") Money sent back to Honduras by persons working in the US or another country.

Ronda A firebreak that encircles a defined area.

Saldo Minutes purchased for one's cell phone or modem.

Sanitario Restroom. At the Monastery, the dry-compost toilet.

Sapote A grapefruit-sized egg-shaped tree fruit with a hard brown rind and deep orange flesh that tastes and feels something like cooked pumpkin.

Semana Santa Holy Week.

Shakers A Christian sect originating in England in the mid-1700's, which practiced communal living and celibacy. They died out in the 20th century.

Sojourner A woman who makes a commitment to live the monastic life one year at a time with the expectation of returning to secular life.

Sor Formal title for a religious Sister or nun. (At Amigas del Señor, we have chosen to use the more familiar *Hermana*.)

Spiritual Formation An intentional formal process to promote spiritual growth in the participants.

Tableta A hard, caramel-flavored candy made from sugar and either grated coconut or milk.

Tajadas Sliced and deep-fried green banana or plantain.

Tamale (full name *nacatamal*) A traditional Christmas and New Year's food made from the starch strained from boiled ground corn, with a filling of meat, rice, and other ingredients, wrapped in a piece of banana leaf and steamed.

Tamalitos A food made of ground raw young corn, seasoned and wrapped in corn husks and steamed.

Tercera edad (Literally "third age") Senior, over age sixty.

Third age > see *tercera edad*

Topogigio A small knotted baggie of frozen Kool-Aid, eaten by biting off one corner and sucking.

Tostadas Corn tortillas toasted on the edge of the *comal* and kept crispy in the oven.

UMC The United Methodist Church. (www.umc.org)

United Methodist Church, The A Protestant denomination based in the US with millions of adherents across the globe.

Unprogrammed Worship Quaker worship in which participants wait in silence upon the Lord, and stand to give spoken ministry when led by the Spirit.

Something Better

Upper Room, The A bimonthly booklet with daily devotional readings written by Christians from around the world and published in 33 languages. (www.upperroom.org)

Vespers (*Vísperas*) Afternoon prayers, held at about 2:30 pm at the Monastery, or the soonest convenient hour when travelling. (See "Vespers" in Ch. 7)

Weekly Review The practice of reading our journal entries from the past week, noticing themes or events that stand out (especially in our spiritual lives), then sharing aloud our reflections without comment from others.

Yearly Review The practice of going over what has happened in the Monastery's life during the past twelve months, sharing aloud by topic during daily sessions in January.

Yuca ("manioc" or "cassava") A starchy edible tuber. (See "Harvesting Yuca" in Ch. 5)

Wornita, a Garifuna, peels *yuca* with her children, 2007

The Sisters walk the main road toward Limón, 2013

Worship Sharing

Creating Community
From: Sister Confianza

At Amigas del Señor Monastery, we try to be a true community, a place where each person can be herself, a beloved child of God. To do so, it is important to create a safe space for individuals to share of their deepest thoughts and feelings. We haven't always succeeded, but making the effort has been a good practice in openness, empathy, and understanding.

The Quakers developed a format that facilitates intimate sharing called "Worship Sharing," which we use for Weekly Review and many of our Spiritual Formation sessions. It works. The following guidelines are slightly adapted from a handout Sister Alegría received at Multnomah Monthly Meeting of Friends in the early 2000's.

Guidelines for Worship Sharing
- We wait in silent worship, in union with each other, and share gleanings from our spiritual journeys.
- Our purpose is to search together in silence for God's truth and inspiration. We also hope to draw closer as a community by sharing deeply our spiritual experiences.
- Each person has the opportunity and is encouraged to share. Unlike Meeting for Worship, you should not feel that you must be prompted by the Spirit before you speak.
- No Friend is ever required to speak. You can participate fully by listening only.
- In order to allow the space for each of us to share, be mindful of the length of your offering. Typically each Friend shares only one time.
- Listen fully to each person's words. Please do not interrupt or comment upon what another Friend has shared.

345

- Allow ample worship between sharings. Hold the gift that each person offers in the Light, without judgment.
- Speak from your own experience, rather than speaking of the experience of others or of abstract ideas.
- Avoid commenting on, or responding directly to, what someone else has said. One may, of course, share on themes or concerns raised by another as they apply to one's own life.
- Speak to the group. Avoid addressing any individual present.
- Please do not repeat elsewhere what you have heard. Worship sharing depends on our respecting and honoring one another.

Acknowledgements

Gracias
From: Sisters Alegría and Confianza

First and foremost, we give thanks to God. We thank God for our lives, for the gift of a monastic vocation, and for basic writing skills that allow us to share our life with others. This book exists because of God.

We also thank God for the many persons who touch our lives, those who support Amigas del Señor, and those who have helped us in putting this book together. We extend our thanks to:

Each other, for determination to make this book a reality, openness to each other's ideas, and willingness to face our history together, laughing, crying, and struggling through the tender parts so we could heal.

Jyl Myers, who printed up and mailed us all of our email updates from 2008-2010 and proofread the final draft of the manuscript. She was seduced by a seashell to come on her first mission trip with Sister Alegría to Honduras in 2000.

Judy Billings, who printed up and mailed us all of the updates from 2011-2013 and is constantly at our side through thick and thin. Friends like her are hard to come by.

Rosalie Grafe of Quaker Abbey Press, for permission to include sections that were previously printed in our first book, Amigas del Señor: Methodist Monastery.

Russ Hanson, who has encouraged—even pushed—us to write this book, offering to walk with us through the self-publishing jungle. His reading of the manuscript produced thoughtful and helpful commentary. He has mailed us gifts, including a memory disk and a memory stick, maple sugar and even gave us a small book-writing grant.

Donna Metcalf, who shared her beautiful oil painting, "Sisters in Christ," and gave us permission to use it for the cover. She says "it represents the intrepid spirit of adventure Christ brings into our lives..."

Acknowledgements

The late Del Shirley, who gave Beth a digital camera to better share her experiences in Honduras.

Alexandra (Sasha) Bosbeer, who took loads of photos to help us out in her visit in 2012. If you look closely, you'll see her name on some of the photos.

Kathleen Jones, who allowed us to use her digital camera in the summer of 2013.

Sara Kettle, who, in 2014, donated to the Monastery the digital camera we still use.

April Hall Cutting, who provided the photos of Sister Confianza's youth, and gave permission to use her tune "God of Grace," which she wrote as an eight-part round for a United Methodist camp.

Jack Donald who shared the photograph of Gus and himself.

Tércio Junker, who notated some of our music on computer amidst a hectic academic schedule.

Rita Brenner, faithful volunteer editor/proofreader (retired English teacher), who helped us keep our grammar in order.

Winnie Thomas, who proofread the final manuscript.

Life-long Friend Richard Grossman, who reviewed the Quaker terms in the Glossary and revised several of them.

Sister Confianza's parents, Craig and April Hall Cutting, for approving her treatment of their relationship in this book.

Alice Knotts, Rick Seifert, Blythe Stanton, and Bob Wood, who read through parts or all of the manuscript and gave helpful suggestions.

Elizabeth Andrew, who shared her writing, experience, and wise counsel.

Dwight H. Judy, who supported our writing efforts upon our first introduction, and made connections for us as we sought a publisher.

Hearts and Hands for Honduras, the mission team based in Sullivan, Illinois, that has provided stationery supplies, encouragement, and financial gifts. They transport gifts from the US to us when they come to Ceibita, Tocoa twice a year.

Yasser Ordoñez, who, while he was the microscopist at Centro de Salud from 2014-2015, let us use his computer every Tuesday, paying him only what he paid for a day of internet connection.

Celeste Ventura, who in 2016 graciously permitted us to use her computer without charge in the hubbub of her family's hardware store in Limón, and occasionally gave us a cool drink or lunch.

Doc and Dee (Marion and Donita) Dodson, who have offered us friendship, housing, food, use of computers and printing when we visit Balfate, Colón. We have had a few two-day writing retreats at their place.

Maritza Miranda and Ruth Hernandez, who cooked good food for us when we stayed with the Dodsons.

Pascual Torres Fuentes, who, as distributor of _El Aposento Alto_ (The UpperRoom) on the North Coast of Honduras, gave us stacks of older copies of the devotional booklet, which we have used in our bus ministry. Selling current and past _Aposento Altos_ on buses helped pay for our increased travel as we worked on this book.

Our many friends in Limón and around Honduras who have allowed us to glimpse another way of living and thinking by sharing their lives with us.

All those who have read our email updates and sent encouraging comments over the years.

And finally, you, for picking up this book and reading our stories.

¡Muchísimas gracias! Many, many thanks!
¡Que Dios les bendiga! May God bless you!

349

The Sisters at Amigas del Señor Monastery, 2012

About Amigas del Señor

Amigas del Señor is a community of women dedicated to prayer and care of the Creation. Founded in 2006, the religious Order is rooted in Western, monastic, Methodist and Quaker traditions. We are nuns living poor among the poor with a regular schedule of worship and physical work. Our contemplative lifestyle is facilitated by the Monastery's location in the foothills on the North Coast of Honduras. Besides our ministry of prayer, we also engage in outward ministries, including volunteering at the local public health clinic and sharing <u>The Upper Room</u> devotional booklet on buses. We invite unattached women to experience life with us.

Learn more at our webpage:
> www.oakgroveunitedmethodist.com/amigasdelsenor

Read current and past updates at:
> http://groups.yahoo.com/group/amigasdelsenor/

Contact us:

We welcome correspondence.
> **By mail:**
>> Amigas del Señor
>> Limón, Colón
>> Honduras

No numbers needed. It takes about a month for letters to arrive.
> **By email:**
>> amigashonduras@gmail.com

We get internet access every couple of weeks.

Donate:

To support the Sisters and our ministries, please make a check out to "Hermiston FUMC," and write "Amigas" in the memo line. Mail to:

> First UMC
> 191 E Gladys Ave.
> Hermiston, OR 97838

Looking southeast over the newly-built main house of
Amigas del Señor Monastery, 2006

Made in the USA
Lexington, KY
09 March 2017